D1527619

Managing Land-Use Conflicts

MANAGING LAND-USE CONFLICTS

Case Studies in Special Area Management

Edited by David J. Brower and Daniel S. Carol

Duke Press Policy Studies

Duke University Press   Durham 1987

Printed in the United States of America on
acid-free paper ∞
Library of Congress Cataloging-in-Publication Data
Managing land-use conflicts.
(Duke Press policy studies)
Bibliography: p.
Includes index.
1. Land use—United States.   2. Soil conservation—
United States.   3. Environmental protection—United
States.   4. Nature conservation—United States.
5. Land use—Law and legislation—United States.
I. Brower, David J.   II. Carol, Daniel S.   III. Series.
HD205.M35   1986   333.73'13'0973   86-19881
ISBN 0-8223-0560-7

Contents

Acronyms

APA	Adirondack Park Agency
BOR	Bureau of Outdoor Recreation
CIP	Capital Improvements Program
COG	Council of Government
COUP	Conference of Upper Delaware Townships
CWA, section 404	Clean Water Act Wetlands Protection Program
CZM	Coastal Zone Management
CZMA	Coastal Zone Management Act
DEC	New York Department of Environmental Conservation
DEP	New York Department of Environmental Protection
DFG	California Department of Fish and Game
EIS	Environmental Impact Statement
EPA	U.S. Environmental Protection Agency
FERC	Federal Energy Regulatory Commission
LCP	Local Coastal Program
MCPB	Montgomery County Planning Board
MOU/MV	Memorandum of Understanding
NEPA	National Environmental Policy Act
NMFS	National Marine Fisheries Service
NOAA	National Oceanic and Atmospheric Administration
NPS	National Park Service
NRA	National Recreation Area
SAM	Special Area Management
SAMP	Special Area Management Planning
TDR	Transferable Development Rights
TNC	The Nature Conservancy
USFWS	U.S. Fish and Wildlife Service

Preface

This effort would have been impossible without the cooperation and help of many individuals. Our authors deserve credit, above their written contributions, for their patience and commitment to the project while the manuscript was under review. We also wish to thank John Banta of the Adirondack Park Agency, Ben Mieremet of the National Oceanic and Atmospheric Administration, and our authors for their participation in the May 1983 roundtable discussion in Washington, D.C., which guided many of our own conclusions about the special area management process. Our greatest gratitude, however, goes to Barbara Rodgers, Lee Mullis, and Carroll Carrozza of the Center for Urban and Regional Studies for their tireless aid in producing this document—over and over. Final thanks to LA and JB, as always.

DJB/DSC
May 1986

Introduction

Perhaps as a natural reaction to the extensive body of environmental legislation passed during the 1960s and 1970s, there has been a growing concern with the costs and complexities of environmental regulation. In many areas these problems have been manifested in lengthy, uncertain, and complicated approval processes for development projects and in conflicting statutory responsibilities for local, state, and federal agencies. These delays and inconsistencies have often been exacerbated by conflicts between uses (that is, preservation or development) and a lack of incentives for cooperation or long-term policy commitments by regulatory agencies.

The management problems brought about by multiple-use demands on special resource areas have led to recognition of the need to deal more effectively with these areas and, more important, have evolved into a number of potentially useful management approaches. These early efforts are ad hoc responses to the common problems of management complexity and use conflicts. However, through these experiences, a growing group of concerned practitioners and others have become convinced of the value of special management tools and techniques and the need to develop and refine such approaches. Some of these unique experiences and resource planning methods are described and evaluated in the case studies presented in this book.

It is our hope to demonstrate how these ad hoc responses are linked by the single process of *special area management* and to identify important issues, concerns, and trade-offs likely to be faced in any future attempts that employ this approach. Moreover, because of the benefits of special area management apparent from the case studies, the concluding chapter will seek to identify important opportunities and constraints in institutionalizing the special area management process beyond its present ad hoc character.

Early responses to resource conflicts

Whenever there are competing demands on a scarce resource, there is likely to be some form of conflict between proponents of each use. This situation is made more complex when governments begin regulating land usage, guided by the assertion that environmental preservation of an area is a legitimate competing "use" for land. Although governments' efforts to assert environmental values have succeeded in slowing the rate of environmental degradation as well as preserving many important natural resources, they have not resulted in any dependable solution to the resource conflict issue that often necessitated their initial involvement. Understanding the history of such conflicts and the search for mechanisms to resolve user conflicts and balance competing interests is therefore essential to understanding the need for special area management.

Beginning late in the 19th century the federal government initiated efforts to preserve unique environmental areas, or to limit development activities where such activities could threaten conservation of surrounding natural resources. The first national park, Yellowstone, was established in 1872. Following Yellowstone's creation, the General Revision Act of 1891 was passed to enable millions of acres of federal land to be set aside as national parks or forests to preserve their natural values and protect them from "forest raiders." Five additional national parks were created by 1900 under this mandate. The act also engendered considerable political conflicts between opponents and proponents of this new conservation movement. Most notably, attempts were made to repeal the 1891 act and impeach President Grover Cleveland when he proposed increasing the national forest system to 50 million acres.

Public lands management in the 1920s and 1930s, through a series of acts restricting overgrazing (Taylor Grazing Act), mineral leasing, and forestry, introduced the now-prevalent notion of multiple-use management of federal land resources. These and other statutes established the principle that the management of federal land would be based on detailed inventories of the existing resources, careful planning, and public participation, with the goal of achieving a careful balance among competing uses. Controversies and resource conflicts have not disappeared under the multiple-use concept, however, but they have been institutionalized within the various planning processes used by the Bureau of Land Management and the U.S. Forest Service.

In the 1960s and 1970s federal and state governments expanded their efforts in environmental protection from merely setting aside unique wilderness areas to actually regulating private land uses to ensure that the surrounding environment was protected. This complex network of laws affected facility siting by requiring federal or state environmental impact assessments or development permits. Facility operations were also affected by water and air protection legislation controlling the levels of pollutants allowed to be discharged into the environment. These laws raised industry's operating costs significantly and have led to many delays in the siting and construction of new facilities in environmentally sensitive areas.

Perceived need for regulatory simplification

In response to these increasingly complex or overlapping environmental regulations, some efforts have been made to consolidate permit programs and to simplify permit procedures. In North Carolina, for example, the U.S. Army Corps of Engineers issues general permits (rather than individual permits under section 404 of the Clean Water Act or section 10 of the Rivers and Harbors Act) to project applicants where plans are already approved by the state's coastal management program. This procedure has cut fourteen days off the average processing time. By focusing solely on reducing the time required to obtain a particular permit, however, permit simplification has failed to address the substantive conflicts and issues that may arise concerning a proposed development.

Regional coordination and management by quasigovernmental agencies have emerged as better approaches both to managing multiple uses within areas and to achieving regulatory simplification. One of the first of these efforts derived from the rapid development of the San Francisco Bay region. An Army Corps of Engineers report, issued in 1959, noted that two to three square miles of wetlands were being filled annually for development, threatening a significant estuarine system. Popular sentiment, aroused by the loss of bird feeding areas and the evidence of increasing pollution in the bay, was strongly in favor of action to preserve the existing wetlands. The result was the formulation of the San Francisco Bay plan, a collaborative effort of local, state, and federal agencies to identify critical areas for preservation and to establish a permit and review system for development. A permanent commission composed of this same range of public and regulatory interests was established by the California legislature in 1969 and has been successful both in reducing habitat loss in the bay and in increasing port activity. Other prominent examples of this type include the Hackensack Meadowlands Development Commission in New Jersey (created in 1968) and the Tahoe Regional Planning Agency (created by the governors of Nevada and California by consent of the Congress in 1970). Though the overall missions of these agencies differ considerably, the creation of each agency represents an attempt to involve several layers of government toward improving management performance and resource protection.

These diverse efforts to deal with resource conflicts, in part engendered by government involvement, can be seen as precursors to the special area management experiences described in succeeding chapters. Many of the lessons learned in the San Francisco Bay area and elsewhere have actually been applied to these newer management efforts. Special area management can therefore be understood as the most recent attempt to deal with the resource conflicts inherent to land-use development and preservation.

What are special areas?

Special areas may most easily be thought of as "storage centers" for resource conflicts. As such, special areas can generally be defined by some or all of the following characteristics:

1. the failure of existing management authorities to achieve their management goals for the area or enhance the area's values
2. the lack of an appropriate management framework
3. user conflicts between preservation and development because of the area's high resource value
4. management conflicts (between local, state, or federal agencies in the same area)
5. a spatial resource system historically identified by agencies and users

Special areas may also be delineated by legislative proclamation (see, for example, the Adirondack Park and Pinelands case studies). Often, the rationale for these new boundaries is to provide management authority broad enough to preserve effectively the existing natural character of an area. Thus, special areas are those areas that are so naturally valuable, or so important for human use, or so sensitive to impact, or so particular in their planning requirements, as to require special area management treatment.

Perhaps of greater importance than any systematic definition for special areas are the management implications for an area once it is defined as "special." The definition of an area is likely to influence the type of management approach employed as well as the constraints that managers will face. Larger areas suggest that a wider range of issues and interests will need to be considered, and management may be constrained by an inability to perform detailed planning. At the same time, though smaller areas may be managed more effectively, the effects of development activities outside the area may be uncontrollable and potentially adverse.

The roots of special area delineation may also serve as a determinant of the management process to follow. Public concern for a region may lead to legislative definition of an area, together with specifically defined management goals and tasks and often *new* management authority. However, where a special area is defined primarily by management fragmentation and complex regulatory processes, management may tend to focus on increasing coordination and cooperation between existing management authorities. Each of these approaches (new agency creation versus increased coordination between existing agencies) implies a different set of constraints regarding public acceptance, implementation authority, and long-term predictability and success. The factors that make an area ripe for special management treatment therefore vary considerably. Determining when special area management is best employed is one important goal of this book and will be reiterated throughout the case studies and conclusion.

Special area management

Special area management (SAM) is the attempt to manage development in complex ecological and administrative settings. Though applicable to many types of resources, most often SAM processes occur in areas possessing valuable natural resources particularly vulnerable to uncontrolled development and so require special management to preserve those qualities that made the area initially attractive. Frequently, these areas are subject to intense political conflicts because competing interests are vying to promote uses that may be fundamentally incompatible. Finally, because special areas tend to overlap political boundaries, special administrative arrangements or new management forms are often created to increase regulatory coordination or to guide development.

Although the case studies presented here represent a wide range of management areas, goals, tools, and outcomes, all the studies do in fact share a common thread of management challenges. Viewed in this light, special area management emerges as a generic process to:

1. resolve management conflicts
2. provide greater predictability and assurance for both conservation and development interests
3. focus and streamline a set of management strategies
4. provide varying outcomes depending on the nature of the special area, the available management tools, and the participants in the process

The third point deserves additional mention, for while the particular management tools, actors, and legal authorities may vary between areas, the attempt to focus management into a single setting is what distinguishes special area management from more traditional management forms. In each case, some type of catalyst will be present to force the resolution of issues and drive the management process beyond its current standstill. This catalyst may be provided through the establishment of a special authority charged to deal specifically with the conflicts and issues facing an area, though such an occurrence is rare and has no guarantee of success (a new authority may merely add one or more tiers of authority to an already complex institutional environment). More often, relevant parties and decision makers are convened to a forum designed to resolve present conflicts as well as anticipate and resolve future conflicts. In many cases these forums are instituted by local groups or individuals frustrated by the failure of top-down planning and regulatory efforts to resolve user conflicts. It is also noteworthy that bringing the parties together is often more difficult than actually resolving the substantive concerns.

The other major distinction between special area management and other management forms is its explicit attempt to increase the predictability of future management and regulatory decisions. The success of special area management efforts hinges on this search for predictability, for by compromising their regulatory discretion or future interests in a special area management plan, parties to the plan must rely on some set of assurances that the agreed-upon plan will be implemented as originally conceived. The case studies illustrate a variety of techniques for providing this predictability (from consensus-building to legal assurances) and for maintaining the integrity of the special area management process through changing circumstances and plan amendments.

Case studies

The case studies that follow represent a diverse set of problems from the fields of coastal management, regional planning, and resource management. However, each of the cases raises issues critical to effective decision-making, and all are linked by common elements of the special area management process, which include:

- adaptation of management forms suitable to special circumstances
- definition of the proper relationship between the public and private sectors, and
- description of the politics and logistics of successful implementation.

The first chapter in the collection, "Special Area Management Planning in Coastal Areas: The Process," by Charles K. Walters, outlines the major elements of the SAM process. This article evolved out of a number of planning efforts that included the author (while with the National Marine Fisheries Service), the most notable being the long-term planning effort still under way at Grays Harbor, Washington. The Grays Harbor Estuary Task Force, composed of local, state, and federal coastal interest groups or regulators, was formed in 1975 to develop an estuary management plan for the harbor. Grays Harbor had been plagued with development versus preservation conflicts, and this planning effort is seen as an innovative attempt to resolve conflicts and improve predictability for permit and regulatory decisions through group consensus-building. Implementation of the plan relies on joint use of existing state and federal coastal regulations. Walters's article outlines the pros and cons of this process and identifies the important constraints and opportunities it presents. The benefits of the Grays Harbor approach were large enough to receive congressional recognition and encouragement in amending the Coastal Zone Management Act in 1980. Readers interested in specific information on the Grays Harbor, Coos Bay, Oregon, and other experiences noted in the chapter are referred to the bibliography on special area management at the end of this volume.

Following Walters's chapter are two related pieces on the subject of environmental mediation, reprinted from *Environment* magazine and a book from the Conservation Foundation. This approach has broad application for special area management and has been used extensively. The notions of consensus-building and consensus decision making have strong relevance to the special area management process.

Another important set of special area management experiences are outlined in the next chapter, "Special Area Management at Estuarine Reserves," by John Clark and Scott McCreary. The U.S. Estuarine Sanctuary Program was set up in 1972 by the Coastal Zone Management Act to preserve a number of representative estuarine types for scientific research and education. This chapter reviews evolving special area management experiences at three designated sanctuaries, Apalachicola Bay, Florida, Elkhorn Slough, California, and Tijuana River, also in California.

Mary Dolan's chapter, "Baltimore Harbor Environmental Enhancement Plan," describes the effort of the Regional Planning Council to develop a plan to improve the aquatic habitat of Baltimore Harbor and reduce the time required to process fill permits for projects requiring mitigation. The emergent goal of this special area management process was to reconcile the state of Maryland's wetlands filling compensation program with federal (Army Corps of Engineers) mitigation requirements.

This case study demonstrates a number of elements important to success in multi-agency planning partnerships, including the presence of preexisting institutional focus on an area, a reliable data base, and the value of a neutral facilitator to guide plan development.

Lindell Marsh and Robert Thornton's case study details another evolving approach for special area management, the development of habitat conservation plans under section 10(a) of the Endangered Species Act. The planning precedent they describe involved a residential development proposal in San Bruno, California, which threatened the habitat of a federally protected butterfly species. A task force of county and federal officials, together with interested environmental groups, developed a plan to preserve butterfly habitat while permitting limited development to occur. Plan agreements were contained in a contract signed by all relevant parties, which includes provisions for amendments in the event that the agreed-upon management plan fails to provide the degree of species protection desired by the U.S. Fish and Wildlife Service (a contract cosigner).

Under this scenario, future plan modifications proposed by the Fish and Wildlife Service will be accepted by all parties if it can be shown that the modifications

1. are necessary for the conservation of a species listed under the Endangered Species Act,
2. cannot be accomplished through the continued implementation of the existing habitat conservation plan, and
3. represent the minimal modifications available that could appreciably improve the likelihood of survival of the affected species.

This habitat plan concept (with its potential for yielding "creative" public-private habitat management partnerships) was specifically encouraged in the 1982 reauthorization of the Endangered Species Act. A similar ongoing attempt to develop a habitat conservation plan in Key Largo, Florida, is also described by Marsh and Thornton. Here seven endangered species are threatened by a proposal to open up development in the northern part of the island. A steering committee of county officials, environmentalists, and state representatives has been convened by Governor Bob Graham to devise a solution to the conflict, using the San Bruno model.

Following the San Bruno study are several chapters dealing with large-scale regional management programs. The Adirondack Park Agency case study by Richard Booth and the Pinelands Commission chapter by Daniel Carol describe the efforts of these regional management agencies to elicit local government participation in their programs. The companion chapters on national recreation areas ("urban parks") by the Conservation

Foundation and on local opposition to the National Park Service efforts in the Upper Delaware River area by Glen Pontier offer a contrast to the Pinelands and Adirondack examples. The chapter by Melissa Banach and Denis Canavan reviews the agricultural and open-space preservation program in Montgomery County, Maryland. Each of these cases serves to further define the common threads in the special area management process as well as illustrate constraints and trade-offs common to these types of management efforts.

The book's concluding chapter attempts to summarize the common elements of the special area management case studies presented here. From that point, the chapter concludes with a discussion of the advantages and disadvantages of trying to formalize what have essentially been ad hoc processes to date.

At the very least, this collection should offer some insight for those interested in natural resource management. More than this, however, it is the editors' belief that the special area management process offers great promise for resolving many important management problems faced by practitioners. Thus, while each area may be faced with a unique set of problems and participants, the tools and techniques of special area management may help provide a solution for areas fragmented by land use conflicts involving private and public sector interests.

Special Area Management Planning in Coastal Areas: The Process

Charles K. Walters

Special area management plans developed in Grays Harbor, Washington, and other coastal areas show great promise in reducing conflicts of development versus preservation. In most of these planning efforts, task forces composed of relevant local, state, and federal coastal interest groups or regulators work together to resolve use conflicts for a special area, preparing a plan to guide future regulatory decisions. The goal of this process is to improve the predictability of regulatory decisions and to trade off development in one part of the area in exchange for long-term preservation of the remaining portion. Certain principles, such as consensus decision making and balanced task force representation, are crucial to the success of the technique. Other elements of the process, such as implementation methods, will vary depending on individual circumstances.*

Competition for use of coastal shorelands and aquatic areas, particularly those adjacent to port areas, continues to increase. Regulatory authorities have developed over the past decade to balance the need for new coastal development against other values such as critical habitat for important fish and wildlife. These regulations have also attempted to ensure that new development, if allowed, does not significantly degrade aquatic systems. Unfortunately, most local, state, and federal shoreline and water development permit procedures designed to guide development have traditionally functioned on a case-by-case basis, with little ability or authority to assess and control accumulative impacts of projects over time and along a shoreline. The need for a more comprehensive approach to coastal environmental regulation has therefore become evident.

The Coastal Zone Management Act provides states the potential to develop longer-range plans for shorelines and aquatic areas, but most state plans are general and policy-oriented rather than geographically specific and they have little project-siting capability. Some coastal manage-

*The author worked for the National Ocean Policy Study, Senate Committee on Commerce, Science and Transportation, at the time this chapter was written.

ment efforts have attempted, however, to integrate land- and water-use planning efforts with review procedures, such as those required under NEPA (National Environmental Planning Act). One such effort, the Grays Harbor Estuary Management Plan, has attempted to integrate all such procedures into a detailed, site-specific, long-range agreement between local, state, and federal bodies. Although the agreement process has encountered some difficulties due to changing federal policies (such as federal wetland protection guidelines), the effort has precipitated positive changes in national legislation for future planning efforts.

Specifically, the Grays Harbor planning effort was instrumental in a 1980 amendment to the Coastal Zone Management Act to encourage Special Area Management Planning (SAMP) efforts, even though no guidance has ever been developed by the agency implementing the Act—the Office of Ocean and Coastal Resource Management. The Grays Harbor SAMP process also influenced changes in the Clean Water Act (section 404, 1982 version), which enabled stratified permit decisions to occur in the plan process and for advanced identification of dredged material disposal sites as well as de-designating sites for dredged material disposal. Other SAMP efforts at Yaquina Bay, Oregon, Lower Willamette River, Oregon, Coos Bay, Oregon, and Kenai, Alaska, discussed briefly in this chapter, have also provided valuable lessons for future SAMP efforts in coastal and estuarine areas.

The geographical areas included in the following discussion are marine, estuarine, and freshwater aquatic areas as well as adjacent shorelines. By compressing all anticipated conflicts into the present, the mediated, consensus SAMP process should provide the predictability needed by development interests for investment purposes and by conservation interests for long-term protection of important ecological areas. The SAMP process requires an open, give-and-take atmosphere, however. In areas of historical conflict between development and conservation interests, it is difficult to initiate and complete such a process. All the ingredients must be there: the right people, the right process, commitment by all represented groups, funding, and a "superhuman" facilitator/consultant. SAMP is not a method that should be attempted everywhere, but it does offer a solution where large-scale conflicts exist between development needs and long-range natural resource productivity. SAMP should be considered where the time and effort can be prorated in the future to provide predictability not otherwise available.

Initiating the SAMP process

Prior to embarking on an estuary planning effort, careful analysis needs to occur on the need for such an exhaustive planning effort. SAMP is not a simple cure-all process. Quite the opposite: SAMP is costly, time-consuming, and stressful as well as politically dangerous for participants. Some analysts have likened SAMP to a high-stakes poker game.[1] If the desire is sufficient, however, the effort can be worth it for all involved. Long-term predictability for all interests is the key benefit.

As part of the original "needs" test to determine if a SAMP is the best solution, a series of important issues or problems usually arise. In the Grays Harbor case, for example, an application to build a site to manufacture offshore drilling equipment generated substantial controversy and eventually provided the impetus for the formation of the Grays Harbor Estuary Management Task Force.[2] Agencies or groups that are expected to be important in decisions on these catalyzing issues should be members of the planning task force. Otherwise, key groups that are not represented on the decision-making body may not accept the SAMP agreements and may litigate or hinder plan progress. One mistake identified by some in the Grays Harbor plan was to exclude a conservation representative from the task force. Continued adverse publicity to the Grays Harbor plan has occurred, largely due to the choice in task force composition.

The public plays an important role in planning processes in coastal areas. Several techniques can be used to secure their participation. One technique is to choose at-large members for the task force representing a balance of public opinion. Another is to have conservation and development groups select a representative. Still another is to utilize balanced representation from existing state Coastal Zone Management (CZM) Citizen Advisory Groups. Whatever technique is chosen depends on the local situation. It is imperative, however, that the size of the task force be kept workable while maintaining a balance between conservation and development interests.

Once the important players have decided that a need exists for a comprehensive, long-term, balanced plan with enough detail for predictability, a lead agency should be agreed upon. The lead agency should be mutually trusted by development and conservation interests. Traditionally, counties or multi-county agencies, such as councils of governments (COGs) or regional planning commissions have been lead agencies in western states, while state agencies have been the lead in gulf and eastern states. Careful thought also needs to go into how the planning effort might be implemented, thus possibly influencing the selection of a lead agency.

Special area management plans developed in states with federally approved coastal management programs may rely, for example, on specific provisions of the Coastal Zone Management Act to ensure that future federal actions or projects will be consistent with the plan's intent.[3]

One of the first agenda items for the task force is to select a facilitator. This task will be one of the most important throughout the process. Although it is extremely important that the facilitator work for the task force, he/she must be imaginative, creative, and able to skillfully guide the group through difficult times. The facilitator must be neutral and trusted by all SAMP representatives. The facilitator must appreciate and understand aquatic and terrestrial natural resources and their requirements, including cumulative adverse impacts and the role of ecosystem-wide planning rather than isolated case-by-case decisions. The facilitator must also understand port, industrial, commercial, and residential pressures and needs.

During the SAMP development effort, there will be a continual need for planning creativity, mediation, alternative courses of action, and caucusing. A complete, retrievable record of decisions will be needed. Since the SAMP process is so long and entails so many complex agreements, task force members will forget exactly what they agreed to. The facilitator will have to build on these agreements each session and will have to continually summarize agreements made to date. All of this dictates a methodical record-keeping system, available to task force members on request. Consultant/facilitator delays because of overcommitment have been a major problem in previous SAMPs. Frank discussions with potential consultants on expectations and deliverables should help alleviate this problem.

Developing the SAMP

A skilled facilitator should carefully structure the agenda of the first session around simple tasks to build cohesion, sort out the players, and establish written and unwritten rules. An aggressive, unseasoned facilitator could begin to dominate the task force at this time, however, and push some task force members in a direction they are uncomfortable in going. A fine line exists between suggesting concepts and alternatives and "pushing the process" in a certain direction. Part of the "sorting out" will be the task force/facilitator role. If the task force is all new to the game, the facilitator could overdirect the task force.

Seating is very important, as is the size and "feel" of the room. The task force seating should be equal around a table or square of tables. Theater seating is not conducive to team-building and should not be used. Task force members should be convinced of their importance in this effort by having an important speaker set the stage. A local, state, or federal elected official (or combination) would be ideal, providing they have been properly briefed.

All agreements must be made by consensus.[4] Consensus is a basic principle of SAMP.

All task force members are equal and should be fully involved. Not to speak out on an issue will be interpreted as agreement. A voting or minority viewpoint may lead to nonsupport of the plan. Since this arrangement may be a new role for some task force representatives, it is important to make sure consensus procedure is well understood by all task force members.

The SAMP process works effectively only if consensus can be reached and task force members can give and take with professional respect for each other. In Grays Harbor, for example, state and federal resource agencies and the Port of Grays Harbor were in warring camps prior to the plan. During the planning process a mutual trust developed enabling informal resolution of a number of issues that arose. Several permits were issued on the strengths of the planning decisions made to that point, even though a lot of give-and-take, caucusing, and mediating was ahead. This good-faith gesture on the part of the agencies was met with equal good faith on the part of the Port of Grays Harbor by not using its known political strength to direct the plan or certain projects as it chose. A phone call is now usually enough to solve issues.

Two additional imperatives should be assumed for estuarine SAMP efforts: use a natural resource base for decision making, and plan for water and shoreline uses that are compatible with long-term resource conservation. Past and existing shoreline uses should not dictate future shoreline and adjacent aquatic area uses without regard for adverse impacts on aquatic resources. Historic shoreline and upland uses were developed when land was inexpensive and resources were deemed inexhaustible. Aquatic productivity has recently become an important factor in many shoreline areas and could be a limiting factor not only in future availability of valuable resources, such as fish and shellfish, but also in water quality and livability in that area. One can no longer afford to ignore the natural resources in an area or impacts of upland uses on those resources.

Once the task force ground rules have been outlined and agreed to, actual planning can begin in earnest. Usually the first step involves the development of the planning boundary—to define the geographic scope of the special area being considered.[5] Sufficient uplands should be included to deal with alternative locations and construction techniques for proposed projects. A railroad line or highway or similar mappable feature works well for the landward boundary of the plan. In addition, decisions should be made for the land-water interface.[6] Jurisdictions change at the land-water interface. State and federal permit authority exists in water and wetland areas. Use of the Clean Water Act's section 404 line or the line of nonaquatic vegetation (or Army Corps of Engineers–Environmental Protection Agency jurisdiction line) is one easy solution.

Another decision to be made is how to deal with the water area of the plan. The Grays Harbor plan divides upland and adjacent areas from water at the ordinary high water line because of state planning laws. The bulk of estuarine waters are a single unit, affected by adjacent shoreline and wetland uses and activities. The best example of planning from the water shoreward is the Lower Willamette River management plan, completed in 1973 for the Portland, Oregon, River and adjacent shorelines. In that case, numerous existing uses were deemed to be nonconforming and to have an unacceptable adverse impact on natural resources and, therefore, were planned for future phaseout. Other SAMP efforts have identified large blocks of water area, identified general uses, and developed policies for specific future uses.

The task force must then develop and agree on general planning and plan implementation procedures. Questions to be answered include:

1. Does the task force expect to make detailed decisions on all future uses along the active shoreline? An alternative is to have general-use areas with specifics to be defined at the permit stage. The degree of predictability will be directly correlated to the detail of decisions made.
2. Are specific biophysical management units to be utilized? In Grays Harbor these units were determined by similar physical, biological, urbanized areas. Some management units (MUs) were less than a mile of shoreline while others were much larger.
3. Is an estuary-wide mitigation-restoration plan envisioned? Early discussion of definitions, procedures, and limitations should occur. "De-designation" under section 404 of the Clean Water Act should be considered.
4. Will there be a dredged material disposal plan developed? If so, advanced designation under section 404 of the Clean Water Act should be considered and procedures understood.
5. Are any endangered species known or suspected? Specific federal and/or state procedures will have to be followed if endangered species are found within the plan area.

6. What will the exact sequence of planning events be? In Grays Harbor, for example, it was agreed to make decisions in phases. The first circuit around the estuary was to determine general planning area boundaries (for five areas). During the next circuit forty-four management unit boundaries were determined, then uses, specific projects, etc. The task force tried to avoid unresolved issues, but those that occurred were left until the circuit was complete to enable system-wide balancing and trade-offs.

7. Where and when will public input be sought? Should the public be briefed at public hearings at key phases in the planning schedule, by mail-out tabloids, or merely through the completed "straw man" draft? Will all planning sessions be open to the public?

All foreseeable implementation procedures such as amendments, plan updates, appeals, plan adoption, the need for an environmental impact statement, and details of plan adoption and commitment should also be addressed up front. The future role of the task force in each of these processes should be agreed to. It is advisable to have the task force involved in all future changes in the plan or it will disintegrate upon the first imbalancing change.

Next the task force may wish to develop a series of large-scale inventory maps for decision making. Most of the information needed for the planning data base probably exists in agency files. A technical subcommittee or subtask force may be necessary to collect such information and, working with the lead agency and consultant staff, to put it into a format usable by the task force. Large charts and maps put on the walls of the meeting room will enhance memories and facilitate decisions.

Each plan will require a different set of inventories, but the following are examples:

1. A number of fish and wildlife inventories:
   −critical habitat such as spawning areas
   −clam beds, oyster grounds, commercial fishing areas, marine mammal haulout areas
   −endangered species sitings and important habitat
2. Ownership—local, state, federal, large corporation
3. Political jurisdictions
4. Land use and public access
5. Historically filled and diked areas
6. Water or wetland areas owned by development interests or proposed for development

7. Corps of Engineers authorized and private channels and dredged material disposal sites

This information can be collected and prepared concurrently with task force meetings.

The heart of the SAMP effort will be the development of management category systems and the delineation of land and water areas into the chosen classification scheme. (This approach mirrors the land-classification efforts undertaken in the Adirondack Park and in the Pinelands; see later chapters.) In Grays Harbor the task force identified eight large planning areas of similar character on the basis of the extent of current development, water quality, physical boundaries, and political jurisdictions. The planning area concept allowed for general descriptions of the area's contribution to the overall system, its existing character, its committed uses (both natural and man-related), its conflicts and assets, and recommendations for future use. Planning areas were too large, however, to allow for meaningful designation of future management objectives for the plan. As such, these larger areas (comprising roughly one hundred square miles) were further subdivided into forty-four management units, using more specific biological, physical, and political criteria.

Using the already-developed guidance from the larger planning area, management objectives for the management unit (MU) were delineated. The Grays Harbor Task Force used an expanded version of the Washington Coastal Zone Management program's management category system for this purpose. The eight categories were:

1. Natural: to preserve and/or restore natural areas
2. Conservancy Natural (CN): to preserve and restore or enhance areas to their natural condition
3. Conservancy Managed (CM): to protect an area for uses that depend on natural systems
4. Rural Agricultural (RA): to protect existing and potential agricultural lands from urban expansion
5. Rural Low Intensity (RL): to restrict intensive development along undeveloped banklines and maintain open spaces
6. Urban Residential (UR): to protect areas in which the predominant use is or should be residential
7. Urban Mixed (UM): areas in which there is or should be a mix of compatible urban uses
8. Urban Development (UD): areas in which predominant uses are or will be industrial and commercial development

Considerable discussion is usually necessary to agree upon activities that may be allowed by permit in each MU. Activities should be as specific as possible. (See table 2.1 for a sample matrix of permitted activities from the Grays Harbor plan.)

If any application of an activity is of concern, the activity may only be conditionally allowed or only under special listed conditions. All terms such as conditional, permitted, special, etc., should be agreed upon and standardized from the beginning of the process.

Enough information has to be developed within the MU to meet the expectations of the task force. If partial or stratified permit decisions are expected, then the information must be included for future reference. Documentation of decisions in the plan is very important to avoid future misunderstandings and challenges. If an environmental impact statement

Table 2.1 Permitted activities matrix (Grays Harbor)

Permitted activities

Management category	RL	CN
STRUCTURES		
Piers, docks, wharves	O	*
Pilings and mooring dolphins		
Bridges	O	*
Causeways		
Outfalls	+	+
Cable/Pipeline crossing	O	*
Boathouses	+	*
Breakwater		
BANK		
Diking	+	
Bulkheading	+	
Groins		
Jetty		
Special project fills		
Bankline straightening		
Bankline erosion control	+	*
CHANNEL		
New access channel		
Channel/Berth maintenance		
Channel realignment		

Permitted activity	O
Conditional activity	+
Special conditions	*

is necessary, documentation should be especially detailed in key decisions. Issues may develop concerning development or conservation proposals in individual management units that appear unsolvable. A systematic trade-off or "balancing" of one proposal for another may be achievable on a larger scale. Issues such as port development, dredge material disposal, mitigation banking, and others may best be resolved by dealing with the entire environmental system.

Occasionally during the process, the task force needs to back away from the individual management unit and look at the whole plan. One technique is to summarize what has occurred each time the circuit of the plan is completed.

It is possible that an issue or two will be unsolvable by the task force. A formal mediation group may be needed at the end of the plan if all issues are not resolved.

Once complete, the draft plan should be submitted to task force members prior to a public draft release. Often the consultant has had to fabricate specific language based on his vague understanding of some complex agreement. Task force members should review such language carefully before public release.

If an EIS is involved in the process, the work should be done concurrently with plan development. An EIS started after plan completion could take an additional eighteen months. Other implementation mechanisms, such as memoranda of understanding with agencies or CZM state plan amendments, local land use plan adoption, etc., should be factored into the time-and-procedure equation. If these are left until the plan is completed, many false starts and delays could occur.

Any plan must be flexible enough to grow, but a plan as time-consuming as a SAMP should not be modified easily or it will cease to be predictable. Procedures for plan amendment should be established using the same task force used for plan development. Some projects may be too controversial—lack sufficient detail—and may be undecided in the plan. The task force should be scheduled to convene every six months for such interpretations. Political pressures should be used to keep the plan on course. If political pressure is used to allow exceptions to the plan, however, the commitment will evaporate.

Positive features of SAMP

Past and present permit processes have precipitated major political and legal conflicts. Through the SAMP process, however—as long as the initial rules of the game for plan implementation and amendment are adhered to—coastal waterway construction permit programs can be greatly streamlined. The degree of permit simplification achievable depends on the extent to which the task force dealt with details of the project(s) in the plan. If the SAMP is done under authority of the Coastal Zone Management Act, the "federal consistency" provision of the act will serve to sort out permit applications for projects inconsistent with the plan. Projects not allowed in the plan, however, should be rejected by local, state, and federal government permitting agencies as inconsistent with the plan. The plan can be amended for such projects, providing the task force agrees and "rebalances" the plan through mitigation, reduction in development options, or similar measures. Plan amendments for such projects should not be easy, however, or the predictability of the plan will be lost.

A second major advantage of SAMP efforts is their potential to reduce future regulatory uncertainty. Development interests need predictability so they can make advanced plans and site investments. SAMP can provide that predictability, providing adequate commitments to the plan are made by all parties.

SAMP efforts are unique in that they can also offer long-term resource protection. Long term conservation and protection can be achieved through a SAMP that might be unachievable in most other forms. SAMP ideally includes systemwide decisions over an area such as an estuary, therefore providing the ability to consider interaction between estuarine ecosystem components (that is, subtidal, intertidal, unvegetated wetlands, vegetated wetlands, etc.). Protection mechanisms developed so far include authority of planning law, zoning, restrictive convenances, fee title transfer, as well as mitigation with the modified area protected under the above restrictions. More effort is needed to develop protective mechanisms.

Closely related to the above point but worthy of discussion is the capability of a SAMP to effectively deal with cumulative impacts of projects occurring throughout the SAMP planning area and over time. This has been the biggest drawback of past and present permitting, reviewing and planning systems. The SAMP is like a Polaroid camera, allowing an instantaneous image of all future proposed habitat and water quality changes. This allows carrying-capacity levels to be considered for new and existing uses in the planning process.

Finally, the SAMP process offers a prime opportunity to plan for future mitigation efforts as well as areas suitable for dredged material disposal. Presently mitigation efforts are case-by-case and appear unplanned to development interests, particularly port authorities. Committee members of the American Association of Port Authorities, for example, have recently expressed interest in developing systematic mitigation plans so that mitigation for specific projects will contribute to an overall scheme, not just serve as a Band-Aid approach that may not be contributing to the ecosystem. It is not advisable to develop a mitigation or dredged material disposal plan without a SAMP. Too many future options are affected by either activity to plan for such a single purpose. These planning efforts can easily be developed within the context of a SAMP, however, and add to its usefulness.

Negative features of SAMP

An up-front realization of the negative features of SAMP is also important. If these features are known, they can possibly be minimized by careful planning and frank discussion.

First, it must be recognized that the SAMP process is complicated, requiring extensive information gathering, decision making, and integration of planning, permitting, and review processes such as those required for environmental impact statements prepared under the auspices of the National Environmental Policy Act (NEPA). The record of decisions must be quick, clear, and well documented. Very complex planning and economic, ecological, regulatory, marketing, legal, and political theories and principles will have to be dealt with by all task force parties. Specific factors will also tend to make each SAMP situation unique.[7]

Second, the SAMP process will require extensive individual task force member commitment. Task force individuals representing agencies or influential groups can expect to meet at least once a month for several years during SAMP development. In addition to understanding the planning, economic, and ecological principles noted above, each member will need to prepare extensively for future meetings. Strategies may have to be devised with allies, package trade-offs may have to be predetermined, caucuses at critical points may have to be planned to avoid a consensus call at a certain time, etc. A complete understanding of the area's resources, from natural systems to developmental potential, is a necessity.

In addition, the process may be very stressful for participants. At many junctures in the process one can expect one's "bottom line" to be crossed, leaving one feeling betrayed and pushed beyond expectations. The "mediator/record keeper/planner" may have to save the day with alternate techniques, methods, etc. Tempers will flare and cooling-off periods may be necessary. Dealing with future opportunity options is stressful, as is making a judgment call beyond one's authority. Procedures can be developed to minimize stress but not eliminate it. Some individuals can be expected to burn out if the SAMP takes more than eighteen to twenty-four months to reach completion.

Fourth, each party to the SAMP may bring (voluntarily or involuntarily) a varying degree of commitment to the plan. Commitment to a SAMP is an important yet elusive concept. Local governments and ports want regulatory agencies to be legally committed to the plan, yet federal law limits the extent to which a federal agency can be committed. While local government and ports are legally committed via state and federal planning law, these laws and policies are sometimes modified politically or loosely interpreted by the implementing body. Regardless of the legal commitment, the policy and therefore the political commitment made by all, coupled with the continuation of the mutual trust established between task force members, are what make a SAMP successful. One of the first SAMPs developed in Yaquina Bay, Oregon, in 1969 has worked extremely well without anyone worrying about legal commitment. The parties openly discuss any problems and mutually solve them.

When all task force members and representative groups have signed off on a plan, support should be sought from local, state, and federal elected officials. A deviation in the plan by any party could then be prevented by political pressure. In many areas, conservation interests have felt that political pressure has worked only against them, however, and not as a stabilizing force for ecological principles. This could change if an attempt was made to fully brief local, state, and federal elected representatives on the importance of a SAMP, its finely tuned balance, and its long-term streamlining capabilities. This could be a major briefing task but would probably be worth the effort.

Finally, since the SAMP process is personalized, one of the potential future problems with any SAMP is the change in commitment due to changing personnel. Memoranda of understanding or letters of intent help, but they cannot be relied on completely. If agencies, local government, or individuals want out, they will find a way. SAMP efforts have failed in some areas. One was attempted for Kenai, Alaska, but was rejected by local government part-way through the process, even though state and federal agencies were supportive. Another failed in Coos Bay, Oregon, because an overzealous local government accepted all agreements made after a four-year process, then kicked out state and federal members and added back in all of the development proposals they could not get by consensus. What is needed is pride in being a part of a good thing and strong personal interest. The stakes need to be made high enough so that parties cannot easily get out. As one alternative, a full task force meeting could be reconvened each year after the plan is completed, even if there were no necessary functions such as amendments, large conditional use proposals, etc. This could serve to enforce the need to maintain commitment to the plan.

Common SAMP mistakes

The following mistakes should be avoided. In some cases these mistakes have impeded the progress or even occasionally threatened the completion of a SAMP.

1. *Allowing the process to take too long.* Eighteen months appears to be the maximum time that should be allowed to prevent loss of interest, commitment, change in personnel, etc.
2. *Drawing* SAMP *boundaries too small, thus eliminating necessary biological-political "trading room".* Trade-offs between developable areas and undevelopable areas will be necessary. If the area is too small, no flexibility will be possible. An ecosystem approach is best.
3. *Omitting key group representation on the task force.* Influential groups that have been omitted may delay or block the plan.
4. *Establishing too large a task force.* Although this might appear to contradict the immediately preceding item, the two are mutually supportive. A delicate balance must be struck between size and composition of the task force. While nine members is an ideal size, certainly no more than fifteen to twenty members should be considered for a task force. If more member representatives are absolutely necessary, various systems such as subcommittees, working groups, etc., might be considered.
5. *Selection of a consultant or lead agency without a development or preservation bias.* Impartiality is a must. All interests must be able to trust the consultant to develop compromise positions and help mediate difficult issues.
6. *Allowing the consultant to dictate task force direction and technique.* The consultant should be responsible to the task force, not vice-versa. Suggestions and alternative scenarios should be suggested by the consultant, but the decisions on procedure and directions should be made by the task force, not the consultant.
7. *Inadequate records kept of task force decisions.* A specific decision by the task force and background information used in the decision may be needed to meet future permit criteria, NEPA statements, and political questions. Members will want varying degrees of record detail,

but complete transcripts should be available on request to task force members.

8. *Allowing too much time to elapse before each member receives task force decisions, meeting minutes, and plan language requested from the consultant.* Often the group will agree in concept on an issue and direct the consultant to draft the specific wording. If too much time goes by (two weeks should be maximum), members forget or question the decision and intent of the language.

9. *Too much time between task force meetings.* Members forget detailed decisions and issues, as all are involved in many other complex issues. Task force meetings should not be more than one month apart, and they should be held more frequently if possible. Anything beyond a month will put each member in the position of coming unprepared or having to extensively reorient himself. Some of the members will not have the ability or opportunity to prepare, and consequently the meeting time will be inefficient and occasionally totally wasted.

10. *Political intimidation of task force members.* A sense of mutual trust is difficult to establish but critical to the success of a SAMP. SAMP efforts have usually evolved out of the need to resolve situations of past conflict. Politically strong members of the task force (often port authorities) have traditionally strong-armed resource agencies and must consciously avoid this technique in the SAMP process. A SAMP should encourage frank, friendly discussion of tough issues. It is not the time to intimidate via the political process.

11. *Changing group or agency representatives.* This results in a lack of understanding of the issues, considerable lost time for the task force in reorienting the new member, changing commitments, and occasionally a total change in an agency position on an issue.

12. *Changing of agency policy.* If the SAMP takes too long, as discussed in (1), agency policy could change during the development of the SAMP. For example, the EPA made major policy changes three times during the Grays Harbor process, leading to delays.

13. *Selecting inadequate meeting facilities.* The amount of effort put into a SAMP will be considerable. Since most task force members will be very busy and their time valuable, several concepts will be important. The meeting rooms should be quiet, with no messages or phone calls taken except at breaks. The seating arrangements should be similar to summit or peace talks. A circular table or rectangular arrangement of tables, placing all members as equals is extremely important. Caucus areas or rooms need to be nearby. Several private phones will be needed for members to check in on legal/policy positions.

14. *Inadequate consultant and staff services.* Time will overtake the effort unless the consultant understands what he must deliver and what help he can expect from task force and lead agency staff. As already mentioned, the task force should meet at least once a month. Between these meetings minutes must be developed, inventory and background graphics and data must be prepared, as well as draft sections of the plan. Expected deliverables must be discussed and agreed upon at the beginning of the effort. If an EIS must be prepared, the funding and drafting agency must be agreed to at the onset of the SAMP.

15. *Adding the NEPA process (EIS preparation) to the plan process.* These processes should be concurrent. Other requirements, such as endangered species consultations, should also be addressed early on and developed concurrently with the plan. Some of these processes could add an additional year to a SAMP.

16. *Inappropriate agency, group, or jurisdictional representatives.* The representatives on the task force should be senior enough within an organization to know and therefore represent their groups on policy issues. They must also have the technical capability to discuss impacts, issues, and future options. A multidisciplinary background is valuable, as issues will be wide-ranging. Fine-tuned negotiating skills will be needed. Credibility, professional trust, and the ability to get along in a very stressful environment are mandatory.

SAMP efforts require consensus on all decisions, therefore each representative must be able to ratify agreements made throughout the process. If issues require the development of new policy or interpretations of existing laws and policies, direct agency consultation must begin at the early stages of SAMP development and continue throughout the process.

17. *Inadequate agency commitment to SAMP.* Although the procedures and agency ability to commit to SAMP continues to change for the better, previous efforts have suffered due to reluctance by EPA and the Corps of Engineers to commit to agreements their task force representatives made under the consensus rule. Changes in this extremely important area will be discussed in the Regulatory Reform section.

18. *Implementation procedures left until the end of the process.* Specifics on amendment procedures and the extent to which local, state, and federal agencies will implement the plan should be agreed to early on. New procedures are evolving and will be discussed under the Regulatory Reform section.

The impacts of regulatory reform on SAMP

The Reagan administration came to power in January 1981 with a determination to remove or modify many regulations or policies that hindered development. Such attempts at regulatory reform, regardless of their particular merits or motives, have served to delay the plan implementation process at places like Grays Harbor. EPA, for example, which had been represented on the Grays Harbor Estuary Management Plan Task Force since the beginning (1975) and had developed a key role in technical and policy assistance, suddenly decided at the uppermost Washington, D.C., level to abandon the planning process. After nearly a year of stalling, EPA decided in 1982 (after congressional prodding) to uphold the plan it had previously agreed to. In February 1983 EPA redrafted Clean Water Act guidelines (section 404) to eliminate a key concept central to the entire Grays Harbor plan agreement—Advanced Designation and Dedesignation of Dredged Material Areas—only to reverse itself later on.[8] Most recently, proposals to use the advanced designation concept have been opposed by environmental groups. Regulatory uncertainty (in part caused by inconsistent attempts at regulatory reform) threatened to destroy consensus in Grays Harbor.

An entire chapter could be developed on the impact of these changing regulatory policies and procedures upon coastal development. The most unfortunate effect appears to be that until the dust settles, all planning efforts must cope with changing federal guidance. This added uncertainty will tend to make SAMP efforts in coastal areas more difficult and time-consuming. The only solution may be to specifically list planning rules rather than to refer to sets of federal guidelines.

Environmental Mediation

Gerald Cormick and Gail Bingham

The growing use of court remedies for personal as well as business or governmental conflict is part of the quarrelsome nature of American society. But it has also been encouraged by the Congress as well as by state legislature and city councils whose members remain tenacious in their belief that every problem has a legal solution. Elaborate rules and lofty goals have been set for both public and private institutions and businesses. Other agencies and individuals also have been given the power to seek court remedies whenever these goals or rules are ignored.

The burdens thus placed on the courts have had some unfortunate consequences, including crowded calendars and significant costs and delays for the disputants. Are there alternatives or supplements to the judicial system as a means of settling social conflicts while still achieving desirable public policy? One method being tried is mediation—the introduction of a third party who attempts to bring together warring factions and get them to develop and agree on a solution to their differences. Beginning in the early 1970s a number of private foundations, especially Ford and Rockefeller, sponsored mediation projects around the nation. The following two chapters by Gerald Cormick and Gail Bingham, reprinted from Environment *magazine and Bingham's* Conservation Foundation *book, respectively, review recent experience in this growing field.*

The myth, the reality, and the future

Gerald Cormick

The first explicit effort to mediate an environmental dispute began in the fall of 1973 when the author and a colleague, Jane E. McCarthy, initiated discussions with parties to a flood-control/land-use planning conflict in Washington state. In December 1974 that lengthy and difficult mediation effort culminated in a unanimous, written agreement between the dozen or so parties at interest. That widely documented and discussed mediation effort has become the prototype for a variety of similar efforts by the Institute for Environmental Mediation and other emerging organizations.[1]

Since 1973, mediators with the Institute have discussed the application of mediation with disputing parties in scores of environmental-economic conflicts. About two dozen complex disputes have been successfully resolved. And, equally important, the Institute is presently exploring with state, federal, and regional governmental agencies ways in which mediation may be made available in a more regularized manner.

Environmental mediation has evolved from an interesting and novel concept to an accepted but often misunderstood part of the environmental decision-making process. Successful efforts to resolve long-standing disputes make good copy; the notion of solving problems to everyone's relative satisfaction is appealing. There is a reservoir of persons acting as consultants in the field of public involvement who see mediation as a possible new vocation. It is hardly surprising, then, that the bandwagon has attracted a large and diverse group of riders. This popularity has been accompanied by claims for mediation and suggested applications of the process that appear to be beyond reasonable expectations, based on experience with the mediation process in other contexts.

Intervention processes

Mediation, a particular approach to conflict resolution used for centuries in international relations and extensively for the past five decades in labor disputes, has become a buzz word used to describe a bewildering array of conflict-intervention processes and styles. A danger we now face is that the overselling of the process and its misapplication by inexperienced intervenors anxious to enter the field will result in costly failures that could broadly discredit the mediation process. This concern has led the Institute for Environmental Mediation to be particularly careful that potential parties to the negotiation-mediation process have a clear understanding of what the process entails, where it is most effective, and what it can reasonably be expected to achieve.

There are a variety of intervenors presently active in environmental-economic disputes, all of whom claim three essential characteristics:

- They are impartial or "neutral" as to the specific disposition of the issues in dispute.
- Their focus and expertise relate to process rather than to scientific or technical knowledge.
- The intervention process that they practice seeks to achieve mutually derived and mutually acceptable outcomes.

However, it has also been found that there are at least three different types of intervention processes being practiced.[2] *Consensus-building* is a

problem-solving approach grounded in small-group process that empha-
sizes the common interests of disputants in jointly defining and solving
problems. *Mediation* is an approach adapted from labor relations that
seeks to identify—through negotiation—the limited but real cooperative
actions possible for mutually interdependent parties having different long-
term interests and objectives. *Policy dialogues* are a problem-solving and
negotiation approach developed on a pragmatic, ad hoc basis by leaders
of environmental groups and representatives of industry. Dialogues are
intended to identify joint positions that can be advocated in the public
policy arena by interest groups that are normally opposed to one another.

While their practitioners may share the three essential characteristics
outlined, each process differs substantially in the basic assumptions that
underlie its development, the means by which the services of the intervenor are made available, the specific activities of the intervenors, and the
process outcomes that can be anticipated. It is critical that the parties and
the intervenor have a clear and consistent understanding of the process
and their relative roles and responsibilities if the always difficult problem
of settling their differences is to proceed to a successful conclusion.

The mediation process

The term mediation, used in its strictest sense, is nothing more or less
than a device for facilitating the negotiation process; negotiations can and
do occur without a mediator, but mediation can never occur in the absence
of negotiation. The Institute for Environmental Mediation uses the following definition when discussing the mediation process: "Mediation is a
voluntary process in which those involved in a dispute jointly explore and
reconcile their differences. The mediator has no authority to impose a
settlement. His or her strength lies in the ability to assist the parties in
settling their own differences. The mediated dispute is settled when the
parties themselves reach what they consider to be a workable solution."

A number of important considerations are implicit in this definition:
(1) Involvement of the parties in the mediation process and their acceptance of the mediator(s) are voluntary. (2) The parties will jointly explore
and debate the issues, both in joint sessions and in caucuses of one or
more of the parties with the mediator. (3) The mediator has no authority
to impose settlement. (4) The mediator facilitates the negotiation process
by assisting the parties to reach a settlement acceptable to them. (5) An
agreement requires the support of all the parties: it is a consensus, not a
majority decision. (6) The mediator shares with the parties the responsibility of ensuring that any agreement reached represents a viable solution

that is technically, financially, and politically feasible to implement.

In environmental-economic disputes the parties are seldom able to proceed directly to negotiation of the issues dividing them. They must first reach an understanding of the framework within which they will negotiate, have some assurance of the good-faith intent of all involved to reach a mutually successful conclusion through accommodation, and have confidence in the skills, objectivity, and independence of the mediator(s).

To mediate or not?

To assist the parties and the mediator in making a determination of when and whether to use the mediation process, the Institute suggests eight questions that should be explicitly and mutually addressed:[3]

1. Are all parties who have a stake in the outcome of the negotiations represented? Is any party excluded that could prevent an agreement from being carried out?
2. Have all of the parties reached general agreement on the scope of the issues being addressed?
3. Are the negotiators for each party able to speak for their constituency? Is there a reason to believe that, if the negotiators reach an agreement, the agreement will be honored by the groups they represent?
4. Have the immediate parties and the eventual decision makers committed themselves to a good-faith effort to reach a consensual agreement?
5. Has a realistic deadline been set for the negotiations?
6. Are there reasonable assurances that affected governmental agencies will cooperate in carrying out an agreement if one is reached?
7. Does the mediator operate from a base that is independent of both the immediate parties and the decision makers with jurisdiction over the dispute?
8. Do all parties involved trust the mediator to carry messages, when appropriate, and to honor confidential remarks?

Clearly, it is impossible for either the parties or the mediator to determine the answers to all of these questions at the outset. Therefore, it is appropriate and necessary that there be extensive exploratory discussions between and among the parties and the mediator before any commitment is made to negotiate the issues.

These discussions should culminate in a clear and mutual understanding of such matters as the parties to be involved; the specific and, perhaps, differing roles of private groups and organizations, government agencies, and elected officials; the scope of the issues to be addressed; elected deadlines for showing progress and achieving agreement; sponsorship and commitments necessary to help ensure implementation; and the projected form any agreement that is reached will take—for example, written contract, proposed legislation, signed joint recommendations. Agreement on at least these items should be achieved before moving to a formal discussion of the issues if unnecessary misunderstandings are to be avoided during the difficult negotiation phase.

Mediation successes

Where these necessary conditions have been met, mediation can be a powerful tool in reconciling even the most difficult situations. During the first ten months of 1981, for example, mediators from the Institute helped conflicting parties reach agreements in five diverse disputes located in four western states.

The Briones Park dispute. A long-standing dispute in northern California over access to and development of a major regional park was settled when negotiators representing the regional park district, local governments, neighborhoods most directly affected by the type and location of park development, and user interests reached agreement on a mutually acceptable development plan.

The Queets Sewer Lagoon dispute. A dispute in Washington state between an Indian tribe, local government, private interests, and federal agencies over arrangements for the protection of a sewage treatment facility that was threatened with imminent destruction by a changing river course. The issue was settled after a relatively brief period of intensive and difficult negotiations.

The Homestake Pitch Mine dispute. In Colorado the Homestake Corporation and seven environmental organizations and coalitions reached an agreement that settled their differences over the operation and reclamation of an open pit uranium mine in the Gunnison National Forest. State and federal agencies concurred with the agreement.[4]

The CREST dispute. In Oregon, Institute mediators assisted two towns, a county, a port authority, four state agencies, and four federal agencies in reaching a mutually acceptable plan for the location, nature, and timing of development, protection, and mitigation for loss of habitat in the estuary of the Columbia River. For years the controversy had pitted development interests against conservation interests.[5]

The Riverside solid waste siting dispute. Institute mediators helped representatives of ten local organizations reach agreement on a package of recommendations to submit to the Riverside County, California, board of supervisors. The agreement recommends a replacement site for two landfills scheduled to close, steps for strengthening county management of solid waste disposal, and programs to recover valuable resources and reduce the need for landfill space. The effort was sponsored by the California State Solid Waste Management Board.[6]

Misperceptions about mediation

There are a variety of widespread misconceptions and misperceptions regarding the mediation process and its application. Dealing with these misunderstandings may be as important as definitions and descriptions in providing real insights into how the process works.

Mediation can resolve differences. Mediation does not lead to a resolution of the basic differences that separate the parties in conflict. Rather, in situations where none of the parties perceives that it is able to gain its goals unilaterally, mediation can help the parties agree on how to make the accommodations that will enable them to coexist despite their continued differences. Labor and management, for example, have never reconciled their basic disagreement over the share of profits that should go to labor versus capital. As the Homestake Pitch Mine dispute demonstrates, environmental coalitions may negotiate standards for revegetation, site reclamation, and water quality maintenance of an open pit mine when they realize it cannot be completely blocked, even though they would never agree that the mine is desirable or even necessary.

A mediated agreement, therefore, cannot be construed as an indication that two or more conflicting parties have resolved their divergent priorities or reconciled their differing perceptions. Rather, it is an indication that, in the immediate situation that confronts them, they have found a solution upon which they are able to agree despite their basic differences. Those who would espouse mediation as a means by which society can forge a new consensus, making future conflicts unnecessary, are doomed to failure and frustration. Mediation can best be seen as a process for settling disputes, not for resolving basic differences.

Mediation can avoid conflict. Conflicts are *settled* through the mediation process. Until the conflict emerges and the parties are confronted with limits to their unilateral options and mutually desire to find some settlement of specific issues, there is no basis for negotiation. It is the conflict that provides the awareness of the problem, the acceptance of the need to find other than unilateral solutions, and even the leadership necessary to represent often ad hoc interest groups. Avoiding the conflict not only makes negotiation unlikely in the short run but may also serve to delay and make more painful the ultimate confrontation.

Mediation is nonadversarial conflict resolution. Since it requires the presence of a conflict, mediation is decidedly not nonadversarial. Indeed, it has been the experience of mediators at the Institute that unless the parties remain mindful of their conflicting interests, they are unlikely to strike a bargain that is viable when faced with the difficult realities of implementation; both the parties and their agreements will be repudiated by their constituents. Established, confident adversaries aware of their own interests make the best negotiators and work out the best agreements.

Mediation is an alternative to litigation. Although mediation is sometimes touted as an alternative to litigation, this claim is intended to appeal to those who see proposed projects frustrated by interminable court delays. It is a much less appealing claim to citizen and environmental organizations who oppose such projects and who see the courts as a critical line of defense. Actual or threatened litigation is often a necessary prerequisite to the willingness of a party proposing some action to negotiate; it is the source of power and influence that brings the parties to the table and to mediation.

Rather than being an alternative to the courts, mediation often relies on them for its viability. While the parties to a conflict may at some point choose to negotiate in lieu of initiating or continuing court action, mediation cannot reasonably be expected to supplant or negate the need for litigation until such time as protesting constituencies are provided with some other basis for their power and influence.

Successful mediation is where the negotiators learn to like, trust, and agree with each other. Statements such as this are usually based on a misunderstanding not only of the mediation process but of the nature of environmental-economic conflicts. Such disputes typically involve a number of groups and organizations, many with large constituencies. The purpose of mediation is to assist representatives of these various organizations and interest groups in formulating a mutually acceptable agreement that will be ratified by their constituents. Where the focus is primarily on the relationships and understandings between negotiators who are at the table, there is a danger that they will begin to like, trust, and understand each other to the point where they forget that their constituents have not had the benefit of the same intensive and cooperative interaction. Solutions that are not politically viable may gain credence in the rarefied atmosphere of cooperative discussions, but they may later be repudiated as a "sellout" by constituents. Some intervention processes have their roots in small group methodologies or the settlement of interpersonal disputes where all of the actors can be gathered around the table and where the intervenor and participants need not be concerned with the need for ratification.

The mediation process works best where the parties have sufficient mutual trust to negotiate in good faith, mixed with a continued realization that agreement among the negotiators is only the beginning. Indeed, for the negotiators to reach an agreement that one or more of the parties' constituents fails to ratify will only exacerbate the conflict. Successful mediation agreements can be concluded even when the interactions merely confirm the breadth of the basic disagreements between the parties.

Mediation is where everyone sits around a big table and negotiates. In mediation the most critical action—orchestrated by the mediator—often occurs away from the table. As has already been outlined, a critical role played by the mediator in environmental conflicts is creating the framework for negotiations: this is likely to take at least as long as the actual negotiation of the issues. During the negotiations per se, the mediator is likely to spend the majority of his or her time in individual caucuses with one group or subgroups of the parties, helping them to explore positions and formulate alternatives, advising on the mediation process, carrying messages, and "trying out" offers on behalf of the parties. Indeed, if the mediator is effective in this part of the task, his or her role in the joint meeting may be minimal. (In one recent joint negotiation, the mediation team spoke less than a hundred words—including a check of whether anyone wanted coffee—during a 3½-hour meeting.)

The mediator should have technical expertise in the issues. It has been the experience of the Institute that where a mediator has personal expertise regarding the issues in a dispute, he or she may be less effective. First, experts have a tendency to rely on their own assumptions and values rather than allowing the parties to teach them about the dispute. Second, there is an inclination to filter information and communication based on their independent assessment of the facts. Third, the discussions tend to move away from the underlying sets of values and perceptions that led to the dispute and end up focusing on technical concerns. This can result in solutions that are technically appropriate yet do not represent a real accommodation of the more basic value differences.

Finally, the greater the technical expertise of the mediator in a subject area, the more the agreement is likely to be a result of the mediator's "leading" the parties, and the less committed the parties will be to the difficult task of implementing the agreement. However, the mediator does have a responsibility to become sufficiently conversant with the issues in dispute and the legislative, legal, and organizational environment within which they occur to be able to communicate effectively with the parties and to assist them in devising viable solutions.

Where the parties to conflict are aware of these common misperceptions and misconceptions of the mediation process, it can provide an additional basis for judging both the appropriateness of the process and the qualifications of the mediator.

Future directions

Our experience to date suggests that mediation can play a role in settling many environmental-economic disputes. However, a number of specific steps must first be taken if mediation is to evolve from an interesting idea to a more broadly available option. (While it is possible to discuss these required actions, this chapter does not argue that experience with the mediation process in environmental conflicts yet justifies a full-fledged national commitment. Rather, continued experiments with more formal application of the process in specific issue areas may be the prudent course.)

Encouraging negotiated solutions. The reluctance of representatives of government agencies to become involved with mediation efforts—as they are apprehensive about a lack of support at higher levels in their agency—is an important factor impeding the development of environmental mediation. A clear statement of public policy that encourages mutual solutions based on the interaction of public and private parties will, at some point, be necessary.

Public policy support for negotiations between labor and management was embodied in executive initiatives and national legislation during the 1930s. In the environmental arena such support might be made clear and effective by such actions as providing special alternatives and funding for mitigation for loss of habitat, where mutual agreement is achieved, between normally disputing interests, or by providing that such agreements "go to the front of the line" for further processing. Of course, to qualify, such agreements would have to fall within the bounds of established laws and regulations.

Establishing a viable power base for all parties. The negotiation-mediation process requires that all parties have sufficient power to influence the action of each other party. Government organizations and private corporations are endowed with such power or influence by our existing political-economic system. Citizen and environmental groups, however, often must develop their power resources on a situation-by-situation basis, through legal challenges and the delay and uncertainty they represent. For mediation to become more broadly and regularly applied, it may be necessary to develop less transitory sources of influence for protesting constituencies.

In the labor-management analogy this power was conferred by a combination of legitimizing the strike and establishing legislative requirements to bargain. In environmental-economic disputes one approach might be to require that government agencies calculate into their benefit-cost ratios the cost of delay in cases where they are unable to demonstrate the broad support of interest groups.

The problem of conferring "recognition". Recognition is often termed a "threshold issue": It frequently requires greater clout to enter the decision-making process than to influence it once entry has been achieved. Labor originally achieved recognition through such economic actions as strikes, boycotts, or even the physical takeover of production facilities. Today, recognition is conferred through representation elections. In environmental-economic disputes recognition is conferred by real or threatened court challenges or political action. The alternative is difficult to perceive.

It might be argued that labor-management history teaches that a more orderly route to the recognition of unions was achieved only after existing authorities realized that such recognition was inevitable. If the analogy holds, we may be approaching the stage in environmental-economic disputes where there is similar inability to avoid dealing with parties who oppose proposed projects. The best approach may lie in some combination of the political process, as applied in union representation elections, and the concept of "standing," as applied by the courts.

Identifying appropriate points for intervention. Most projects or proposals that become environmental disputes require a lengthy decision-making, permitting, and public involvement process. Typically legislation providing for mediation of labor-management conflicts identifies a point after extensive negotiations should have occurred but before the direct economic action is permitted. The mediation agency is informed of the status of the negotiations and may intervene. The intent is to avoid interfering with negotiations between the parties while recognizing the public interest in avoiding unnecessary disruptions.

Similarly, in environmental disputes it may be possible to identify points in the decision-making process where a mediator has an opportunity to confidentially discuss with the parties the current status of a dispute and possible alternatives for settling it. It may be possible to build into such a system a provision that particular actions—such as filing for administrative or court review—automatically trigger consideration of the use of a mediator. There are two critical factors that must be recognized here: first, mediation must avoid becoming just another hoop for the parties to jump through before they get down to serious consideration of their differences; second, an actual mediation effort, beyond initial discussions of the process and whether it is appropriate, must be kept voluntary.

Provision of mediation services. Here again, the labor-management analogy provides a useful point of departure. Virtually all mediation services are supported and/or provided by state or federal governments as a matter of public policy. Except in unusual circumstances, the parties do not directly pay for mediation services, either singly or jointly.

There are a number of reasons why a similar reality will operate in environmental-economic disputes, including: (1) the disparate nature of the conflicting parties and their differential ability to finance the cost of mediation services; (2) the absence of any preexisting relationship through which the parties could agree to share the cost of mediation services; and (3) the inordinate amount of time that a mediator must routinely spend developing a possible negotiating relationship without any assurance that a particular dispute will, in fact, progress to negotiation of the issues.

Of paramount concern in the long-term provision of mediation services for environmental disputes is where such services should be located. Here the labor-management analogy suggests the need for some entity independent and insulated from operating departments and agencies. Unlike the labor-management sector, where disputes occur and services are provided at either the federal or state level, many environmental conflicts involve combinations of local, state, and federal concerns and agencies. For this reason the Institute has been particularly interested in exploring the use of regional and joint state-federal bodies as an appropriate location for environmental mediation services.

Realizing the potential

It is both possible and desirable to explore further these and other initiatives on an experimental basis in order to determine their viability further. It must be recognized, however, that unless such experiments proceed with the support of all those parties and interests involved in environmental-economic conflicts, they are unlikely to succeed.

The mediation process holds exciting potential for settling difficult environmental-economic conflicts. Where appropriately applied by capable mediators, it has resulted in innovative and mutually beneficial agreements. Where misapplied, it can exacerbate already thorny situations. The next few years will determine whether and how this potential will be realized.

Resolving environmental disputes: a decade of experience

Gail Bingham

Negotiation, mediation, consensus-building, policy dialogue—these and related approaches through which parties can resolve their differences voluntarily are becoming increasingly important in settling environmental disputes. *Resolving Environmental Disputes: A Decade of Experience* documents the development of these dispute resolution alternatives and assesses whether the results have met initial hopes and expectations. What are the different approaches to environmental dispute resolution? What have these approaches sought to achieve, and how successful have they been? What kinds of disputes have been resolved? Who have the parties to these disputes been? How much do these dispute resolution processes cost? How much time have cases taken to be resolved? What other lessons have been learned to date?

The book is intended for anyone interested in finding better ways of addressing controversial environmental issues. It is written particularly for the men and women in government agencies, private corporations, and public interest groups who are responsible for making decisions that affect the environment and who often find themselves in dispute.

As used in this chapter, the term *environmental dispute resolution* refers to a variety of approaches that allow the parties to meet face to face, with the assistance of a mediator, to reach a mutually acceptable resolution of the issues in dispute. Although there are differences among the approaches, all are voluntary processes that involve some form of consensus-building, joint problem-solving, or negotiation. Litigation, administrative procedures, and arbitration are not included in this definition because the objective in those processes is not a consensus among the parties.

The interest in alternative approaches for resolving environmental disputes seems to come largely from dissatisfaction with more traditional decision-making processes. Specific complaints about these processes are legion, but mostly they are related to the same problem—the frequent inability of traditional decision-making processes to deal satisfactorily with the real issues in dispute. When disputes are not adequately resolved, dissatisfied parties may attempt to prolong the dispute, hoping to change the outcome, using whatever means are available. In environmental disputes the parties often have many such opportunities—through administrative appeals, perhaps in several different regulatory agencies, through litigation, and through political action. The parties often also have the clout to use such opportunities, although the result may be only a stalemate.

Although environmental dispute resolution processes are often characterized as being alternatives to litigation—with the presumption that litigation is bad—in this chapter voluntary dispute resolution processes are viewed as additional tools that may or may not be more effective or more efficient under certain circumstances. In this view litigation and other traditional decision-making processes remain important options. Disputes over environmental issues are so varied that no single dispute resolution process is likely to be successful in all situations. Depending on the circumstances, the parties may prefer to litigate, to lobby for legislative change, to turn to an administrative agency, or to negotiate a voluntary resolution of the issues with one another. This is a complicated strategic decision that is, and should be, affected by the experiences and resources of the parties, as well as by their calculation of how well their interests will be served by different approaches.

The growth of the environmental dispute resolution field

In 1973 Daniel J. Evans, then governor of the state of Washington, invited mediators Gerald W. Cormick and Jane McCarthy to help settle a long-standing dispute over a proposed flood control dam on the Snoqualmie River. In the decade following that precedent-setting invitation, mediators and facilitators have been employed in over 160 environmental disputes in the United States. Compared to 1973, when only two individuals were beginning to develop a mediation practice for environmental disputes, there are now organizations and individuals in thirteen states, the District of Columbia, and Canada offering environmental dispute resolution services. Others, elsewhere, are attempting to establish a similar practice.

In addition, and relatively recently, the practice of environmental dispute resolution has grown beyond the resolution of disputes on a case-by-case basis to the institutionalization, by statute, of procedures for resolving environmental disputes. Statutes in Massachusetts, Rhode Island, Virginia, and Wisconsin authorize or even require negotiation of hazardous waste facility siting disputes. A statute in Virginia specifies procedures for negotiation and mediation of intergovernmental disputes triggered by annexation proposals; in mid-1984 the Pennsylvania legislature was considering a bill that would authorize mediation of any local land-use or zoning dispute.

The track record of the field has grown with time. At the end of 1977 nine disputes had been mediated. Another nine were mediated in 1978, and eighteen more were mediated in 1979. By mid-1984, mediators had been involved in over 160 disputes. Environmental dispute resolution organizations also provide services that are not reflected by the number of cases in which they have been involved. Many conduct training courses in the effective use of environmental dispute resolution techniques. All provide consultation and technical assistance to parties in disputes wishing to explore the feasibility of an alternative approach in a particular controversy. Other services offered include newsletters, conferences, and consulting to various organizations, particularly government agencies, wishing to develop an organizational capability for more effective dispute resolution.

Among the cases that comprise the cumulative track record of the environmental dispute resolution field, there is striking diversity. The primary issues involved in these cases fall into six broad categories. Some cases involve site-specific disputes over a particular project or plan; others involve disputes over questions of state or national environmental policy.

1. *Land use.* About seventy site-specific and sixteen policy-level land-use disputes have been resolved with the assistance of a mediator. They have involved neighborhood and housing issues, parks and recreation, preservation of agricultural land and other regional planning issues, facility siting, and transportation.

2. *Natural resource management and use of public lands.* Mediation has been used in twenty-nine site-specific and four policy-level controversies, involving fisheries resources, mining, timber management, and wilderness areas, among others.

3. *Water resources.* Among the sixteen site-specific cases and one policy-level case that involved water resources, the issues in dispute included water supply, water quality, flood protection, and the thermal effects of power plants.

4. *Energy.* In this area ten site-specific and four policy-level cases involved such issues as siting small-scale hydroelectric plants, conversion of power plant fuel from oil to coal, and geothermal development.

5. *Air quality.* Odor problems, national air quality legislation, and acid rain were the topics of six site-specific cases and seven policy dialogues.

6. *Toxics.* National policy on the regulation of chemicals, plans for removal of asbestos in schools, pesticide policy, and hazardous materials cleanup were among the issues discussed in five site-specific cases and eleven policy dialogues.

When people think of environmental disputes, they commonly think of cases in which environmental groups challenge proposals made by private industry. Most environmental dispute resolution cases do not fit that model, however. Many mediated environmental disputes have involved only public agencies. In others, citizen groups were engaged in disputes with their local government, or a mix of government agencies were in dispute with one another and a variety of interest groups.

- Environmental groups were at the negotiating table in only 33 percent of the site-specific cases documented by the Conservation Foundation.
- Private corporations also were involved in 33 percent of the cases studied.
- Surprisingly, environmental groups and private companies were involved in negotiations with each other in only 18 percent of the site-specific cases studied.
- Federal and state agencies and units of local government were involved in 81 percent of the cases.
- Local citizen groups were involved in 44 percent of the cases.

For the most part, environmental dispute resolution processes have been used on an ad hoc basis. Recently, however, efforts to encourage and routinize the practice have emerged. Negotiation and mediation procedures have been written into statutes governing hazardous waste siting, annexation, and coastal zone management issues. The Administrative Conference of the United States (ACUS) adopted a resolution in 1982 recommending that federal regulatory agencies incorporate negotiation into the rule-making process under certain circumstances, and three federal agencies have experimented with negotiated rule-making. In 1984 ACUS recommended that greater use of negotiation be made in the cleanup of abandoned toxic waste sites. In New Jersey the state supreme court commissioned a special study and is now sponsoring an experimental effort to explore ways in which the courts can encourage the voluntary resolution of environmental issues, among others, that frequently come before the courts in that state. In addition, the National Institute for Dispute Resolution announced support in mid-1984 for statewide offices of dispute resolution in four pilot states—Massachusetts, New Jersey, Wisconsin, and Alaska.

How successful have environmental dispute resolution processes been?

Although people's strategies for resolving environmental disputes may vary depending on their views about social conflict and the characteristics of the dispute itself, individuals and groups care about similar factors.

They care about the outcome and the extent to which it satisfies the real issues in dispute, as they see them. They care about the process—how much they will be able to influence a decision, the fairness of the process, and its efficiency. And, to the degree that the parties have or wish to have a continuing relationship, they care about the quality of that relationship and their ability to communicate with one another.

An assumption inherent in environmental dispute resolution alternatives is that the parties are good judges of what the real issues are and whether they are resolved adequately. Another is that the voluntary nature of the process, both in deciding whether to participate and whether to concur in an agreement, allows the parties to exercise their judgment freely. In theory, therefore, environmental dispute resolution processes allow broader attention to the real issues in dispute because the parties set the agenda and because they decide what the terms of the agreement will be. Thus, the first and most simple measure of how successful these processes have been in resolving the issues is how often agreements have been reached.

A test of how well the agreements reached have resolved the real issues in dispute is whether the parties supported the agreement through the implementation process. It is during implementation that other problems with the adequacy of a dispute resolution process may emerge. Were all the parties with a stake in the issues involved? If not, an agreement may still have been reached, but it may not have addressed the issues of concern to unrepresented parties. These parties may take action to block the implementation of the agreement. Does the agreement satisfy community norms of fairness? Were the parties well informed during the process so that the agreement is technically sound? Was a mechanism established for dealing with unanticipated events after the agreement was reached and the negotiations terminated? How were the parties able to handle disputes that may have arisen during the implementation process?

Intangible factors are also likely to be important to parties in dispute. Sometimes, as part of reaching an agreement, and sometimes in spite of not reaching an agreement, the participants report that the process itself was valuable. They may feel that they have gained valuable insights into their opposition's point of view on the issues and have created more open lines of communication. For example, in one policy dialogue sponsored by the Conservation Foundation, the parties reported more than a dozen instances in which one or another of them contacted others on issues outside the scope of the dialogue group's discussions. They had not done so in the past, although many had been involved in these issues for many years. Even when parties have decided not to participate in mediated negotiations, studies have shown that in many cases they believe that the contacts by the mediator have helped them to clarify the issues and to better understand the dynamics of the dispute, thus helping them to deal with one another more effectively through more traditional decision-making processes.

In 133 of the 162 cases documented by the Conservation Foundation the parties' objectives were to reach agreement with one another. Of these cases, one hundred involved site-specific issues and thirty-three involved policy issues. The success with which the parties were able to reach agreement is shown in table 3.1. Overall, agreements were reached in 78 percent of the cases. Little difference between site-specific and policy-level disputes was evident in the cases examined. The parties were successful in reaching agreement in 79 percent of the site-specific cases and in 75 percent of the policy dialogues. When the parties at the table had the authority to make and to implement their agreements, they were able to reach an agreement in 82 percent of the cases. When the agreements took the form of recommendations to a decision-making body that did not participate directly in the negotiations, the parties reached agreement 74 percent of the time.

Reaching an agreement does not mean that it sticks. The problem with litigation and administrative proceedings usually is not that decisions are not reached, but that these decisions are frequently appealed. In theory, if the parties themselves have voluntarily agreed to a decision, they are more likely to be satisfied with it. Thus, agreements reached through an environmental dispute resolution process should be more likely to be implemented. How well is this claim borne out in practice? For site-specific disputes, of those cases in which agreements were reached and implementation results

Table 3.1   Success in reaching agreements

		Site-specific dispute		Policy-level dispute	
		Object of the process			
	All cases	To reach a decision	To agree on a recommendation	To reach a decision	To agree on a recommendation
Agreement	78% (104)	81% (52)	75% (27)	100% (4)	72% (21)
No agreement	22% (29)	19% (12)	25% (9)	0% —	28% (8)
Total	100% (133)	100% (64)	100% (36)	100% (4)	100% (29)

are known, the agreements were fully implemented in 80 percent of the cases, partially implemented in 13 percent, and not implemented in 7 percent. There has been more difficulty in implementing the results of policy dialogues than in implementing agreements reached in site-specific disputes. Of the policy dialogues in which agreements were reached and implementation results are known, agreements were fully implemented in 41 percent of the cases studied, partially implemented in 18 percent, and not implemented in 41 percent.

What affects the likelihood of success?

There are few absolutes in predicting whether parties involved in any specific dispute will be successful in reaching agreement, or whether they will be successful in implementing an agreement if they reach one. There are several principles, however, that appear to increase the likelihood of success. Some of these principles are based on qualitative observations, others are backed up by more quantitative analysis, but all remain hypotheses that will require further study.

The parties must have some incentive to negotiate an agreement with one another. The willingness of all parties to a dispute to participate is a major factor in the success of a voluntary dispute resolution process, if one expects an agreement reached to be both fair and stable. But the parties are unlikely to participate, let alone agree to a settlement, if they can achieve more of what they want in another way. However, it is difficult to assess the importance of such incentives, because mediators generally do not convene negotiations unless the parties are at least somewhat interested in attempting to resolve the dispute.

The way the negotiation or consensus-building process is conducted also appears to be an important factor in whether agreements will be reached. Mediators often refer to the difference between "interest-based" negotiation as opposed to "positional" bargaining in discussing what makes negotiations effective. In particular, the ability (and willingness) of the parties to identify the interests that underlie one another's positions, and to invent new alternatives that satisfy these interests, helps enormously in resolving disputes. At times, however, the parties can find no common ground regardless of their skill in negotiating with one another, even if they had the assistance of a mediator. Again, it is difficult to evaluate how well a negotiation or consensus-building process is conducted.

The likelihood of success is less clearly affected by the number of parties involved in the dispute, the issues themselves, or the presence of a deadline. There is no evidence that a larger number of parties makes reaching agreement more difficult. In fact, the average number of parties for cases in which the parties failed to reach an agreement was lower than the average number of parties in cases in which agreements were reached. Also, the evidence does not show that the issues in dispute have a significant effect. More study, done perhaps at a more detailed level, may show different results. The influence that the kind of issue has on the likelihood of success also may be linked to other factors such as whether the particular dispute has precedent-setting implications. Finally, it appears that the presence of a deadline does not affect the likelihood of reaching an agreement.

The most significant factor in the likelihood of success in implementing agreement appears to be whether those with the authority to implement the decision participated directly in the process. When those with the authority to implement decisions were directly involved, the implementation rate was 85 percent; when they were not, only 67 percent of the agreements reached were fully implemented. Agreements were not implemented in about 7 percent of the cases in both categories. The difference in the implementation results is that when those with the authority to implement the recommendations were not at the table, the terms of the agreement were more likely to be modified. Agreements were partially implemented in 27 percent of the cases in which those with the authority to implement the agreements were not at the table as compared with 7 percent of the cases in which those at the table had the authority to implement their agreements.

Few factors are absolute preconditions for success. In many situations the combined positive effect of some factors can offset potentially negative factors. Also, many factors may be subject to modification by the parties and the mediator before and during the dispute resolution process. If no deadline exists, the parties may be able to create one. If one side does not have sufficient incentives to negotiate, another may raise the ante with assurances about implementation, mitigation, or compensation offers contingent on an agreement, or with reminders of ways the dispute could be escalated. If there are an overwhelming number of parties, coalitions may be possible. If those with power to implement the agreement are not direct participants in the process, the mediator may be able to provide an appropriate link between the parties and the eventual decision maker.

The most important reason for a relatively high success rate in dispute resolution efforts probably is that the mediators conducted dispute assessments at the beginning of each case as a first step in helping the parties decide whether to proceed with a voluntary dispute resolution process and, if so, what the nature or the ground rules of the process should be.

Environmental disputes are so varied that different forms of assistance will be appropriate in different cases, depending on the circumstances and the wishes of the parties. Mediators spend time discussing the possibility of a voluntary dispute resolution process with each of the parties, identifying and bringing to the parties' attention those conditions that may make it difficult to resolve the dispute, and helping the parties decide how they wish to proceed. Logically, this initial screening, if done well, will improve the likelihood that, once an informed decision has been made to negotiate, the parties will be successful in reaching an agreement. Until comparable samples of negotiated settlements without the assistance of mediators are available, however, this will remain a hypothesis.

Are environmental dispute resolution processes really cheaper and faster than litigation?

Perhaps the single most common assertion made about environmental dispute resolution processes—indeed, about alternative dispute resolution processes generally—is that they are cheaper and faster than litigation. There has been little empirical evidence to support this assertion, however. Actually, very little information exists about how long it takes either to mediate or to litigate environmental disputes. Further, there are several conceptual problems in making comparisons between environmental dispute resolution alternatives and litigation.

Most individuals and organizations involved in environmental disputes can cite at least one occasion in which the parties became so locked in a legal stalemate that there seemed to be no way out. These stories have helped build the case for the weakness in relying solely on litigation for settling disputes, but they also may have oversimplified the image both of litigation and of environmental dispute resolution alternatives. A lawsuit that goes to trial may take a very long time, but few lawsuits go to trial. Some mediated environmental disputes are not necessarily fast if the issues are complex. In addition, although mediators generally charge less than attorneys, this does not necessarily mean that one can be substituted for the other. It is also important to consider other costs associated with resolving disputes. The costs of preparing for negotiation, for example, may be as high or higher than the costs of preparing for some kinds of litigation, particularly for public interest groups.

A simple comparison of the costs of litigating a complex dispute that later was mediated, although striking, can be misleading. First, it is unrealistic in many situations to begin counting the costs of mediation at the time that parties agreed to negotiate if the previous period of contention, litigation, or clarification of relative power contributed to the parties' willingness to negotiate a voluntary settlement. A simple comparison of costs also leaves out a major part of the equation—the nature and quality of the outcome. A more efficient process may not be more desirable if it leads to significantly poorer decisions in the view of one or all of the parties. The other major conceptual problem in asking whether environmental dispute resolution processes are really cheaper and faster than litigation is the problem of finding comparable samples of cases.

Environmental disputes, on the average, do take longer to resolve through litigation than do civil suits generally, although the median durations of both are relatively short. Data compiled for the Conservation Foundation by the Federal Judicial Center show, for example, that the median number of months from filing to disposition of all civil cases in U.S. District Courts terminated in the twelve-month period ending 30 June 1983 was seven months, whereas for the same period the median duration of all environmental cases was ten months. For cases that went to trial, the median duration of civil suits generally was nineteen months; for environmental disputes, it was twenty-three months.

More interesting than the median duration of these lawsuits, however, is the range among the cases: 10 percent of all civil litigation in this sample took more than twenty-eight months from the time of filing to disposition; 10 percent of the environmental litigation took more than forty-two months. For those cases that went to trial, 10 percent of the environmental cases took longer than sixty-seven months—or over 5½ years—not counting any possible appeals to a higher court. It is likely, therefore, that it is the threat of protracted litigation, not the length of the standard case, that creates the popular conception that mediation is faster than litigation.

In documenting environmental dispute resolution cases, some information was available about how much time the dispute resolution process took. This information is not complete, but one can get some idea about the duration of cases. Not only is this information incomplete, it is definitely not comparable to the statistics about litigation given above. Keeping that in mind, the median duration of the environmental dispute resolution cases in this sample was between five and six months, and 10 percent of the cases took over eighteen months to resolve. Information about the costs of these cases is too sparse to report with any confidence.

Looking ahead to the next decade

During the next ten years it will be important to identify and to put into practice mechanisms that will encourage the use of environmental dispute resolution processes that will increase the likelihood that disputes will be resolved successfully, and that will protect the parties from potential abuses of these processes. To accomplish this without losing the flexibility that is an inherent part of the strength of voluntary dispute resolution processes will be a challenge. In addition, several important questions remain unanswered. How will the services of mediators be funded? Can citizen groups and public interest organizations afford to use these processes? To whom are mediators accountable, to whom should they be accountable, and how should such accountability be maintained?

In the future the institutional mechanisms for implementing environmental dispute resolution processes are likely to include: a continuation of the role that independent mediators now play in responding to the needs of parties on an ad hoc basis; court-referred or court-linked programs; mediation services provided by local, state, or federal agencies; and the incorporation of voluntary dispute resolution procedures into state or federal statutes. These options are not mutually exclusive, but the choices do have important implications with respect to who pays the mediator, to how these processes become more widely available, to the flexibility of the approach, to the accountability of the mediator, and, ultimately, to how successful voluntary dispute resolution processes will be as an innovation in public decision making for environmental issues.

During the first decade in which mediators have helped parties to environmental disputes resolve issues directly with one another, the mediators' services have been paid for principally by foundation grants. Corporate donations, government contracts, in-kind support from citizen groups and public interest organizations, and fees have made up the rest. For the most part, however, the mediators' services have been free of charge to the parties. The question of how these services will continue to be paid is pressing. Foundation officials and others in the field raise a legitimate question: has this first decade of experience established the value of mediation services sufficiently that someone, the government or the parties themselves, is willing to pay for them? The data compiled by the Conservation Foundation begin to provide a basis for making such an evaluation. In the years to come, additional case experience along with the addition of institutional mechanisms to encourage the resolution of environmental disputes will create a framework for a more detailed assessment of environmental dispute resolution processes.

Special Area Management at Estuarine Reserves

John R. Clark and Scott T. McCreary

The national estuarine reserve program, established by the Coastal Zone Management Act, is designed to preserve a number of representative estuarine types for scientific research and education. Adjoining land-use activity often threatens to disturb and degrade estuarine areas designated by the program. As a result, special area management processes have evolved at several estuarine sanctuaries to ensure that these areas can be maintained at near baseline conditions. An array of management tools—including strict local regulation, watershed repair, land acquisition by private conservation groups, and wetland restoration—complement state acquisition in the sanctuaries at Elkhorn Slough, California, Apalachicola Bay, Florida, and Tijuana Estuary, California. These tools are implemented by state and local resource managers, usually with bargaining and negotiation among other key actors.

After many years of debate, Congress passed the Coastal Zone Management Act in October 1972 (Public Law 92-583), thereby authorizing a new federal role in land preservation. This role enabled the Department of Commerce "to grant funds to coastal states for planning, land purchase, and interim management of Estuarine Sanctuaries" as defined in section 315 of the act.

In creating the National Estuarine Sanctuary Program, Congress sought to preserve certain estuaries at near "baseline" ecological conditions for scientific study. The success of this "preserve for science" initiative has varied greatly among the seventeen sanctuaries so far established. Some

*John Clark was on sabbatical leave from the Conservation Foundation when he prepared this chapter. His research was conducted in part with financial assistance from the Washington Sea Grant program under grant No. NA81AA-000-30 from the National Oceanic and Atmospheric Administration. Scott McCreary was program manager with the Coastal Conservancy of the state of California when he prepared this chapter. Federal legislation reauthorizing the Coastal Zone Management Act enacted on 7 April 1986 renamed the National Estuarine Sanctuary System as the National Estuarine Research Reserve System. The three major estuarine areas examined in this chapter—Elkhorn Slough, Apalachicola, and Tijuana River—while identified in the text by their former status as national estuarine sanctuaries, are now officially referred to as national estuarine reserves.

are functioning estuarine field laboratories, while others have attracted little scientific interest. But the process of creating these sanctuaries has provoked some imaginative techniques for special area management. These initiatives are the subject of this chapter. Particular attention is given to the following federally designated national estuarine sanctuaries: Apalachicola River and Bay, in the Florida Panhandle; Elkhorn Slough, in central California; and Tijuana River Estuary, in southern California near the international border with Mexico.

Estuaries as special needs

The term "estuary" means a protected, or sheltered, shallow coastal water body that has a free connection to the sea and has waters that are diluted by runoff from the land but are still salty (greater than 0.5 parts per thousand salinity, the threshold of human taste). Thus, estuaries serve as mixing basins where ocean water is mixed with freshwater from rivers.[1]

Following this definition, Great South Bay (New York) would be classified as an estuary but Long Island Sound would not; Mission Bay (San Diego) would be classified as an estuary but Puget Sound would not. Such huge systems as Chesapeake Bay and San Francisco Bay are sometimes classified as estuaries, but, from a management point of view, either one would be more usefully considered to be a composite of the smaller estuaries of the bay that are associated with specific river entrances. In its generic "National Estuarine Pollution Study," the Department of Interior identified 881 different estuarine systems along the U.S. coastline.[2] In a 1980 study on estuary management the senior author identified 140 estuaries as being of "current high National interest."[3]

Coastal bays and other estuary types are the richest of coastal waters. They not only produce an abundance of fish and shellfish but also serve special needs of the migratory nearshore and oceanic species that require a shallow protected habitat for breeding or as sanctuary for their young. The wetlands—marshes and swamps—that border estuaries provide habitat and food for estuarine life as well as cleanse the water, stabilize the shore, and buffer coasts from impacts of flooding. Also vital to ecologic balance are the tide flats, oyster bars, and submerged grass beds on estuary floors.

Because of their high species diversity and habitat value, healthy estuarine ecosystems have special importance for scientific research and nature education. However, estuaries' resource-carrying capacities can be reduced when functioning wetlands, salt marshes, grass beds, reefs, and other vital areas of the basin floor are seriously altered or degraded. Carrying capacity also suffers when sediments accumulate on the bottom of the basin, causing shoaling and lowered water quality. Special management attention may therefore be needed to preserve estuaries' important resource values.

The federal catalyst

The coastal zone management initiative recognizes that coastal resource management has to embrace land and water issues jointly and concurrently. It is clear that land, or "dryside," developments can have a strong effect on water, or "wetside" resources. The thorniest issues in coastal management have been those of controlling impacts from the dryside. These include industrial pollution, sewage discharge, conversion of wetlands to developable real estate, obstruction of water circulation by causeway construction or marinas, excessive sedimentation caused by watershed development, and diversion of freshwater inflow. One of the primary goals of the Coastal Management Act was to bring dryside land development under control through a joint land-use regulatory undertaking with the states.

While the coastal zone management program was thought to have a good potential for success in dryside controls, neither Congress nor any of the outside proponents — for example, the Woods Hole Coastal Zone Workshop[4] and the National Estuary Study[5] — believed that adequate protection for *research estuaries* could be guaranteed by regulation. That is why Congress decided to create a special estuarine sanctuary program.

Under this program the National Oceanic and Atmospheric Administration (NOAA) — the administrator of the CZMA — offered matching grants to states for planning, acquisition, and the first five years of managing the approved sanctuaries. NOAA also offers matching grants to fund research in estuarine sanctuaries. NOAA set up standards to ensure that the sanctuaries would be representative of the ecological variety of estuaries by classifying the U.S. coastline into biogeographical zones and allowing one sanctuary per zone. Since most zones embraced several states, this set up some competition between states for the sanctuary to be approved for a particular biogeographic zone.

The primary purpose of the National Estuarine Sanctuary Program was to forestall ecological degradation of certain designated estuaries.[6] This program would hold a representative sample of estuaries and associated islands or upland areas at near "baseline" conditions and thereby encourage long-term scientific research where natural variables predominated over development-linked variables. Specifically it would set aside estuarine areas "to serve as natural field laboratories in which to study and gather data on the natural and human processes occurring within the estuaries of the coastal zone."[7]

To accomplish this goal, Congress reasoned, it was necessary, through purchase, to gain proprietary control over some of the dryland and transition areas immediately adjacent to the selected estuaries to prevent pollution from unregulated land runoff (silt and chemicals) and physical disruption of ecologically essential fringing wetlands. In authorizing funds for such purchases, Congress set in motion several state-operated programs that started with simple combinations of land purchase (fee simple) and water quality protection (regulatory) but have since progressed to include the creative techniques for coupled land and water area protection that are discussed in this chapter.

Estuary identification and selection process

The process for identification of candidate sites for federal estuarine sanctuaries normally involves three steps: (1) federal criteria are set by NOAA; (2) candidate areas are nominated by individual states; and (3) NOAA selects from the nominations. Throughout this process, however, the presence or absence of local political support and active participation of the local scientific community plays an important part in the success or failure of a proposed site.

In the first stage—drawing up federal criteria—NOAA was free to establish a system for identification and selection of sanctuaries according to a congressional mandate that it must "distribute its funds to those sanctuary proposals that represent major types of estuarine systems and reflect regional differentiation and a variety of ecosystems so as to cover all significant natural variations."[8]

In its guidelines NOAA defined a qualified estuarine sanctuary as "an area which may include all or the key land and water portion of an estuary and adjacent transitional areas and uplands, constituting to the extent feasible a natural unit, set aside as a natural field laboratory to provide long-term opportunities for research, education and interpretation on the ecological relationships within the area."[9]

To provide a framework for "regional differentiation," NOAA also chose the biogeographic classification developed by the pacesetting Woods Hole Coastal Zone Workshop (May 1972).[10] This classification divided the U.S. coastline into eleven zones. (Table 4.1 displays these eleven biogeographic zones and important subgroupings.) NOAA guidelines did not directly address the goal that a "variety of ecosystems" be represented by the designated sanctuary sites. The federal guidelines did indicate, however, that priority should be given to selection of areas with high habitat and

Table 4.1   The eleven major estuarine sanctuary biogeographic classifications (with important subgroups).

ACADIAN
 1. Northern Gulf of Maine (Eastport to the Sheepscot River)
 2. Southern Gulf of Maine (Sheepscot River to Cape Cod)

VIRGINIAN
 3. Southern New England (Cape Cod to Sandy Hook)
 4. Middle Atlantic (Sandy Hook to Cape Hatteras)
 5. Chesapeake Bay

CAROLINIAN
 6. Northern Carolinas (Cape Hatteras to Santee River)
 7. South Atlantic (Santee River to St. John's River)
 8. East Florida (St. John's River to Cape Canaveral)

WEST INDIAN
 9. Caribbean (Cape Canaveral to Ft. Jefferson and south)
10. West Florida (Ft. Jefferson to Cedar Key)

LOUISIANIAN
11. Panhandle Coast (Cedar Key to Mobile Bay)
12. Mississippi Delta (Mobile Bay to Galveston)
13. Western Gulf (Galveston to Mexican border)

CALIFORNIAN
14. Southern California (Tijuana River Estuary to Pt. Concepcion)
15. Central California (Pt. Concepcion to Cape Mendocino)
16. San Francisco Bay

COLUMBIAN
17. Middle Pacific (Cape Mendocino to the Columbia River)
18. Washington Coast (Columbia River to Vancouver Island)
19. Puget Sound

GREAT LAKES
20. Western Lakes (Superior, Michigan, Huron)
21. Eastern Lakes (Ontario, Erie)

FJORD
22. Southern Alaska (Prince of Wales Island to Cook Inlet)
23. Aleutian Islands (Cook Inlet to Bristol Bay)

SUB-ARCTIC
24. Northern Alaska (Bristol Bay to Demarcation Point)

INSULAR
25. Hawaiian Islands
26. Western Pacific Islands
27. Eastern Pacific Islands

species diversity. In other words, NOAA preferred nearly natural areas with a minimum of human disturbance.

At the second stage of selection the various states—following current NOAA criteria—devise their own systems for selection of candidate sanctuaries. The states that had a prior system for identifying or classifying estuaries as "critical areas" were highly influenced by the experience in their nomination procedure. All three of the cases examined in this chapter had been specially recognized by the states prior to and apart from the later estuarine sanctuary selection process. Apalachicola Bay had been identified as a Critical Area under Florida's Environmental Land and Water Management Act of 1972, as well as an "Estuarine Preserve" under an earlier Florida act. The two California sanctuaries (Elkhorn Slough and Tijuana River estuarine sanctuaries) were identified for special protection through a series of planning exercises. First, both were identified as priority areas for acquisition in a 1974 Department of Fish and Game report. Second, both were covered by policies of the state's 1975 Coastal Plan requiring that estuaries be specially protected. Third, both were covered by policies in the 1976 Coastal Act that require preservation of environmentally sensitive habitat areas and that the biological quality of coastal waters and estuaries be protected. Fourth, Tijuana estuary was designated for protection under the Local Coastal Program for the Tijuana River Valley, which had been approved and certified prior to sanctuary nomination. The scientific evidence and public support built up through these advance critical area designation programs was, in the authors' opinion, essential to their later successful establishment as estuarine sanctuaries.

At the third stage of selection, NOAA confirms that the state-selected candidate meets federal criteria and conforms to NOAA's program, implementation schedule, and budgeting strategy. If the preacquisition grant application is approved, NOAA provides a planning grant to formalize the sanctuary proposal. Normally the state's lead agency for coastal planning is the grant recipient and may either undertake the preacquisition planning or award a grant to another agency or subcontractor. The formal sanctuary proposal, at a minimum, has to specify boundaries, a management structure, and a program for research and education. In order to comply with the requirements of the estuarine program requirements and the National Environmental Policy Act (NEPA), these elements of the plan are incorporated in a draft Management Plan and Environmental Impact Statement (EIS). This document serves as a blueprint for sanctuary establishment, guiding future activities in land acquisition, facility development, and the management of research and education programs. The draft EIS is presented at a public hearing in the affected community, comments are received, and a final EIS is prepared to incorporate appropriate changes. The lead agency for the state prepares a land acquisition and development grant, as well as an application for first-year operation and maintenance funds, using the final EIS as the basis for the proposal. NOAA then awards grants for operations and land acquisition and development, along with a series of conditions to guide the expenditure of funds by the state.

Sanctuary designation and political processes

Regardless of the scientific merits of a candidate site, a significant degree of bargaining and negotiation among interest groups and agencies normally accompanies sanctuary establishment. Although nominations of sanctuaries described in this chapter were motivated by a sincere commitment to estuary protection, key actors bring a host of other goals to the process. As the three cases will demonstrate, there are generally three ingredients for successful nomination: (1) support by the scientific community; (2) support from some faction of local citizens; (3) support from legislators or agency directors who control allocation of matching funds and other key functions needed for sanctuary implementation. For these reasons the scientific endeavor of identifying natural research laboratories always becomes political in the end.

Since estuaries are fundamentally reserves for science, support by the scientific community is crucial to successful nominations. In this regard, scientists have a dual role as neutral investigators and important political actors. Scientists who support successful sanctuary nominations may gain important recognition that can in turn facilitate research funding and an opportunity to help guide future resource management.

Estuarine sanctuaries, like other types of protected areas, can be imagined as overlays placed on existing land- and water-use practices. Without local, grass-roots support, a sanctuary is unlikely to succeed. Usually local environmental groups support sanctuary designation. Some resource users (such as fishermen) may support a sanctuary proposal if they believe the sanctuary can forestall a threat to their livelihood (or oppose it if they fear that their traditional activities will be restricted). Depending on the attitude of the community, some local political leaders have enhanced their popularity by championing sanctuary designation (as in Apalachicola Bay) or calling it an unwanted government intrusion (as in Imperial Beach, next to Tijuana River Estuary).

Other local interests may oppose sanctuary designation for a variety of reasons: (1) objections by local officials to perceived loss of tax base; (2) fears by property owners that they will be forced to sell their property by coercive means; (3) knee-jerk reaction against intervention of state or federal governments (often encompassing the other concerns). Although these concerns are not always based on factual information, they must be addressed carefully. In the cases reviewed, local objections were addressed in several ways: offering concessions in acquisition and management policies, providing direct representation of local interests within the management structure, and incorporation of nonprofit organizations to represent local interests and complement the formal sanctuary management structure.

Case histories in estuarine protection

Estuarine protection efforts at Elkhorn Slough and Tijuana River, California, and Apalachicola, Florida, provide useful insights into the wide variety of preservation tools that have been employed in support of the estuarine sanctuary program. The case studies also illustrate, however, that unit resource management of the entire estuarine system—including associated uplands—is crucial to long-term success.

The primary question—how much land must be preserved to ensure that the estuarine sanctuary's condition will not be degraded—has been a difficult one to answer because quantitative data documenting cause and effect relations between land use and estuary conditions are scarce. As such, the determination of sanctuary management priorities has rested on the answer to several unique questions. For example, should most of the money be spent to purchase transitional wetlands to protect the "edge zone," the vital rim of the estuary? Or should priority be given to holding key parcels in the watershed in their natural state to decrease the potential for soil erosion and runoff pollution from farm chemicals? How much can local or state land-use regulation be depended upon to solve these problems? What level of local administrative capacity exists? How much compliance with land-use regulations and management policies can be expected? These questions should be addressed before preservation methods are selected.

In each of our example cases, sanctuary proponents have recognized the importance of managing estuarine sanctuaries as unit resource systems, consisting of four major ecological zones:

1. *Aquatic area:* water and the submerged bottomlands, to mean low water (mean lower low water in California)
2. *Transition area:* tideflats, wetlands, and floodlands (up to the 100-year flood boundary)
3. *Shorelands:* upland terrain of the entire watershed (down to the 100-year flood boundary)

4. *Drainage system:* the entire surface hydrologic network (creeks, perennial streams, ephemeral streams) that drains the watershed into the aquatic area

Unit resource management effectively couples the land side of the estuarine ecosystem together with the water side, thereby creating a unified zone of watershed, shoreline, and waterbody.[11] Implementing unified management has turned out to be a difficult undertaking, but some success is being experienced at each of the case sanctuaries.

The Elkhorn Slough National Estuarine Sanctuary

The Elkhorn Slough estuarine sanctuary is distinguished from others in the national system by the scope of the watershed protection and erosion control efforts under way in a local/state program for land-use management that embraces forty-eight square miles of shorelands, or 68 percent of the estuary's watershed. This watershed program may become a leading example of a functioning watershed regulatory program on behalf of estuarine ecosystem management in the United States. Rigorous enforcement of the program, which specifies target amounts of land disturbance in each of several subwatersheds, should arrest excessive rates of siltation and secure the slough as a stable and satisfactorily functioning system. Success in the watershed, together with resolution of remaining problems in the "transition zone" and "aquatic zone," would make Elkhorn Slough a prime example of estuarine unit resource management.

The Elkhorn Slough estuarine ecosystem is located on Monterey Bay, roughly midway between the cities of Santa Cruz and Monterey. The estuary curves west and south for approximately seven miles from its head, draining seventy square miles of hilly uplands and cultivated marine terraces. It opens into the Monterey Canyon offshore, through an inlet adjacent to Moss Landing, a small, maritime-oriented community (see figure 4.1).

Elkhorn Slough proper consists of a channel that tends to be fairly shallow, reaching depths of about 15 feet and a width of 700 feet at its western end near the inlet. Of its seven-mile length, the western three miles is fully tidal, the flow being enhanced by a U.S. Corps of Engineers navigational dredging program. Vestiges of formerly extensive eelgrass beds are found near the slough's mouth.

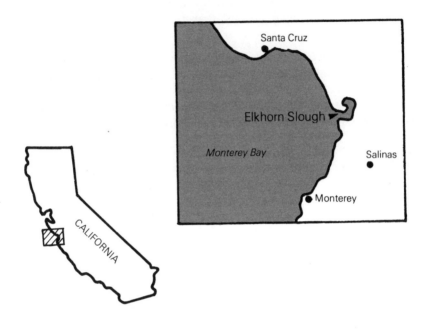

4.1   Elkhorn Slough Estuarine Sanctuary Regional Location Map

Tidal action affects the lower end of Elkhorn Slough strongly, but the upper end of the slough tends to stagnate, particularly in summer. About half of the marshland in the slough is partially or entirely cut off from the tides by dikes and tide gates. The amount of freshwater discharged into the slough changes with the seasons—the mean annual rainfall is approximately twenty inches, but nearly all of the rain comes in winter, as is characteristic of most estuaries; but in other seasons the salinity remains close to full ocean strength, which is unusual in estuarine systems.[12]

Water quality in Elkhorn Slough has suffered from activities associated with land use in the watershed. High coliform bacteria counts have been recorded in the estuary, primarily as a result of agricultural runoff and septic tank leachate. Sewage effluent, historically a problem, has largely been corrected. Portions of the estuary are filling rapidly, mostly from sediment eroded from croplands and roadcuts. The problem is exacerbated by poor farming practices that cause severe disruption of the soil surface and excessive pesticide use that has contaminated sediments in portions of the slough. The Pacific Gas and Electric oil-fired power plant near the inlet discharges steam generator cooling water into the channel, increasing water temperature by six degrees and jeopardizing planktonic biota that are entrained with the intake flow. These negative impacts on the ecosystem must be corrected sooner or later through mitigation or restoration programs.

The transition zone of the slough encompasses tidal flats, marshes, beaches, and floodplains, amounting to about 2,075 acres.[13] The slough's salt marsh, one of the largest south of San Francisco Bay, is dominated by the perennial *Salicornia virginica* (pickleweed), which account for more than 90 percent of the marsh's vegetative cover. The Wildlife Conservation Board—the acquisition arm of the California Department of Fish and Game—has purchased approximately three hundred acres of diked salt ponds adjacent to Highway 1 from the Monterey Bay Salt Company. Nearly half of the former tidal marshlands had been modified by diking, primarily for livestock grazing, and fingers of grazed grasslands are intertwined with diked pasture or tidal marsh. (The Department of Fish and Game has recently restored tidal action to former pastures in the sanctuary in an attempt to re-create tidal wetlands.)

The shorelands of the Elkhorn Slough watershed consist of rolling hills and swales drained by a network of intermittent systems. Nearly three-quarters of the 41,081 acres of shorelands are used for pasture and agriculture.[14] The estuary is set among rolling hills that steepen to the south and east. Elevations of three hundred feet are reached within one-quarter mile of the estuary's eastern bank, with lower elevations to the west and north. The oak woodland and grassland watershed of the hills east of the slough are used for livestock grazing and intensive strawberry and kiwifruit cultivation. Low-density residential development is scattered throughout the foothills east of Elkhorn Road and is expanding on the north and east of the slough. Shorelands north and south of the estuary support crops such as artichokes, brussels sprouts, cabbage, beans, lettuce, melons, sugar beets, and strawberries. The shorelands are also used for industrial and commercial purposes. Moss Landing Harbor, at the mouth of Elkhorn Slough, has a yacht club and docking facilities, as well as the Moss Landing Marine Laboratories and the community of Moss Landing. The structures of the Pacific Gas and Electric power plant and the Kaiser refractory plant visually dominate the south harbor.

The shorelands of the Elkhorn Slough watershed are drained by a network of small, intermittent swales and streams. There are no permanent ponds or lakes. Average rainfall varies from eighteen to twenty-one inches annually, with most precipitation in the winter months. Because infiltration rates are high on the permeable Aromas sands (the dominant soil type), surface runoff is primarily limited to periods during and briefly following storms. Creeks and swales are dry between April and October (although persistent riparian vegetation indicates subsurface moisture). Discharge rates are high during periods of peak winter runoff, but average annual runoff averages only 2,300 acre-feet.[15]

The politics of sanctuary establishment

In February 1978 the California Coastal Commission nominated Elkhorn Slough as the state's first choice to become part of the Coastal Zone Management Act's national estuarine sanctuary program. This selection followed an intensive search by state coastal staff to identify the estuaries most suitable for designation. Protecting Elkhorn Slough was not a new idea in 1978, however. For example, in 1976 the area was given "highest priority" for acquisition by the State Wildlife Conservation Board and listed as one of five "wetland projects" for which State Bond Act Monies were appropriated (AB 2133, chapter 462, Statutes of 1976). None of the other areas considered for estuarine sanctuary designation were so listed. In addition, the Nature Conservancy (TNC) had been slowly acquiring wetlands since 1968 and already owned hundreds of acres around Elkhorn Slough. Moreover, the U.S. Fish and Wildlife Service briefly considered plans to buy all transition lands on the northerly-westerly side of the slough.

Another factor in Elkhorn Slough's selection, apart from strong conservation interest, was that the State Coastal Commission's regional staff for the Monterey area pushed for a sanctuary nomination more aggressively than any of the other five regional staffs. Scientists affiliated with the Moss Landing Marine Laboratory situated on Elkhorn Slough also lent their support, giving the proposal both a scientific credibility and a local voice in favor of designation. In this case and the others discussed, scientists definitely became important political actors through their advocacy on behalf of sanctuary designation. Also, competitive California sanctuary proposals weakened. For example, although a few members of the scientific community (notably estuarine scientist Joel Hedgpeth) supported Tomales Bay,[16] their influence was overshadowed by local interests who (mistakenly) feared a loss of hunting and fishing opportunities. Resources Secretary Huey Johnson therefore earmarked the funds needed to match the federal planning grant to Elkhorn Slough.[17]

While nomination of an estuarine sanctuary land receipt of federal planning funds is simple procedurally, the politics of sanctuary development after the nomination has been accepted is considerably more complex. Most delay is caused by local community concern over the possible consequences of designation. The process of negotiation with various interests before, during, and after designation may become quite drawn out.

On one side, sanctuary proponents argued that Elkhorn Slough's wildlife habitat is one of the most important remnants of coastal estuary, salt ponds, and salt and brackish marsh still remaining in California. Thousands of water-oriented birds depend on this stopping place to feed and rest. American avocets, blacknecked stilts, and snowy plovers are permanent residents in the area. Caspian and Forster's terns have established colonies on dikes and islands. A nesting colony of Caspian terns in Elkhorn Slough is the only one in central California except for those in South San Francisco Bay.[18]

Other proponents recognized the research potential of Elkhorn Slough if designated an estuarine sanctuary: "The Elkhorn Slough Estuarine Sanctuary will be a priceless asset to the teaching and research programs of California State universities and colleges and to Moss Landing Marine Laboratories. It will serve as a primary study area of the environment essential to the nurture and success of countless species of birds, plants and animals dependent on its stability. An opportunity to utilize this area for demonstration of the nature of California's formerly pristine environment will come only once."[19]

The sanctuary was opposed by some commercial and industrial interests, including the Moss Landing Harbor District, Pacific Gas and Electric Company, Kaiser Refractories, commercial fishermen's organizations, and some landowners. Much of the dissent stemmed from political rivalries and philosophical disagreements that preceded the sanctuary nomination process. The term "sanctuary" itself also rekindled an ongoing struggle between preservation and development interests.

The harbor district was concerned that the sanctuary might restrict harbor operations and future expansion. Pacific Gas and Electric worried that establishment of the sanctuary might lead to controls on future placement of transmission lines from its Moss Landing power plant or to pressures against its extensive use of Elkhorn Slough for cooling purposes (cycling of estuarine water through steam generators on their production of commercial chemicals from seawater). Fishermen were falsely alarmed by rumors of state-federal control over fishing activities. Farmers and other landowners, including real estate speculators, were concerned over restrictions on the use of their land, the possibility that condemnation would be used, and that low prices would be paid for lands to be purchased for the sanctuary. Moreover, the county of Monterey, though strong on open space protection, did not have a vigorous track record of enforcement of land-use controls prior to the 1976 Coastal Act. Local landowners were unaccustomed to strict government oversight.

Through the environmental impact review process, local hearings, and informal consultation, sanctuary proponents came to understand and satisfy most opposition to the sanctuary. For instance, the water area of the slough was excluded from the sanctuary. However, there were still some political battles in the implementation of the proposal.

Implementation and sanctuary management

In July 1978 the state of California successfully applied to NOAA for a "preacquisition grant" for an Elkhorn Slough Sanctuary (award: $29,438). Matched by the state (50:50), the grant was used to determine preliminary boundaries, estimate real estate costs, formulate a preliminary management plan, and draft a research-education agenda. After completing the planning stage, the state received a $1,042,000 grant from NOAA, matched by $1,888,000 in state funds, for the acquisition of approximately 1,510 acres of wetlands and shorelands. Lead agency for acquisition was the State Wildlife Conservation Board. The California Fish and Game Department manages the slough as an ecological reserve.

The sanctuary was officially designated in June 1980 for the following purposes:

1. to protect, maintain, enhance, and restore the quality of the estuarine ecosystem in perpetuity
2. to enhance research that will provide knowledge to the general public and assist local decision makers in dealing with coastal development
3. to enhance, restore, and maintain optimum populations of migratory birds and indigenous flora and fauna, with special protection provided for rare and endangered plant and animal species

An advisory committee provides additional guidance in identifying key parcels of land for acquisition and policy direction for restoration and education programs at the sanctuary. Members of the Elkhorn Slough Estuarine Sanctuary Advisory Committee include the Monterey County Board of Supervisors, the California Fish and Game Department, the California Coastal Commission, the Moss Landing Laboratory, the University of California Sea Grant Program, the U.S. Fish and Wildlife Service, the Moss Landing Harbor District Commission, the Nature Conservancy, the Moss Landing Commercial Fisherman's Association, and the Property Owners' Subcommittee. Such interagency advisory committees are common features at all estuarine sanctuaries. (At Elkhorn Slough the advisory committee also formed a separate private organization, the Elkhorn Slough National Estuarine Sanctuary Foundation, to receive dedications of land or funds in exchange for tax considerations.) The California Department of Fish and Game (DFG) acts as lead management agency.

Well over one thousand acres of transitional land on the southerly-easterly side of the slough has been acquired by the Wildlife Conservation Board for the DFG as the core area of the ecological reserve through fee-simple acquisition and purchase of easements to help reduce estuarine pollution from upland areas. Although a substantial area was still in private ownership until quite recently, a coordinated effort of the Wildlife Conservation Board, the Nature Conservancy, and the Packard Foundation has made great strides toward creating a buffer around the whole shoreline of the estuarine commons to protect the integrity of the ecosystem.[20] The Nature Conservancy held five parcels as of 1985 and was actively pursuing additional acquisition and restoration-enhancement plans. The Nature Conservancy could acquire these additional parcels more quickly than the DFG and then sell them to DFG when state funds are available.

Effective protection for the estuary from runoff pollution and siltation also derives from a unique county-sponsored management program that is developed and implemented in conjunction with the California Coastal Commission. Monterey County's land-use management program includes some protection for all four elements of the Elkhorn Slough ecosystem —aquatic, transition, shorelands, and drainage system. The county requirements specifically provide for (1) setbacks along all watercourses of the land drainage system, (2) protection of riparian, wetland, intertidal, and other aquatic areas from future dredging, filling, and other adverse activities, (3) general protection and restoration of estuarine habitats and estuarine circulation, and above all (4) a program of development control and zoning to reduce the rate of erosion of soil from the watershed that had been filling the estuary with silt.

One supporting element of the program is the innovative erosion control study created by a team led by Thomas Dickert of the University of California at Berkeley with funding from the federal Sea Grant program. Dickert and his graduate student colleagues classified the shorelands of the watershed by erosion sensitivity and then suggested a program of controls that the county could use to prevent land uses that were the most erosion-producing. To organize the work, the shorelands of the Elkhorn Slough watershed were subdivided into thirty-seven subwatersheds. Extensive field research was conducted within each subwatershed and in the transition area and drainage system.

The elements of research were (1) time-series analysis of changes in transition and aquatic area habitat structure, (2) hydrologic studies of rainfall, runoff, channel flows, silt loading (bedload and suspended silt), (3) study of the effects of soil type, slope, and vegetation, and (4) study of the effects of soil disturbance and impervious surfaces. From this data base quantitative estimates were made (for each subwatershed) of erosion potential, soil transport through the drainage system, and soil deposition as sediment in transition and aquatic areas of the estuary.[21]

These research findings targeted a maximum allowable yearly erosion rate for each subwatershed, based upon the probable natural rate of soil loss that occurred in the subwatershed before significant disturbance. A "zero degradation" goal was proposed. Measures are being designed to return the shorelands to soil erosion rates existing in the "natural state" of the shorelands (using a benchmark of fifty years ago, which is as far back as useful records go). This goal is to be accomplished by enforcement of restrictive performance standards on development governing "off-site impacts" of soil losses, coupled with watershed management incentives.

Once these techniques were devised by the University of California at Berkeley research team, close cooperation with State Wetlands Coordinator Eric Metz and regional staff of the Coastal Commission ensured their translation into policies of the local coastal program for north Monterey County.

Even the most carefully conceived land-use planning and zoning are not sufficient to reverse watershed erosion and restore lost habitat values in the Elkhorn Slough complex. As a sequel to watershed analysis and the local coastal program (certified June 1982), the State Coastal Conservancy (SCC) has become involved in project implementation. Currently the SCC is working closely with the county, the regional commission staff, and the Moss Landing Harbor District to draw up two overall restoration plans: one for Elkhorn Slough—Bennett Slough, and a second for neighboring McClusky and Moro Cojo sloughs. Costs of the plans alone are estimated at $60,000 to $75,000 each for the Elkhorn Slough (phase I) and McClusky Slough–Moro Cojo Slough. The SCC funds are matched by the county's harbor district.

Along the shorelands of Elkhorn Slough the county and the State Coastal

Conservancy have identified twenty-two candidate restoration projects. The proposed actions range from removing exotic vegetation ($5,000) to major debris removal and installation of water control structures ($200,000). Other actions may include removal of silt, reconfiguring of topography, replanting, and removal of dikes.[22]

A combination of regulatory and restoration approaches is to be used to reduce watershed erosion and sedimentation of the Elkhorn Slough complex. The regulatory component builds on the findings of the Dickert study. Control of residential development in the shorelands is to be accomplished by the county's Local Coastal Program (LCP), which limits the density of development to one dwelling unit per 2.5 or 5 acres, or lower densities in some cases.[23]

The LCP also designates fifteen subwatersheds where erosion has already exceeded the target amount identified by the Dickert study. In these areas, farmers are to provide offsets for any new land clearing by reducing existing erosion. Which method to employ is left to the landowner's discretion except that the owner has to get a use permit to open new agricultural land. Permits are to be denied unless a full offset is proposed and certified by the U.S. Soil Conservation Service.

Currently, the Soil Conservation Service is working with landowners and lessees to reduce severe erosion rates on strawberry fields. Another federal agency, the Agricultural Stabilization and Conservation Service, may also help fund erosion control measures, but only up to a maximum amount of $3,500 per year. Since the underground pipes and outlet basins needed to control erosion would cost up to $70,000 for a sixty-acre spread, and many strawberry growers do not own the land they till, the prospects for immediate erosion reduction are not bright without funding assistance. The State Coastal Conservancy estimates also suggest that some erosion-control projects could take ten to fourteen years to complete.[24]

To accelerate the pace of erosion control and watershed restoration, the Coastal Conservancy is now exploring alternative cost-sharing concepts with the Monterey Coast Resource Conservation District. For small farms where the federal government pays 70 percent of erosion control, the Coastal Conservancy could add a 20 percent increment, leaving the landowner with a 10 percent obligation and a stake in the project ($500 per year). On the larger acreages, the Coastal Conservancy could match the federal grants of $3,500 per year and shorten the time needed to implement full-scale projects. Under both scenarios, funds would be disbursed as a grant to the Monterey Coast Resource Conservation District, which would contract with individual farmers and monitor project compliance.

As of February 1985 the Coastal Conservancy had identified seven candidate growers for the erosion control, based on their proximity to Elkhorn Slough or major tributary creeks. Total costs for the erosion control are estimated at about $560,000. It should be stressed that the erosion control program would carry a very large political benefit: it would demonstrate to growers that they have an important stake in the overall management of the sanctuary and its watershed.

Case summary

After many years of interest and effort by state and federal agencies and the public to find a way to protect the Elkhorn Slough ecosystem, designation as a national estuarine sanctuary provided the catalyst for successful action. While a program to acquire all needed transition land and to gain better aquatic area authority is early in its implementation period, it would appear that the present momentum will guarantee a successful conclusion. Without the sanctuary designation, the extraordinary coupling of estuary protection with innovative land-use control and restoration in the shorelands could not have come about.[25] As a complement to designation, resource management at Elkhorn Slough has benefited from a combination of a strong institutional framework, committed individuals in key positions, and a sustained research effort on estuarine and watershed issues.

One cornerstone of the Elkhorn Slough program is the California Coastal Act of 1976, which (1) established policy standards for the protection of "environmentally sensitive habitat areas," (2) required that "biological productivity of coastal waters, wetlands, and estuaries be maintained," (3) required every coastal jurisdiction (county, city, or port district) to implement a "local coastal program," including a land-use plan consistent with statewide policies, and (4) specifically extended the boundary line for coastal land-use regulation far inland to include critical shorelands around major estuaries like Elkhorn Slough. Also important were personal involvement on the part of the staff of the Central Coast Regional Commission to save the Elkhorn Slough estuary, particularly Lester Strnad; the efforts of Thomas Dickert's team to establish a scientifically sound basis for land-use controls throughout the watershed; and the continuing estuarine research interest of the local Moss Landing Marine Laboratory.

More recently, the Elkhorn Slough Foundation and the flexible programs of the State Coastal Conservancy have picked up where the early guidance of the Coastal Act left off. The foundation is helping to build and sustain local support, while the Coastal Conservancy's unique mandate has helped fill important gaps in expertise and funding.

Tijuana River National Estuarine Sanctuary

Federal sanctuary designation brought to reality a long-term effort to protect the Tijuana River estuary in San Diego, California. In the later 1960s a group of citizens fought tenaciously against the proposed channelization of the Tijuana River for flood control purposes. Many of these same people were roused again to oppose plans for marina development in the estuary, which had been favored by the city council of Imperial Beach, a small community bordering the northern edge of the estuary. In the early 1970s the State Fish and Game Department identified Tijuana estuary as one of nineteen acquisition priorities for coastal wetlands. Then in 1975 the California Coastal Plan reinforced the need to protect the estuary. Despite these and other recognitions, it was not until the area was designated as the Tijuana River National Estuarine Sanctuary that the entire estuary and surrounding shorelands were finally secured from urban encroachment and agricultural degradation. The methods by which the State Coastal Conservancy is working to assemble adjacent shoreland property, initiate restoration activities, and address water quality problems (with the help of a local land trust and a university foundation) are the distinguishing features of the Tijuana River National Estuarine Sanctuary.

The Tijuana River estuary lies just above the Mexican border in south San Diego (see figure 4.2). The Tijuana River extends eleven miles eastward where it receives the drainage from a watershed of 1,731 square miles (in both the United States and Mexico) via two connecting intermittent streams. The estuarine system extends 1½ miles east from its ocean inlet and three miles north and south behind a broad, sandy ocean beach. Freshwater inflow to Tijuana estuary fluctuates significantly from year to year as a function of seasonal rainfall and release of water from upstream dams. Mean annual discharge for forty-four years of record (through 1980) is 29.1 cubic feet per second, 21,080 acre feet per year, concentrated from January to April.[26]

In total, the estuary embraces 546 acres of tidally influenced area (aquatic and transition components), 147 of which are tidal channels and 368 are mudflats and marshlands. A notable feature is the presence of *Spartina foliosa* (cordgrass), a species absent in more disturbed sites in southern California. *Spartina* dominates at the lowest elevations, with

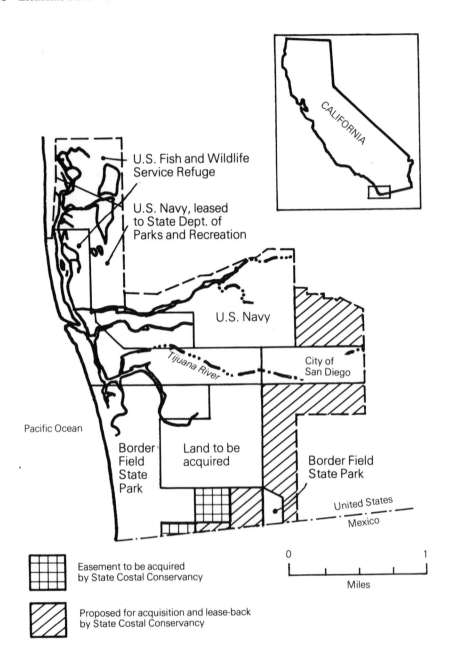

U.S. Fish and Wildlife
Service Refuge

U.S. Navy, leased
to State Dept. of
Parks and Recreation

CALIFORNIA

U.S. Navy

Tijuana River

City of
San Diego

Pacific Ocean

Border
Field
State
Park

Land to be
acquired

Border Field
State Park

United States

Mexico

Easement to be acquired
by State Costal Conservancy

Proposed for acquisition and lease-back
by State Costal Conservancy

0   1

Miles

4.2   Tijuana River Estuarine Sanctuary Regional Location Map gradation into succulents (pickleweed) and salt cedar abundance as elevation increases.

The waters and bottom communities of Tijuana estuary provide habitat for twenty-nine fish species and nineteen families, including an abundance of small gobies and sculpins as well as important recreational species of bass and flatfish. Recently completed research has documented very high densities of larval fish in the channels of the Tijuana estuary relative to offshore areas, demonstrating the importance of the area as a nursery. The fifty-four invertebrate species in Tijuana estuary reflect adaptations to a variety of substrate, salinity, and tidal conditions.

The sanctuary is the southernmost U.S. stop in the Pacific flyway, as the channels, mudflats, and sandy beaches of Tijuana estuary are used by a variety of migrating species. Shorebirds account for the largest portion of the migration. Migratory waterfowl are common in winter months, notably the Pintail, Cinnamon Teal, American Widgeon, Surf Scoter, and Ruddy Duck. Sandbars attract flocks of terns, including Forster's, Elegant, Common, and California Least. Sand dune and river mouth areas provide nesting sites for the endangered Least Tern. About twenty species of shorebirds use the tidally influenced portions of Tijuana estuary on a fairly regular basis. Four species—the Willet, Dowitcher, Western Sandpiper, and Marbled Godwit—account for over three-fourths of the individuals counted.

Politics of sanctuary establishment

Local conservationists were convinced that California's coastal regulatory program—as effective as it was in guiding the use of private property—could not deliver the high level of conservation necessary to protect the ecological integrity of the Tijuana estuary.[27] Unlike virtually all other major wetlands in San Diego and throughout southern California, the Tijuana estuary is neither bisected by a major road or freeway nor reduced in size from diking, dredging, or filling. However, the pressures for urban development extending south from San Diego and north from the Mexican border town of Tijuana were a cause for concern. In addition, surveys by the Soil Conservation Service showed that much of the surrounding agriculture would require especially careful husbandry to protect the estuary from excessive sedimentation.

Besides the concern over both agricultural preservation and sedimentation risks to the estuary, local interests were motivated by the concern that over three-quarters of the Tijuana River's watershed lies in Mexico and the river must pass through Ciudad Tijuana—the fastest-growing city in the Northern Hemisphere—on its way to the estuary. A special concern was the chronic overflow of sewage from a connector linking Tijuana and a sewage plant in San Diego. Environmental interests and scientists felt that national sanctuary designation would provide important negotiating leverage in moving toward binational resolution of long-existing water quality issues. A coalition of local and state interests decided to explore the potential of NOAA's estuarine sanctuary program to create a forum for solution of regional planning issues and to fund essential purchases of private land in the lower Tijuana Valley. Because the Southern California Region of NOAA's biogeographic classification had as yet no sanctuary, proponents were able to advance the Tijuana River estuary as an active candidate. The California Department of Fish and Game was particularly adamant that such a southern California site be chosen, and the Tijuana estuary also earned the support of marine and estuarine scientists.

A preexisting Local Coastal Program (LCP) for the Tijuana River Valley —adopted by the city of San Diego and certified by the California Coastal Commission in 1980—created a strong foundation of land-use regulation favorable to estuarine protection. The LCP discouraged subdivision of farmlands for residential development, required strong control on use of pesticides, established a 100-foot buffer strip of undisturbed land around wetlands, and imposed other firm environmental controls. These controls curbed a tendency toward speculative interest in the remaining private land surrounding the estuary that had blossomed when plans for marina development were actively considered by the community of Imperial Beach. LCP policies also put public landholders on notice that environmental protection was a priority for their parcels.

The nomination and program design for Tijuana River estuary were also accompanied by a strong consensus-building effort. First, Coastal Commission staff invited nominations from dozens of organizations. Seven sites were nominated and screened by an ad hoc review panel of staff representing six resource agencies. The findings of this ad hoc selection committee were reported to the Coastal Commission, resulting in a unanimous vote for nomination of Tijuana estuary.

In the next phase of work, the Coastal Commission and staff of NOAA's Sanctuary Programs Division (including the second author) prepared an array of acquisition strategies and a management framework. Concurrently, a twelve-member advisory committee was recruited, composed of private landowners, staff of landholding agencies, scientists, and environmentalists. The advisory committee worked through the alternatives in two day-long workshop sessions. The outcome was near unanimity on both acquisition priorities and an appropriate structure for a management authority (the Tijuana management authority has subsequently taken time to refine priorities based on a closer look at environmental-ecological criteria). Largely as a result of collaborative working relationships built up during the designation and design phase, political opposition to the sanctuary was minimal. The U.S. Fish and Wildlife Service and the California Department of Parks and Recreation generally saw the sanctuary as a complement to their existing interests. The U.S. Navy was already managing a portion of their wetlands and clapper rail habitat in compliance with the Endangered Species Act. The city of San Diego also supported the sanctuary.

Two key landowning interests supported the sanctuary. The San Diego Gas and Electric Company, with landholdings amounting to two hundred acres, came to its position after recognizing that its goal to build a power plant adjacent to the wetland was unlikely to materialize. The combination of declining forecasts for energy demand and strict land-use controls rendered the company's site "surplus" for corporate purposes. Farmers in the area also began to support the sanctuary after the winter floods of 1979 and 1980 removed from production much of the lowlands once used for agriculture. Matt Marshall, a farmer with a background in environmental management, advanced the concept of acquisition of fallow agricultural land followed by leaseback to willing farmers.

The major voice against the sanctuary was the mayor of Imperial Beach, Brian Bilbray (Bilbray is now a state assemblyman). Though not strictly opposed to conservation, Bilbray was convinced that economic development and cleanup of sewage pollution should come first.

At the public hearing on the EIS for the sanctuary, testimony was overwhelmingly supportive. Of approximately forty-six speakers, just five opposed the sanctuary. Eleven of twelve members of the advisory committee delivered positive statements.[28]

Implementation and sanctuary management

While the orientation of the program is definitely one of preservation, protection, and utilization, the intent of sanctuary designation is to foster uses of the estuary and Tijuana Valley that are compatible with the long-term maintenance of a diverse and productive estuarine ecosystem. Since the designation itself does not confer any new regulations, maintaining the Tijuana River National Estuarine Sanctuary at near-baseline condition can be accomplished only with the cooperation and support of the government agencies and private groups with jurisdiction or interest in the area. But the area's success depends on the ability to successfully couple estuarine conservation and preservation of viable agricultural land through acquisition, and, where appropriate, a leaseback arrangement.[29]

Sanctuary designation is also a logical mechanism to unify and catalyze the many resource-planning initiatives already under way in the lower Tijuana Valley and estuary. It is singularly well suited to bridging the gap between stewardship of public land, regulation of private land, and protection and management of natural resources that are not confined to particular property boundaries. Conceived as a program for cooperative resource management, the estuarine sanctuary links together existing state, federal, and international efforts already under way. The sanctuary will provide a single umbrella for public lands in the Tijuana estuary now held and managed by the U.S. Fish and Wildlife Service, the Department of Parks and Recreation, the U.S. Navy, and the city and county of San Diego. An immediate consequence of the sanctuary will be stabilization of the entire mosaic of wetland and salt marsh in open space-resource conservation and preservation of the open character of the lower Tijuana Valley east of 19th Street.

As proposed, the sanctuary would encompass 2,531 acres. Of this, 1,646 acres were already in public ownership—a 505-acre National Wildlife Refuge (for protection of the endangered Light-Footed Clapper Rail) operated by U.S. Fish and Wildlife, a 681-acre state park, 340 acres of Navy land, and 120 acres owned by the city of San Diego. It was determined that these lands could be included as part of the sanctuary complex because the agencies holding ownership would enter into written agreements to manage them according to sanctuary needs. The remaining 885 acres were privately owned, with agriculture being the dominant use.

Based on initial estimates of land value, the California Coastal Commission requested and received a grant of one million dollars from NOAA, to be matched equally by state funds. The State Coastal Conservancy, an agency with the authority to structure acquisition and other land transactions, and to restore disturbed habitat areas, agreed to provide state matching funds. In December 1981 the Coastal Conservancy formally allocated $1.03 million and soon thereafter began land appraisals under a special interagency agreement with the California Coastal Commission—the state agency designated to receive the federal funds.

Deciding it would be wasteful of funds and agricultural capacity to buy and remove all agricultural land from production, the Coastal Conservancy proposed a mechanism for acquisition and leaseback of the agricultural lands by which the lessors would agree to operate according to high levels of conservation. These agreements would "provide an initial infusion of capital" to the lessors (the present landowners) that would stimulate land restoration and management activities to bring the area to the fullest productive use compatible with good soil conservation practice. Lease fees would be based on income derived from the property, and the revenues would be directed back to management of the sanctuary.

A complementary effort to the acquisition program was the restoration of twenty acres of degraded high marsh habitat in the northern portion of the estuary. Under a grant from the Coastal Conservancy's "Nonprofits Program," the Southwest Wetlands Interpretive Association (SWIA) constructed vehicle barriers to protect sensitive plants. A series of test plots were revegetated using experimental aeration techniques, but arid conditions and vandalism have hampered the success of the revegetation.[30] Ecologist Joy Zelder (San Diego State University) and several graduate student colleagues contributed their expertise (often at no cost). The Southwest Wetlands group trained and fielded volunteers to assist with replanting.

Tijuana River Estuarine Sanctuary is managed by a Sanctuary Management Authority, with the Department of Parks and Recreation as the administrative lead. Other original members of Tijuana River National Estuarine Sanctuary include the U.S. Navy, the U.S. Fish and Wildlife Service, and the cities of San Diego and Imperial Beach. Both cities were required to appoint representatives with formal training or practical experience in resource management. In spite of the fears of some agency staff, both cities appointed representatives with a strong commitment to estuarine protection. To increase the representation and enhance the political attractiveness of the original sanctuary proposal, a subordinate advisory group was also included in the institutional design. Members were to include the Coastal Commission, Coastal Conservancy, the government of Mexico, and water quality agencies. A third tier of the management structure was to include subcommittees for water quality, agriculture, and education.

In 1986 a formal management plan was adopted by all participating management agencies. The plan details changes in the management structure included in the 1981 EIS.[31] The subordinate advisory committee, which had never met, was abolished. The Management Authority has been expanded to include other key players: the Coastal Conservancy, the Coastal Commission, the county of San Diego and the sanctuary manager. Finally, the U.S. Navy has opted to withdraw from the Management Authority.[32]

The subcommittees will continue as an integral part of the management structure. The research and education subcommittee, under the leadership of Joy Zedler, has been particularly active. The group is working closely with the Management Authority to design research and interpretive facilities for the sanctuary.

To date, the Coastal Conservancy has acquired eight parcels totaling about 317 acres. An important land acquisition that recently took place was the purchase of 200 acres of wetland fringe from San Diego Gas and Electric (SDG&E). Coastal Conservancy land acquisition staff are hopeful that the sale will persuade other reluctant landowners to sell.

Another 1985 event was the official groundbreaking of a model sewage treatment program in the Tijuana Valley, east of the sanctuary. The project, researched with Coastal Conservancy funds by the Southwest Wetlands group and water quality engineers, is a modified secondary treatment process that uses biological processes to accomplish a higher level of sewage treatment at lower cost than conventional systems.

A number of new restoration and research projects are getting under way within the sanctuary. In October 1985 the San Diego State University Foundation was granted some $228,000 in Coastal Conservancy funds, matched by $215,000 from the state's environmental license plate funds and $75,000 from NOAA to initiate restoration planning and development of research facilities.

In all, four different restoration projects are getting under way with Coastal Conservancy funding. One focus of the restoration is the mouth of the estuary itself. Temporary dredging measures, completed without the benefit of careful topographic and hydrologic analysis, failed. The funding will enable the preparation of technically sound enhancement plans. Second, the analysis will evaluate the linkages between upstream riparian resources and wetland resources and suggest additional purchase or restoration measures that may lie outside the current sanctuary boundaries.

A third focus for restoration is a damaged riparian zone along Monument Road within sanctuary boundaries. Debris and exotic species will be removed, to be replaced with species that are naturally dominant in this habitat area. The fourth restoration will be to reintroduce saline and freshwater pool habitats in the transition area between damaged wetland habitats and abandoned agricultural land. Nursery plots will be established to supply plant materials for other areas in the sanctuary or elsewhere in the region.

Also being initiated is the Estuarine Research Lab (PERL), a facility that goes a long way toward upholding the research mission of the sanctuary. On abandoned agricultural land purchased from private owners, the Conservancy will fund construction of two replicate experimental marshes — small enough so that hydrology, salinity, and nutrient fluxes can be controlled and monitored. Holding ponds, experimental channels, and trailers housing research equipment will complement the replicate wetlands. No other facilities of this type exist on the West Coast.

Another contribution of the Coastal Conservancy has been allocation of about $28,000 to build a walkway and stabilize an eroding street along the urban edge of the sanctuary on South Seacoast Drive. This project implements a portion of the access plan for the sanctuary and complements a much larger city-sponsored improvement effort to place utilities underground and improve beach access and parking. The design solution, endorsed by all the management agencies, is curbing and guttering with a "self-contained toe" that does not encroach into the wetland. Since the project provides access and prevents resource damage, the Coastal Conservancy was able to act quickly where other agencies were more constrained in offering a speedy response.

Case summary

Tijuana estuary represents an exciting experiment on several fronts: land purchase, experimental restoration, and watershed management. Several factors strongly contributed to the success of the sanctuary venture. A local citizens' organization concerned with education, whose core members had opposed the marina (and a channelization project), campaigned vigorously for the sanctuary. A very active estuarine research program, led by Dr. Zedler at San Diego State University, provided a strong technical foundation to the sanctuary nomination.[33]

Representatives of the Commission of the Californias, a body established to link Baja California and the state of California, expressed strong interest to help in matters affecting the Mexican portion of the watershed and associated pollution issues, as did members of the U.S. Consulate in Tijuana. The agencies with existing land holdings in the area — the Parks and Recreation Department, the U.S. Fish and Wildlife Service, and the U.S. Navy were all extremely cooperative in working toward a joint management effort for the lower Tijuana Valley.

Most recently, some resource managers concerned with the Tijuana estuary have begun to explore International Biosphere Reserve designation for the wetlands complex, the lower Tijuana Valley, and portions of the watershed on the Mexican side of the border. According to staff of the Man and the Biosphere (MAB) Program in the United Nations Education Science and Cultural Organization, such a designation would result in the first binational reserve in the global Man and the Biosphere program. Although biosphere reserve status confers neither funding nor custodial involvement in resource management, several other benefits could result. First, elevating the international status of the Tijuana estuary could provide leverage in binational efforts to clean up sewage pollution. Second, the designation could give local estuarine scientists and managers access to a global network of professionals working on comparable problems. This could stimulate additional funding for Tijuana estuary research. Third, reserve designation of areas on both sides of the international border could prompt much greater Mexican involvement in ongoing management of freshwater inflows and water quality. Fourth, with a biosphere reserve in place, officials from Mexico and Baja California might be inspired to better integrate riverine and estuarine management concerns with infrastructure planning for water supplies, waste treatment, and transportation.

Apalachicola Bay Estuarine Sanctuary

Apalachicola Bay in the Florida Panhandle is the location of the most extensive management effort in the nation to conserve a near-pristine estuary. One of the most productive estuarine systems in North America, Apalachicola Bay receives waters from a drainage basin that extends into Alabama and Georgia. An enormous amount of research, administrative effort, and political activity has been invested over fifteen years to bring a comprehensive management plan to fruition. The major catalyst was the designation of the bay and the lower Apalachicola River, along with a great amount of transition area, as a national estuarine sanctuary.

The Apalachicola sanctuary is distinguished by emphasis on intensive coordination between local, state, and federal regulatory programs to aid in land acquisition efforts and to help conserve the resources of the bay. The sanctuary proposal for Apalachicola was successful largely because an extraordinarily energetic scientist, Robert J. "Skip" Livingston, has devoted his career to understanding the ecology of the Apalachicola system and because the fishing people of Apalachicola came to understand that only through an ecosystem approach to resource management could their livelihood and their way of life be sustained.

The Apalachicola sanctuary is located in Franklin County, Florida. The county, situated in Florida's Panhandle, consists of nearly 350,000 acres —primarily forest and managed for harvest, or lands along the coast, lower reaches of the rivers, and barrier islands that are subject to pressures for residential and commercial development. (Exceptions are those

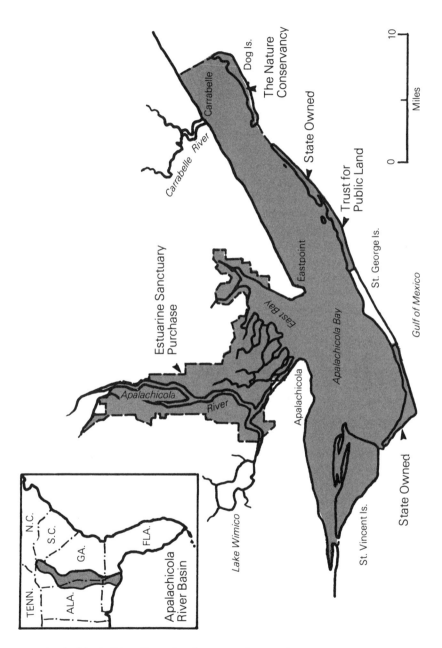

4.3   Apalachicola River Estuarine Sanctuary Regional Location Map

areas under the stewardship of the National Forest Service and the U.S. Fish and Wildlife Service.) Several factors account for the concentration of development on the coastline: Franklin County's terrain, its limited road network, and the dependency of its population on access to water. The population numbers about eight thousand. The county is the logical caretaker of the tremendously productive estuarine ecosystem made up of St. Vincent Sound, Apalachicola Bay, East Bay, and St. George Sound. Because nearly all of the county's residents derive their income directly or indirectly from natural resources produced within its borders, resource protection is not a luxury, it is an integral part of daily life. Not only commercial fishing but many other major sectors of the county's economy —recreational fishing, forestry, coastal tourism and recreation, and construction of second homes—are closely linked to the natural resource base.

The sanctuary includes the bay with its associated tidal creeks, marshes, and bayous, portions of the Apalachicola barrier islands. It encompasses approximately 193,000 acres, of which 135,000 acres are prior state-owned submerged lands and 58,000 acres are transition area (tidal and floodlands) and shorelands. There is a good chance for expansion to include additional adjacent lands.

The watershed terrain is a mixed forest area, with pine plantations for pulpwood culture, some urban areas (including Atlanta, Georgia), and limited agriculture. The valley of the lower part (the Apalachicola River, which runs through six Florida counties) is lightly developed.

The drainage system is extensive. The major conveyance of freshwater is the Apalachicola River, which runs free from the Jim Woodruff Dam and navigational locks at the Georgia border 105 miles south to the bay. Its mean annual flow is about 23,000 cubic feet per second. It is fed by the Flint and Chattahoochee rivers, which flow into a 37,500-acre impoundment behind the dam. It carries the drainage from 19,600 square miles of watershed land (17,000 above the dam, 2,500 below). The river flows between natural berms that separate the channel from the floodlands during low river stage. It widens after it is joined by the Chipola River and becomes tidal and increasingly saline. It serves as a barge route from the Gulf of Mexico to upriver industries in Alabama. Various sloughs lead back into the hardwood bottomlands that are inundated each year. When they drain, great quantities of leaf detritus are carried downstream to enrich the bay.[34]

The transition area surrounding the coastal basin varies from swamp to marsh (the marshes are widest on the inland edge of the bay) to sandy beaches with low dunes to earthen banks. Tidal amplitude is less than one meter. Flood risk is low except during hurricanes.

The coastal basin, Apalachicola Bay, is shallow, with an average depth of about ten feet; the bottom varies from coarse sand to fine mud. Oysters occur in concentrated reefs; submerged grass beds occupy 9,400 acres of the bay. Crabs, fish, and shrimp move between the bay and the ocean using the inlets as major pathways, and all three use this bay as a major nursery area, as they do in so many estuaries of the Gulf of Mexico (for example, crabs migrate hundreds of miles north along the Florida coast to spawn here).[35]

Seafood harvesting and processing is therefore the principal economic asset of Franklin County, which surrounds most of Apalachicola Bay. Franklin County accounts for 90 percent of the total harvest of oysters in Florida and 10 to 12 percent of the state's catch of shrimp and blue crab. Together with finfish such as mullet and sea trout, the harvest and its resulting "multiplier" effect contribute $75 million or more annually to this sparsely populated county's economy.[35]

The water component also includes the brackish part of the Apalachicola River (the lower twenty miles) and the bay proper. Salinity ranges from 0.5 to about 30.0 parts per thousand. Industrial pollution is negligible, but sewage from ill-functioning septic tanks and obsolete treatment plants has been a recurring factor in the vicinity of small cities and shoreline settlements. Sewage treatment capacity has improved considerably since 1980, however.

The ocean component interacts via five inlets (four natural and one man-made) through and around the outer boundary of barrier islands. Salinity varies from about 20.0 to 33.0 parts per thousand. The continental shelf slopes vary gradually (about 2 m/km), and the coast is characterized as medium energy.

Politics of sanctuary establishment

As described by McCreary,[37] local seafood dealers—the economic backbone of Franklin County—were the first to press for permanent protection of the bay through NOAA's estuarine sanctuary program, encouraged by Robert Livingston. The Apalachicola fishermen and seafood dealers feared more than a loss of livelihood; they were concerned that a traditional way of life would be swept aside. Two activities in the Apalachicola region were of special concern: channelization of the Apalachicola River and new developments along Franklin County's barrier islands and beaches.

The local interests were joined by the Florida Department of Environmental Regulation and developed a formal sanctuary proposal with technical assistance from the Conservation Foundation (Washington, D.C.).[38] Sanctuary designation, it was agreed, was the logical technique to permanently foreclose efforts to dam or channelize the Apalachicola River. Establishing the sanctuary would foster research on the ecology of the system that would ultimately benefit the seafood industry and would secure key upland parcels in the immediate drainage of the estuarine basin.

Another important local actor in the designation of Apalachicola Bay National Estuarine Sanctuary was Robert "Bobby" Howell. His support for the sanctuary was strong and consistent. Although Howell's official position was clerk of court, he functioned effectively as Franklin County's chief executive officer and counselor to the commissioners. Howell was a native of Franklin County and had excellent contacts with a variety of state agencies and powerful legislators. He worked closely with Robert Livingston, the Department of Environmental Regulation, the Department of Natural Resources, and with the Conservation Foundation in developing the initial sanctuary proposal. Opposition to the sanctuary came primarily from upriver navigation interests and major landowners on St. George Island with plans for large second-home developments.

Barge operators in Georgia and Alabama were concerned that the sanctuary could block what they saw as needed navigation improvements. A cost-benefit analysis performed by Steven Leitman for the Florida Department of Environmental Regulation (DER) persuaded the U.S. Corps of Engineers that a major channelization was not cost-effective. However, barge operators insisted that additional efforts were needed to maintain the authorized navigation channel. They applied pressure through the governors' offices in their respective states. Florida Governor Bob Graham backed the sanctuary but agreed to meet with the other governors. The result was a set of conditions agreed upon by all three states: (1) Florida would issue a five-year dredging and spoil disposal permit to the Corps to complete maintenance dredging agreements along the entire length of the Apalachicola River; (2) Corps of Engineers' navigation requirements were incorporated into the five-year plan; (3) Florida would undertake, with the Corps and the states of Georgia and Alabama, a study of water resources in the Apalachicola-Chattahoochee-Flint rivers system; (4) the states would reconvene to initiate a long-term spoil disposal plan when the five-year permit expired; and (5) Florida was to work out a memorandum of understanding with the Corps of Engineers to increase the availability of the congressionally authorized nine-foot by 100-foot channel. Then, Leitman facilitated a second set of negotiations among the Corps of Engineers and the six affected Florida counties.

The land development proposals that most worried the Franklin County commissioners were those sponsored by John Stocks and Gene Brown —partners in Leisure Properties, Ltd. The company had acquired a considerable part of St. George Island and had major plans for residential and resort development. For part of the island the firm had successfully negotiated a "development order" under the regional impact process administered by the Department of Environmental Regulation. But the agreement covered only a small part of Leisure Property's holdings, leaving future land use unresolved for some of the island—with some of these areas adjacent to shellfish beds and other areas subject to major flood hazards. Stocks and Brown had been battling with Franklin County's commissioners for several years, trading charges in the courts and in the pages of the *Tallahassee Democrat* and the *Apalachicola Times*. For the seafood dealers, the sanctuary was yet another way to gain leverage over development of St. George Island.

Sanctuary designation in Apalachicola has a particularly long history. A portion of Apalachicola Bay was designated by the state as an aquatic preserve in 1970, a designation that extended minimal new protection to its waters. Legislation adopted in 1972 gave the state authority to intervene in land-use management by designating "Areas of Critical State Concern." By 1977 state planners decided that local governments in the area were unprepared to handle the complex, time-sequenced regulatory procedures that apply to critical areas. Instead they caused the formation of an Apalachicola Resource Management and Planning Program, a partnership of local and state interests. The program was instrumental in securing designation of the bay as a national estuarine sanctuary,[39] with help from the State Department of Environmental Regulation, the Department of Community Affairs, and Franklin County representatives. Also in 1977 a symposium was convened to review the ecology of the bay system.[40]

Implementation and sanctuary management

The Apalachicola Bay National Estuarine Sanctuary was officially designated in September 1980. The concept of protection of bay resources was a coupled dryside-wetside program, combining regulation with acquisition.

The Sanctuary Management Committee has six voting members appointed as follows: a representative of the Franklin County Commission, a local "resource user" (fisherman), a scientist, and a representative from each of three state departments—natural resources, environmental regulation, and game and freshwater fish commission. Various other state and federal agencies are represented as nonvoting members of the committee to provide for coordination.

Initially, the committee's charge was to include a review of all permits. This has not occurred, although the committee has tried to discover and influence permit applications upriver, including Georgia and Alabama, where the largest part of the Apalachicola watershed lies. The committee hopes to accomplish this task by maintaining contact with all agencies having purview over the Apalachicola River basin.

In the planning phase, existing state and federal regulations that protect the aquatic part of the sanctuary were linked with local land-use controls in the transition and shorelands zones to effect a comprehensive regulatory program. Because the Conservation Foundation provided technical input to both the sanctuary plan and the local land-use plan, and because most sanctuary proponents participated in both planning efforts, a unified approach was facilitated. It remains for the Sanctuary Management Committee and the sanctuary staff to ensure continuing coordination among the various regulatory entities.

The sanctuary is fortunate to have so much of the surrounding land in public ownership for protection and park purposes. Because the Florida DNR is both the administrative agency for the sanctuary and represented on the management committee, the prospects are good for the sanctuary's ability to influence the management of the surrounding state-owned lands —about 32,000 acres so far. The sanctuary will also coordinate management of another 7,000 to 8,000 acres of transition land in the East Bay area when acquired (with federal sanctuary funds matched by the state).

The continuing cooperation of the U.S. Fish and Wildlife Service, owners of another 12,300 acres of land (the St. Vincent National Wildlife Refuge), is expected. Cooperative management of these lands secures a considerable part of the sensitive transition area surrounding the estuary.

Two smaller parcels of special importance have been purchased by private land conservation groups for subsequent resale to the sanctuary. Most of Dog Island was purchased by the Nature Conservancy with assistance of local landholders, securing the eastern end of the bay and allowing expansion of the sanctuary past the Carabelle River. The Nature Conservancy purchase came at a time when a developer was about to exercise an option to purchase a major portion of the island, and the state was unable to intercede.

A subdivided parcel on St. George Island, identified as "Unit 4," was purchased from the principal developer of the island (in a "bargain sale" transaction). This was a critical purchase, providing a level of protection for nearby oyster beds that could not be guaranteed with land-use regulations. The parcel surrounds a key wetland-creek area through which Unit 4 drains to the estuary. It was believed that even the minimum land runoff from an intensively developed subdivision—200 lots in 77 acres —would be enough to require closure of the oyster beds to fishermen during much of the year.

The Trust for Public Land, which purchased Unit 4, acted in a situation where the state was hindered politically and administratively. Preexisting transactions had established much higher land values per acre ($18,000 +) than the state was accustomed to paying for transition lands. In addition, the state's previous investments in Apalachicola were large relative to expenditures in other parts of the state, generating pressure to purchase land elsewhere. The purchase of Unit 4 illustrates the value of the involvement of nongovernmental organizations using flexible tools to acquire sanctuary bufferlands.

Recognizing the county's strong interest in protection of estuarine resources and the imminence of sanctuary designation, the Conservation Foundation was asked to prepare a special shoreline strategy as a key element for the county's general land-use plan. The strategy concentrated on (1) physical protection of the transition zone and submerged bay habitats, (2) control of pollutants originating on the land, particularly from residential sources, and (3) guiding development in hazard-prone areas, including special standards for construction and limitations on the rate of growth for the area.[41] A major element of the strategy was the critical shoreline zone, an "overlay zone" that would prohibit septic tanks in shoreline lots adjacent to estuarine resources (oyster reefs, scallop beds), require maintenance of a vegetation buffer, and prohibit logging in the areas adjacent to the shoreline. The purpose of these controls was to reduce to the minimum the effect of land-use practices on water quality over the oyster beds and the bay in general. Also, it would prevent significant physical disruption of the sensitive transition area. The recommended shoreline zone controls were adopted by the county commission, with the exception of the growth control provision, and were in effect at the time of this writing.

The county was most agressive about controlling septic tanks because oysters become easily polluted by human waste and because state-federal regulations require closing down the beds when the pollution index reaches a certain point (70 MPN of coliform bacteria).

Specific controls recommended for septic tanks included the following:

1. Establish a policy of strict septic tank control in the critical shoreline zone, consisting of all land within 150 feet of mean high water along the rivers, bays, and sounds of Franklin County, where it is presumed that due to factors of soil, groundwater, and proximity to surface waters, no septic tanks should be allowed.
2. Require denial of all septic tank applications in pollution-sensitive segments of the critical shoreline zone. These segments are designated "pollution-sensitive" due to their physical proximity to productive oyster beds.
3. Require the environmental health director to establish beyond a reasonable doubt, prior to granting a septic tank permit in the critical shoreline zone, that the systems will operate properly and will not allow the introduction of sewage effluent into groundwater or surface waterways.

Franklin County initiated advanced ecological land-use controls along with its efforts to establish a sanctuary and to otherwise preserve the Apalachicola ecosystem for economic and research purposes. That it took even this first step, and in a fashion that integrated a variety of state and federal ecological policies and regulatory programs, was remarkable in the context of north Florida politics and attitudes. Prior to 1970 there was virtually no regulation or guidance for land use or resource management in the area.

The land-use program, as well as the sanctuary, were supported by innumerable studies, conferences, task forces, scientific workshops, and governmental committees. The result of all such considerations is that conservation of the bay and its resources and seafood harvests should have priority over all conflicting uses, including incompatible land uses and anything that would degrade the inflow of the Apalachicola River and other tributaries. Toward this goal, land-use regulations are to be integrated closely with the purchase of tens of thousands of acres of key transitional land to achieve the desired level of protection.

Prior to the preparation of the shoreline strategy, Franklin County had no planning staff. Day-to-day administration of land-use regulation was initiated by James Floyd, former planning commissioner and retired staffer of the Game and Freshwater Fish Commission. He approached the job with a working knowledge of the county's natural resources, but many interests were concerned that his implementation was less vigorous than needed to protect the resources of Apalachicola Bay.

Although land acquisition for the estuarine sanctuary proceeded during the early 1980s, and elements of the shoreline strategy were at least partially implemented, state interest during a period of eighteen months in 1983–85 produced a series of recommendations to further strengthen the Apalachicola Bay program.[42] DER staffer Pam McVety and DER consultant Steve Leitman were instrumental in this effort. Local circumstances aided the work of the task force. DNR increased the frequency and sophistication of its shellfish monitoring, detecting high levels of coliform bacteria even more frequently than in past years. These findings resulted in closing the bay, which in turn wreaked havoc with the fragile Franklin County economy. Local pressure for improved sewage treatment and stricter shoreline development was stepped up.

These trends culminated in June 1985 with the passage of the Apalachicola Bay Area Protection Act (House Bill 1202), a package of legislation with several important elements (State of Florida, 1985). The legislation was supported by the leadership of the Florida House and carried by a central Florida representative, to avoid underscoring statewide interest in the Apalachicola Bay region. Bobby Howell supported the bill, but James Floyd opposed it as an unnecessary complication and intrusion into local affairs. The preamble to the bill noted the bay's importance as "a National Estuarine Sanctuary, a Florida Aquatic Preserve, an Outstanding Florida Water, a Florida Class II Shellfish Harvesting Area, and an International Biosphere Reserve." A key principle of the bill would ensure that "growth and diversification of the local economy shall be fostered only if it is consistent with protection of the natural resources of the Apalachicola Bay area through appropriate management of the land and water systems." Other principles are those of water quality, management of stormwater discharges to minimize impacts, protection of coastal dune systems, and preservation of wildlife and aquatic habitats.

Other elements of the bill included:

– designation of all of Franklin County as an area of special state concern, enabling state oversight of local land-use planning
– adoption of a 150-foot critical shoreline zone and high-hazard zones, first recommended by the Conservation Foundation (The bill also requires mapping of pollution-sensitive segments of the shoreline zone within twelve months—another CF recommendation. The county will not permit wastewater discharge systems in pollution-sensitive segments of the bay, except for "onsite wastewater systems that will not degrade water quality in the river or bay.")
– $3.58 million for sewage treatment in Apalachicola, Carrabelle, and Eastpoint
– $1.2 million for floodplain mapping of the Apalachicola River Basin
– funding for about seven staff members to carry out local planning

assistance with a Department of Community Affairs field office, coordinate federal and state involvement, conduct shellfish monitoring, wildlife habitat research, and establish educational programs at the National Estuarine Sanctuary Program headquarters

A complementary effort to the 1985 legislation is the prospective purchase of up to 90,000 acres of riverine floodplain in the six counties between the Georgia border and the bay. Approval of these purchases is wending its way through the land acquisition program of the Department of Natural Resources. If successful, this huge acquisition would complete the most extensive purchase of an entire estuarine ecosystem anywhere in the United States—a truly extraordinary accomplishment.

The Apalachicola sanctuary has served to catalyze and coordinate a massive land purchase around the shores of north Florida's largest bay and gained extraordinary leverage on its small investment. The resources of Apalachicola Bay and adjacent waters became the focus of extraordinary interest by state, federal, and private interests. Intensive study and consideration by these interests have identified seafood and other bay resources as having extensive statewide and nationwide significance. The county reacted responsibly to its obligation to state and national interests by doing all it could to conserve the productivity of the bay.

Sanctuary designation, together with substantial state and federal investments in public land acquisition, engendered a series of negotiations and land-use planning exercises that otherwise would not have occurred. For example, resolution of appropriate techniques and timing for maintenance dredging of the Apalachicola River occupied Florida's Department of Environmental Regulation, six of its counties, and the Corps of Engineers for several months. However, by satisfying this condition of sanctuary designation, the state of Florida solved a problem dating back to the late 1960s.

Final comments

The National Estuarine Sanctuary Program, enabled under section 315 of the Coastal Zone Management Act, was originally conceived to protect natural estuarine areas as laboratories for teaching and research. More recently, some sites in the sanctuary program have become models for testing innovative combinations of land regulation, purchase of public land, and resource management to protect a single ecosystem.[43] Although care must be taken in extrapolating from specific sanctuaries to broader principles, we believe that several lessons can be gleaned from the three case studies.

A major lesson to be learned about estuary conservation from the estuarine sanctuary experience is the value of designation. The sanctuary program's success in California, Florida, and elsewhere has to be attributed more to the power of designation than to the power of the federal grant monies. Grants of one or two million dollars that have to be matched 50/50 by the state do not, by themselves, provide sufficient motivation. Therefore, we are persuaded that federal recognition through sanctuary designation is the most important factor.

The power of designation is that it identifies a specific unit resource as the subject of conservation. That is, it recognizes that run-of-the-mill environmental resource protection programs and even coastal management programs operating under statewide and nationwide general standards are not sufficiently responsive to the very specific needs of estuary conservation. It recognizes that estuaries have to be singled out for conservation programs tailored to meet their own needs. Sanctuary designation effectively places agencies on notice that an area has been singled out for research and special protection and therefore deserves the best efforts of each government entity with management responsibility.

A second lesson is that estuary conservation can be enhanced by coordinated use of land purchase and regulation. A strategy that combines these two approaches will usually succeed much better than the separate use of either an expensive purchase approach or a repressive regulatory approach. It is of interest that both Monterey (Elkhorn) and Franklin (Apalachicola) counties were willing to adopt extremely restrictive land-use controls to protect estuarine water bodies. Whether full implementation will live up to the broad policy goals remains to be seen.

Third, sanctuary designation can attract favorable attention from private land conservation organizations. In both the Elkhorn Slough and Apalachicola sanctuaries, the Trust for Public Land or the Nature Conservancy played an important role in securing portions of key estuarine or surrounding buffer areas.

A fourth lesson to be learned is that it is possible through the unit resource approach—as best exemplified by Elkhorn Slough—to manage shorelands and waters together to achieve the single goal of estuary regulation. Regulatory, financial incentive, and restoration approaches used in concert appear to be most useful. The idea of coupled land and water management has been the elusive goal of the nation's coastal zone management program for the past thirteen years. The estuarine sanctuary program has provided new hope that this goal can be achieved.

Fifth, it is also evident that coupled estuary-shoreland resource management programs are a good testing ground for a variety of proprietary land management experiments, including both the participation of private, nonprofit land conservation groups and perhaps acquisition of property rights short of fee-simple purchase. NOAA intends that each estuarine sanctuary embrace as much of its ecosystem as possible, but it provides only $2.75 million annually for land acquisition and site development. This forces the states to find approaches that can "leverage" the federal contribution. Each federal dollar must be matched by a state dollar, but this state dollar takes several forms. Loans or grants from the lead coastal agency or budget allocations by another agency are the most common

Table 4.2 Distribution of major responsibilities for sanctuary implementation: Federal, state, and local government and the private nonprofit sector

Federal responsibilities	Responsible federal agency		
	Elkhorn Slough	Tijuana estuary	Apalachicola Bay and River
Prepare guidelines for sanctuary nomination	*National Oceanic and Atmospheric Administration (NOAA)	*National Oceanic and Atmospheric Administration (NOAA)	*National Oceanic and Atmospheric Administration (NOAA)
Review nomination and provide matching funds for land acquisition, management, and interpretive facilities	*NOAA	*NOAA	*NOAA
Prepare management plans	−NOAA	−NOAA, +USFWS +U.S. Navy (USN)	−NOAA
Enforce use restrictions	U.S. Fish and Wildlife Service (USFWS)	*USFWS, +USN	−DNR
Design and construction of interpretive facilities	−NOAA	+USFWS, +USN −NOAA	
Planning/implementation of related activities	—	+U.S. Boundary and Water Commission	−Army Corps of Engineers

Table 4.2—continued

State responsibilities	Responsible state agency		
	Elkhorn Slough	Tijuana estuary	Apalachicola Bay and River
Screen candidates and prepare nomination and grant proposal	*California Coastal Commission (CCC)	*California Coastal Commission (CCC)	*Florida Department of Natural Resources (DNR)
Receive grant funds	*Department of Fish and Game (DFG)	*CCC	*DNR
Provide state matching funds and in-kind services	*DFG	*State Coastal Conservancy (SCC) + CCC, + Dept. of Parks and Recreation (DPR)	*DNR
Establishment management policy	*DFG	*DPR, *SCC (land), − CCC, − DFG	*DNR, *Dept. of Game and Freshwater Fish (GFF)
Prepare formal management plan	*DFG	*DPR, + SCC, + CCC, + DFG, + USFWS	*DNR, *GFF, *Dept. of Environmental Regulation (DER)
Implement management plan and policy	*DFG	*DPR, *SCC, *CCC	*DNR, DER
Enforce use restrictions	*DFG	*DPR	*DNR
Design interpretive facilities	*DFG, State Architect (SA)	*DPR, *SCC, *SA, − DFG, − CCC	*DNR
Establish guidelines for adjacent land use	*CCC	*CCC	*Dept. of Community Affairs
Employ sanctuary manager	*DFG	*DPR	*DNR
Implement resource enhancement projects	*DFG, *SCC	*SCC	
Construct interpretive center	*DFG	*DPR, − SCC	*DNR
Operate interpretive center	*DFG	*DPR	*DNR

Table 4.2—continued

Local responsibilities	Responsible local agency		
	Elkhorn Slough	Tijuana estuary	Apalachicola Bay and River
Prepare and adopt complementary land use plans	*Monterey County	*City of San Diego *City of Imperial Beach	*Franklin County
Establish management policy	+Moss Landing Harbor District	*City of San Diego *City of Imperial Beach	*Franklin County
Prepare management plan	−Moss Landing Harbor District	+City of San Diego +City of Imperial Beach	*Franklin County
Implement management plan and policy	−Moss Landing Harbor District	+City of San Diego +City of Imperial Beach	*Franklin County

Private nonprofit and other nongovernment organizations	Participating organization or interest group		
Acquire land with sanctuary boundaries	−The Nature Conservancy	−The Nature Conservancy	+The Nature Conservancy, +Trust for Public Land
Restore degraded habitats	−Elkhorn Slough Foundation	*Southwest Wetlands Interpretive Association (SWIA)	—
Management and stewardship	−Elkhorn Slough Foundation	+SWIA	—
Public education and public relations	+Elkhorn Slough Foundation	+SWIA	−Seafood Dealers Association
Acquire land adjacent to sanctuary boundaries	+Elkhorn Slough Foundation	+The Nature Conservancy, +SWIA	—

Table 4.2—continued

Local responsibilities	Participating organization or interest group		
	Elkhorn Slough	Tijuana estuary	Apalachicola Bay and River
Develop model sewage treatment program		*SWIA	
Represent research and education	*Moss Landing Marine Lab	*San Diego State University	*Florida State University
Represent interests dependent on sanctuary resources and adjacent lands in policy setting	+Ranchers +Industry adjacent to slough	+Dairy, row crops, and equestrian	*Seafood dealers

Key to symbols: *Agency or organization plays a primary or lead role, + Agency or organization plays a strong secondary role, − Agency or organization plays a supporting role.

form of state match, but other eligible sources include in-kind services, land donations, bargain sales, or the purchase of land by private, non-profit organizations such as the Nature Conservancy, the Trust for Public Land, or a local land trust.

A sanctuary must also have the support of key public agencies and state legislative committees. Sanctuary designation and implementation require a variety of government functions: environmental analysis, negotiation, and funding for land acquisition, land and recreation use planning, day-to-day management and administration, interpretive center design and construction, education, and resource enhancement. Few, if any, states house these functions in a single agency. Sanctuaries may impinge on federal landholdings and acquisition programs run by groups like the Nature Conservancy. Only through intensive discussions and negotiations among agencies and private groups can this handful of disparate strands be woven into a single management fabric. Table 4.2 summarizes the distribution of major responsibilities among agencies and private interests for implementation of the three sanctuaries. The table indicates whether the actors played a lead or supporting role.

Another lesson is that bargaining and negotiation among key interests during the nomination phase set the stage for smooth sanctuary implementation. This does not mean that the core principle of estuarine protection or strong scientific evidence should be discounted in favor of political expediency. Rather, it means that multiparty discussion may often produce more elegant and more democratic management prescriptions than might be imposed by a single agency.[44]

It is also apparent that even relatively pristine estuaries can benefit from habitat restoration activities. The early evidence from Tijuana estuary and Elkhorn Slough suggests that restoration may best be accomplished through a partnership of scientists, state agencies, and local interests. In many states restoration is a policy goal for wetlands, but it takes a backseat to acquisition and environmental permitting.[45] The work of the California Coastal Conservancy is offered as a tentative model of a government program that can foster affirmative restoration.[46] In fact, some agency staff in the states of Florida and New York have expressed interest in borrowing aspects of the Coastal Conservancy model to help foster wetland restoration and the involvement of nonprofit organizations in special area management.[47]

Finally, the original sanctuary concept should not be regarded as cast in concrete. Midcourse corrections are to be expected, even encouraged. The revision of the management structure at Tijuana estuary, the regulatory contribution of the shoreline strategy and new legislation for Apalachicola Bay, and the wetland and watershed rehabilitation planned for Elkhorn Slough all strengthen the estuarine sanctuary. More changes are likely in the future.

The case studies offered here provide a sort of intermediate progress report of the status of the estuarine sanctuaries program. As the program continues to evolve, we hope research interest on the successful implementation of individual sanctuaries will continue. With the advent of more protected area programs in the developed and developing world, the sanctuaries discussed here could help suggest models for linking estuarine protection with other resource management goals. We encourage comparative analyses of the U.S. Estuarine Sanctuaries Program and the experience of other nations.

Additional references

Bella, D. A., and Klingeman, P. C., 1973. *General Planning Methodology for Oregon's Estuarine Natural Resources.* Corvallis: Oregon State University.

U.S. Bureau of Sport Fisheries and Wildlife and Bureau of Commercial Fisheries, Washington, D.C.: U.S. Government Printing Office. 1970.

California Coastal Conservancy, 1981. Staff Recommendation: Tijuana River Estuarine Sanctuary, December 1981.

Clark, John R., 1982. "Assessing the National Estuarine Sanctuary Program. Action Summary." Report submitted to the Office of Coastal Zone Management, NOAA, 54 pp.

Clark, John R., et al., 1980. "California Coastal Catalog," The American Littoral Society, Special Publication No. 10, 195 pp.

The Conservation Foundation, 1980. *Proposed Ordinances: Franklin County, Florida Shoreline Development Strategy.* The Conservation Foundation, Washington, D.C., 63 pp.

The Conservation Foundation, 1981. *Franklin County, Florida: Shoreline Development Strategy—Supplement.* The Conservation Foundation, Washington, D.C., 41 pp.

Good, James W., 1982. "Oregon Estuarine Planning and Management." Proceedings of the Seventh Annual Meeting of the Coastal Society. October 1981. pp. 213–26.

McCreary, Scott, 1982. "Legal and Institutional Opportunities and Constraints in Wetland Restoration." In *Wetland Restoration and Enhancement in California.* Tiburon Center for Environmental Studies and California Sea Grant Program, pp. 39–47.

McCreary, Scott T., 1985. "The Costs of Coastal Restoration: An Analysis of Wetland, Stream, and Watershed Projects on the Coast of California: Final Report to the California State Coastal Conservancy," June 1985.

Nordby, Christopher S., 1982. "The Comparative Ecology of Ichthyoplankton Within Tijuana Estuary and in Adjacent Nearshore Waters." M.S. Thesis, Department of Biology, San Diego State University.

Personal communication. Susan De Treville, Consultant, California State Coastal Conservancy, January 1985.

Personal communication. Robert Livingston. Professor, Florida State University, June 1985.

Personal communication. Pam McVety. Florida Department of Environmental Regulation, June 1985.

Personal communication. Carolyn Ruesch, The Trust for Public Land, February 1983.

Personal communication. George Stafford, Director, New York Coastal Zone Management Program, July 1985.

Personal communication. Jane Robertson and Jon Celicia, Division of Ecological Services, UNESCO. Paris, France, June 1984.

Sorensen, Jens, Scott McCreary, and Marc Hershman. 1984. *Institutional Arrangement for Management of Coastal Resources.* Research Planning Institute, Inc., in cooperation with U.S. National Park Service and U.S. Agency for International Development.

The Trust for Public Lands, 1982. "North Florida Oyster Beds Saved by TPL." TPL Update No. 7.

Baltimore Harbor Environmental Enhancement Plan

Mary Dolan

The Baltimore Harbor Environmental Enhancement Plan has helped eliminate the delay caused by duplicative state and federal mitigation requirements for wetlands filling in Baltimore Harbor. Under the plan, individuals granted the right to dredge and fill in the harbor are required to develop new wetland areas or otherwise mitigate the loss elsewhere in the harbor. This mitigation is worked out at roundtable sessions with the Environmental Enhancement Task Force, based on the information developed in the plan. The Regional Planning Council of Baltimore, an areawide planning agency, provided a forum for reconciling differing state and federal policies and procedures.

Plagued by delays in the dredge and fill permit process, federal, state and local agencies have joined forces to overcome inconsistencies between applicable state and federal regulations. The resultant special area management effort, embodied in the Baltimore Harbor Environmental Enhancement Plan, has made both economic development and environmental improvement easier in Baltimore Harbor.

The Baltimore Harbor Environmental Enhancement Plan was initiated by the Regional Planning Council to speed up the fill permit process for appropriate harbor uses and to assure that mitigation for those projects takes place in the same geographic area. The Regional Planning Council functioned as a neutral third party in the plan's development, providing background research on environmental policy issues and documenting the consensus of the plan development process. Because the council's powers are only advisory (it cannot enact or enforce regulations), it was therefore able to provide an impartial forum that enabled interested agencies and parties to reach a meaningful agreement on the future of Baltimore Harbor. This agreement promises to reduce unnecessary delays in useful harbor development projects while assuring adequate environmental mitigation.

Need for the plan

The Baltimore Harbor Environmental Enhancement Plan is the result of a continuing effort to reduce confusion and delay in the dredge and fill permit process. These delays have been due to differences between state and federal compensation requirements for wetland losses. Achieving a federal-state consensus took nearly nine years.

In 1975 the U.S. Army Corps of Engineers and the federal environmental agencies contributing to the Corps' permit process requested that the state prepare a comprehensive plan to guide permit decisions in the harbor. An advisory committee, consisting of appropriate federal, state, regional, and local agency representatives as well as business and industrial interests in the harbor, was formed to guide the preparation of the Baltimore Harbor plan. This plan examined and evaluated the economic development needs, the transportation needs, and the environmental aspects in a study area encompassing the entire shoreline of the Patapsco River estuary (Baltimore Harbor). Based on the results of this evaluation, recommended harbor development patterns were specified for the study area. Within this context, local and state governmental agencies agreed on general policies to guide dredge and fill activities in the harbor. These included a listing of conditions under which fill could be permitted in the harbor, alternatives for dredge spoil disposal, and the ultimate use of diked disposal areas. Maryland state policy at this time required monetary compensation for the taking of any state wetlands or submerged lands through wetland filling. Subsequently, federal mitigation guidelines were established, requiring the development of substitute resources for federally approved fill projects if the fill was used for purposes other than erosion control.

The resultant differences between federal and state mitigation requirements led to confusion and delays for development projects in the public interest. Although both levels of government had developed reasonable policies to address the loss of resources, it was difficult for a project application to meet both the financial compensation requirements of the state as well as locate appropriate substitute wetland resources to meet federal mitigation requirements. Separate permit procedures were also in place, which often added months or years before projects received full state and federal approval. This confusion and delay had to be resolved in order for the permit process to function more effectively. The Regional Planning Council, acting as a neutral party, devised a three-phase process which (1) determined the feasibility of resolving these conflicts between state and federal requirements, (2) developed a plan with recommendations for revising the process, and (3) facilitated the implementation of these revisions. This process is the subject of this chapter.

Special area identification—Baltimore Harbor

The tidal portion of the Patapsco River is traditionally the area that has been called Baltimore Harbor. This includes parts of Baltimore City and Anne Arundel and Baltimore counties. The Baltimore Harbor plan delineated a shore impact zone including the land surrounding the harbor that might be most directly affected by the water and waterfront activities. The planning area encompassed the estuary of the Patapsco River, including the shoreline from Bodkin Point in Anne Arundel County around to and including Hart-Miller Islands at the end of the Patapsco River Neck (see figure 5.1).

Baltimore Harbor is an international port serving both bulk and containerized cargo markets. It ranks among the busiest in the United States and second only to New York on the Atlantic Coast. The port provides either directly or indirectly 4 percent of the jobs in Maryland and pays approximately $300 million in state and local taxes. This economic development is often at odds with environmental goals in Baltimore Harbor when dredging or filling is necessary for expansion.

The Patapsco River is an integral part of the Chesapeake Bay estuary. Due to certain characteristics of circulation, the Patapsco River acts as a sink for toxics and nutrients, resulting in a polluted environment within the river itself. This pollution is the accumulation of many years of industrial development in the harbor as well as runoff from upstream development. Yet, conditions are improving. Environmental regulations, including those having to do with mitigation, have resulted in a more beneficial environment for aquatic organisms. Ecologically as well as economically, the Patapsco River estuary should be considered as a unit. Thus, the area defined for the Baltimore Harbor Environmental Enhancement Plan includes the waters encompassed by the Patapsco River estuary. The study area includes the tidal portions of the Patapsco River and slightly beyond the river's mouth from Black Marsh on the north to Bodkin Creek on the south.

Sociological factors add to the harbor's importance. The Baltimore metropolitan area consists of 2.2 million people, with approximately 17 percent (363,000) of them living within two miles of the harbor. As water quality improves and more facilities are built for recreation and shoreline access, more of these people are choosing to enjoy their leisure time on or near the waters of the Patapsco estuary. The national focus on Baltimore's

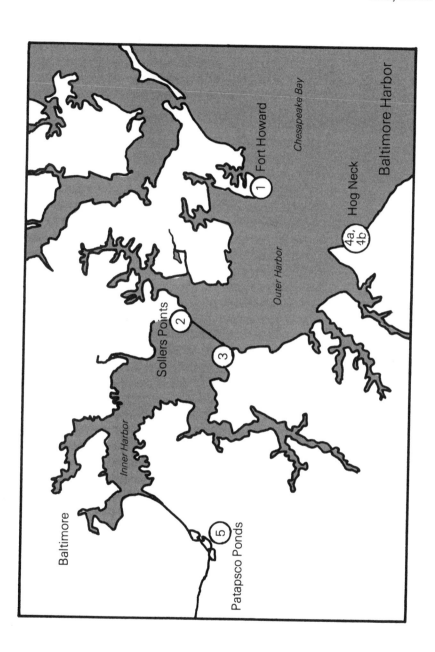

Fort Howard

Chesapeake Bay

Baltimore Harbor

Hog Neck

Outer Harbor

Sollers Points

Inner Harbor

Baltimore

Patapsco Ponds

5.1   Baltimore Harbor Location Map

Harborplace has drawn more people than Disney World, many of them tourists from other states. Continued improvement of the harbor (both economic and environmental) will educate many about the compatibility of responsible development and environmental enhancement. Deterioration would only reinforce perceptions that a healthy environment cannot coexist with a productive economy.

These economic, environmental, and social needs clearly give Baltimore Harbor special area status. The need to address these three sometimes competing needs resulted in the Baltimore Harbor Environmental Enhancement Plan.

Existing policies and authorities

The federal government requires that a permit be obtained for dredging or filling in waters of the United States from the U.S. Army Corps of Engineers, under section 404 of the Clean Water Act (consistent with section 404 B(1) guidelines) and section 10 of the 1899 River and Harbor Act. The state of Maryland, under the Wetlands Act, requires a wetlands license for fill in state wetlands and a wetlands permit for fill in private wetlands. Tidal wetlands lying below the mean high water line are state wetlands; those lying above the mean high water line, subject to regular or periodic tidal action and supporting aquatic growth, are private wetlands.

Before receiving approval, each dredge or fill permit application to the Corps of Engineers and the Water Resources Administration for projects within Baltimore Harbor (in excess of that necessary to control erosion and maintain access) should meet the following criteria:

1. Projects should be water dependent (considering the scarcity of developable shoreline in the harbor). The only exceptions considered are existing non-water-dependent uses which must demonstrate that there are no feasible alternatives to the proposed fill.
2. The proposed project must meet a demonstrated public interest (that is, net increase in employment, tax base, taxes, public access, etc.).
3. The proposed project must be the most practicable alternative considering both environmental and economic resources (to be determined by public interest review).
4. The project must minimize, to the maximum extent possible, the amount of dredging and/or filling and the total adverse environmental impacts that can be expected.

In addition to meeting these criteria, information for many other considerations and components of the environmental impact determination must be provided by the applicant. When this information is assembled, each reviewing agency determines (on a case-by-case basis) if the proposed project satisfies the criteria. In cases where the agency reviews find projects that are questionable, a roundtable meeting is held with the applicant to determine what changes can be made in the project to meet the criteria listed above. Any exceptions, such as the existing uses mentioned in criterion number one above, must demonstrate to the reviewing agencies a high degree of public interest or benefit. If this is not demonstrated, the permit will probably be denied.

Once the criteria are met, mitigation or compensation for the area to be filled is negotiated. The federal agencies require mitigation in the form of replacement or substitute resources, such as wetlands creation, wetlands restoration, fish reefs, etc. The Corps of Engineers prefers mitigation that would essentially offset any impact on the site. This includes reducing the filled area to the absolute minimum necessary to accommodate the water-dependent use and then to mitigate the fill. If replacement or substitute resources are proposed for mitigation, they should be as close to the project site as possible and ideally duplicate the resources lost. However, this is generally not possible in Baltimore Harbor, and a compromise is worked out.

State guidelines are somewhat different. If a wetlands permit or license is approved by the Board of Public Works (made up of the governor, comptroller and treasurer of the state of Maryland), it is their policy to assess monetary compensation, usually employing a guideline of one-third the fair market value of the land created. This money has been deposited in the Wetlands Acquisition Fund, which is most often used to consolidate wetlands holdings in state wildlife management areas on the eastern shore of the Chesapeake Bay. This system was never expected to replace resources lost in the harbor but only to compensate for the taking of state lands. A system of fees to compensate for the lost resources has never been established due to the difficulty of evaluating the loss.

Joint processing of state and federal permits (combining the staff review meetings for the Corps of Engineers permits and state wetlands licenses) has increased the coordination of projects requiring both permits. In addition, an informal agreement has been reached between the two levels of review. If the federal agencies have worked out a satisfactory mitigation plan to replace the state's resource values on a particular project, the state will usually waive the requirement for monetary compensation in connection with the wetlands license on the same project.

The process of developing a satisfactory mitigation program, however, can add a considerable amount of time to the permit process. The average time to process permits requiring mitigation is currently between six and sixteen months (when the applicant response time is subtracted from the total time) between application and issuance of permit.

Two cases illustrate the basic operations of this permit process: the Fort McHenry Tunnel for Interstate 95 and Atlas Machine and Iron Works.

Construction of the Fort McHenry Tunnel necessitated the placement of a large volume of dredged material somewhere within the harbor waters or at an upland location. A task force of agency representatives involved in the permit process was convened by the applicant (Interstate Division for Baltimore City) and their consultants to review potential placement sites and their design. Although the need for the tunnel was well established, the dredged material placement site preferred by the applicant was a 140-acre fill in the harbor. Other alternatives had to be examined and evaluated and their relative suitability, cost, and environmental impacts established. The harbor fill site proved to be the best alternative when environmental and economic factors were considered. Mitigation of the open water fill was included in that alternative. The nature of the mitigation, which includes marsh creation and studies of dredged material rehandling, was negotiated after the permit was granted. However, working with the task force, the applicant was able to secure the needed permits on the condition that such mitigation would be undertaken. This process, including the preparation of an environmental impact statement, took over two years.

The Atlas Machine and Iron Works Company submitted an application to the Corps of Engineers in May 1970 for the construction of a three-acre fill for a new steel fabrication plant with marine facilities on its property in Curtis Bay. After an eighteen-month stalemate, a roundtable meeting was called and the applicant modified its original proposal and resubmitted a compromise plan, taking into consideration the desires of the environmental agencies. The plan specified that the applicant would reduce the fill area by one acre and develop a marshland and a tidal pool nearby in direct compensation for the project. This process took over two years.

Once fill permits have been approved, the Maryland Port Administration requires a separate review for dredging, filling, or structures in harbor waters. This review, usually about two weeks, checks on three criteria: first, that the design is adequate and certified by a professional engineer; second, that the project does not infringe on adjacent property owners' riparian rights; and third, that the project does not present a hazard to navigation.

Land uses in Baltimore Harbor are governed by the local jurisdiction. The General Development Plan for the Baltimore Region and the development plans for each jurisdiction are coordinated to provide a regional development strategy. Economic development agencies are present in all three jurisdictions and work with the Maryland Department of Economic and Community Development and the Maryland Port Administration to encourage new and expanded operations in Baltimore Harbor. Because of the scarcity of land in Baltimore Harbor, the alternative of fill in harbor waters is a fairly frequent request. Indeed, filling for purposes other than shoreline erosion control rarely occurs outside of Baltimore Harbor. The long history of cooperation between levels of government with respect to dredging and filling in Baltimore Harbor has led to a coordinated process, with everyone understanding the needs and directives of the various agencies. The time-consuming aspect of case-by-case analysis and development of a mitigation program is the most serious drawback to the permit process. The Environmental Enhancement Plan was prepared to address these difficulties.

Assessment of area capability and use capacity

Past uses have made Baltimore Harbor much more valuable as an economic unit than as an environmental unit. The environmental capacity of the harbor has long been exceeded, and polluted conditions are the result of both upstream development and harbor uses. Continued economic growth is limited both by economic factors and by environmental factors. The economic factors include those that affect the location and type of development. The availability of appropriate land and markets, as well as transportation and other infrastructure, limit the uses that can be accommodated. Virtually all large parcels of land with proximity to deep water have been developed for industry (including terminals) or recreation. The largest part of the harbor shoreline is bounded by broad expanses of shallow water. These sites require costly dredging and dredged material disposal to accommodate water-dependent industry. One recent project, a coal export terminal, planned to extend an enclosed conveyor 6,500 feet to a dredged embayment off the main channel. Even with the conveyor, approximately 530,000 cubic yards of dredged material would have to be placed either within the harbor or upland. (Overboard disposal of material dredged from the harbor is prohibited in Chesapeake Bay.) Therefore, development is limited to expansion of existing facilities (which often requires filling) or filling adjacent small parcels to make them large enough for development.

Environmental constraints on the capacity for economic development include those that are in force throughout the state. In addition to these standards, regulations result from the harbor's location within an air quality nonattainment area. The degraded nature of the existing water quality is not sufficient to rate a designation of lower than Class I (water contact and aquatic life). Effluent limitations are the same as those imposed on most other segments of Chesapeake Bay.

Limitations on the environmental enhancement potential of Baltimore Harbor include those resulting from both past and current use of the harbor for economic development. The legacy of the past lies in the sediments of Baltimore Harbor. Large amounts of man-made organic materials, sewage sludge, and heavy metals reside in the clay sediments, leaving a thick, dark, oily muck that covers a large part of the harbor bottom. These sediments limit the growth of bottom-dwelling organisms and thus limit those in the food chain that feed on those organisms. Current use continues to deposit toxic materials in the harbor but at a much reduced rate than in the past. Recent sediment samples show a gradual reduction in toxics since the late 1940s in the top layers of sediment. Nonpoint sources, such as storm drains and overland runoff, continually contribute a large amount of sediment, trash, and chemicals to the harbor. Enhancement activities must consider the location of both point and nonpoint sources for mitigation to be successful. In addition, continued heavy use of the harbor by ships and tugboats makes it a very difficult environment for enhancement activities subject to erosion. Storm winds add to the erosion in some areas of the harbor.

Although there are very serious limitations on the harbor's capacity for enhancement, it is still a part of Chesapeake Bay, and the bay would benefit directly from any cleanup or enhancement of the harbor's ecosystem. The overall poor condition of the environment in the harbor is highlighted by small areas of habitat that continue to be productive, although affected by pollution. Planned deepening of the harbor channels from forty-two to fifty feet will probably increase the exchange and flushing of Baltimore Harbor, thereby making the connection to the Bay still longer. This only highlights the need for continued environmental enhancement that will also benefit the harbor itself. Increasing recreational use and continued water quality improvements accentuate the need for habitat enhancement within the harbor.

The Environmental Enhancement Plan proposes a staging concept that recognizes the degraded nature of the existing habitat in Baltimore Harbor yet allows for continued environmental improvement over time. It is important that the types of mitigation recommended for an area have a reasonable chance of success. Certain types of mitigation will enhance the environment to the point where others may then be initiated. The plan recommends that the site review process include such a stepwise approach. This would concentrate enhancement activities in the areas of the harbor that have better water or sediment quality. As water quality standards are met over time, areas previously degraded could then be enhanced.

Goal setting for the special area

The Baltimore Harbor Plan and Baltimore Metropolitan Coastal Area Study encouraged the continuing review of fill project permits in Baltimore Harbor. Case-by-case analysis of these projects revealed the need for a better process that would reduce the amount of time a project was delayed yet increase the chances that appropriate mitigation would be developed for the project. The Regional Planning Council (an advisory planning agency of the Maryland Department of State Planning serving the Baltimore region) asked the responsible agencies whether a study to improve the process was desirable. Once the agencies involved indicated their interest in an Environmental Enhancement Plan, funding was secured through the Maryland Coastal Zone Management Program under the Special Projects Grants.

The Regional Planning Council received a $4,000 grant from the Coastal Resources Division (Tidewater Administration, Department of Natural Resources) to perform a feasibility study over a year's time. The council convened a task force of the appropriate environmental and economic agencies at the federal, state, and local levels. This group, the Environmental Enhancement Task Force, immediately began the work of investigating the background, regulations, and policies that have been described in the previous section. An interim report recognized the need for continued economic development, including filling Baltimore Harbor, and the need for continued environmental resource replacement and enhancement where possible. This resulted in the following objective: to facilitate economic development by speeding up the fill permit process and improving the aquatic habitat of the harbor. The Environmental Enhancement Task Force concluded that it was both possible and desirable that the permit process be facilitated and agreed that they were willing to cooperate and implement the plan once it was developed. Task force members helped to develop the interim report and a scope of work for preparation of the Environmental Enhancement Plan. On this basis, a grant for $31,000 was received from the Coastal Resources Division to prepare the plan.

Selection of management tools and techniques

The scope of study for the Environmental Enhancement Plan included three main parts: an assessment of existing conditions, an assessment of the potential for environmental enhancement for various locations, and an implementation program. The Environmental Enhancement Task Force oversaw the preparation of the plan, approved the final draft, and developed the implementation program.

The outline for the Environmental Enhancement Plan was based on the scope of work mentioned above. Ecological Analysts, Inc., and Land Design/Research, Inc., were selected to perform the first two parts for $23,000. The task force reviewed information developed by the consultants and by the project manager in draft form as it was prepared. This allowed the plan to be prepared relatively efficiently, and differences in agency perception and policy could be addressed as quickly as possible.

The first section was the assessment of existing conditions, which examined such issues as water quality, circulation patterns, sediments, natural shoreline, and wetlands. This work was performed largely by the consultants with the help of the Task Force. The task force helped identify sources of information and selected those of most relevance to be used as primary sources for the consultant review and projection of future conditions. Unfortunately, the most comprehensive data for Baltimore Harbor were collected in the early 1970s. Information from the EPA Chesapeake Bay Program was not yet available at the time the plan was prepared. Although this program has yielded much data since the completion of the study, the assumptions upon which the plan was prepared did not have to be changed as a result. Existing information such as prepared plans, reports, and available aerial photography were used extensively in the assessment. No new data were generated during the plan preparation due to the limited budget.

The scope of work called for ranking potential enhancement sites in the harbor, so ranking criteria were developed by the task force in the early stages of the program in order to define the data needs and reduce the amount of information developed by the consultant. There were no particular scientific or political problems in choosing these criteria other than the above-mentioned limitations on the data. The study area was defined (as described earlier) to include the traditional harbor area and a small area around the mouth of the harbor that had a definite enhancement potential. The task force also explored the need for obtaining certain types of data. Extensive work would have been involved in mapping all the information that was available. For instance, effluent information was available from all pollutant discharges within the harbor; however, funding limitations did not permit the mapping of the exact locations of these discharges.

The potential for enhancement of the aquatic habitat of Baltimore Harbor was established through an inventory of the shoreline and its suitability for particular types of enhancement activities. These activities were selected by the task force based on environmental conditions existing in the harbor as defined by the assessment mentioned above. These enhancement activities include wetlands construction, wetlands rehabilitation, shoreline cleanup, shore erosion and sediment control, submerged aquatic vegetation establishment, and fish reef establishment.

Once the task force agreed that these activities were appropriate to enhance the harbor, the consultant identified characteristics from the shoreline inventory that were particularly important to each type of activity. Values were assigned to the criteria developed during the assessment phase based on the importance of each to a particular enhancement activity. The sites were then screened to determine portions of the harbor shoreline that were not to be considered for enhancement projects. These included commercial or industrial uses with heavy shipping activity (and areas under construction or proposed for such use) as well as sites previously selected from mitigation projects and areas excluded for historical reasons. A matrix was then prepared to analyze the inventory of sites with respect to various criteria. Using the values assigned in the previous step, each reach of shoreline was given a score with respect to the following criteria: water quality, sediment quality, water depth, wind exposure, ship wake frequency, improvement potential, public access, and ownership. Improvement potential was a subjective measure that allowed some flexibility for evaluating the sites where conditions were ideal to develop enhancement. Of the thirty-eight sites evaluated, five were selected by the Environmental Enhancement Task Force for the development of conceptual plans. These five sites were selected to provide a range of sizes, types, and location of enhancement activities. In addition, the sites selected were considered to have a better than average chance for success. This would be due to the ownership of the adjacent property and the environmental conditions presently existing at the site.

Once the enhancement sites were identified, the task force considered alternative means for plan implementation. Two main implementation mechanisms were considered. The first was the spending of public monies through the capital improvement program process. The task force considered it important that enhancement activities be included in plans for shoreline parks and shoreline stabilization activities. Because many members of the task force represented the local planning agencies, the incorporation of these activities into those plans was fairly routine. The task force also assumed that existing programs for water quality improvement could supplement these local efforts.

The second means of implementing the Environmental Enhancement Plan was through changes in the dredge and fill permit process. This offered a logical place to start because both federal and state governments required some form of mitigation or compensation for filling of water in Baltimore Harbor. However, the complex nature of these requirements (as described above) indicated the need to improve the efficiency of the process. The task force asked for two major changes that would make the process considerably more efficient. First, an up-front fee system would remove the responsibility for designing, constructing, and managing a mitigation project from the hands of a developer and place it in the hands of the Maryland Department of Natural Resources. Then, if a satisfactory fee system could be adopted, these fees could be accumulated or banked and applied to the enhancement of the harbor in a manner consistent with the Environmental Enhancement Plan.

Improving the dredge and fill permit system

Historically, the harbor has been zoned for industrial and commercial uses along its shoreline. The Baltimore Harbor Plan, adopted in 1975, gives specific guidelines for breaking down the types of industrial and commercial uses permitted in harbor zones. Water-dependent and backup activities are identified, as well as various intensities of residential development. Residential areas are generally set back from the immediate shoreline, which is almost exclusively devoted to industrial or commercial uses. A considerable amount of open space is also reflected in the Baltimore Harbor Plan. Public agencies are acquiring this land when it becomes available. The planning process reinforces land-use control and encourages the use of enhancement activities in conjunction with open-space development and shoreline stabilization. In addition, the use of state funds for fisheries enhancement and water quality improvement can be channeled into the harbor to implement some of these enhancement activities.

The Baltimore Environmental Enhancement Plan itself focuses more directly on facilitating the permit process as an assured means of implementation. This is because regulations already exist requiring mitigation and because the funding source could be developed simply through the state compensation process. The Environmental Enhancement Plan made six specific sequential recommendations regarding changes in the permit process that would accomplish this goal. After the plan was endorsed, the implementation process involved a series of negotiations that modified or eliminated some of these recommendations. Each is presented below and is accompanied by the actions taken after the plan was published.

1. The Maryland Board of Public Works should consider recommended mitigation projects in lieu of or in addition to monetary compensation for state wetlands, especially in Baltimore Harbor.

The Maryland Board of Public Works has agreed to consider mitigation (in the form of projects from the Environmental Enhancement Plan) in lieu of monetary compensation for state wetlands; however, the board will not necessarily substitute mitigation for compensation. Monetary compensation is a fee for the transfer of property interests in submerged lands. The board will retain the flexibility to charge compensation on a case-by-case basis.

2. Mitigation projects for Baltimore Harbor should include projects from the Enhancement Plan.

The Corps of Engineers (and other federal agencies), the state, and local permitting agencies have agreed to advise applicants of the Baltimore Harbor Enhancement Plan when they receive a project they believe may need mitigation. They will also offer to bring the proposal to the Environmental Enhancement Task Force for further discussion of potential mitigation projects if the applicant so desires.

3. Where monetary compensation is appropriate, federal and state environmental review agencies should recommend a fee system based on the cost of replacing the resources, giving a comparative analysis of this system with the cost determined by the present formula for computing compensation utilized by the Board of Public Works.

Monetary compensation, when deemed appropriate by the Board of Public Works, will continue to be assessed by the state as a reimbursement for the transfer of property interests. Federal permitting and permit review agencies will not consider monetary compensation in lieu of replacing the resources (mitigation) even if that fee is accumulated in a special fund used by the state for that purpose. Federal agencies are very concerned that it might appear that applicants can purchase permits. This concern eliminated the need to determine a fee schedule or to compare it with the formula used by the Board of Public Works.

4. Priorities for the Department of Natural Resources' Wetlands Acquisition Fund, the Fisheries Research and Development Fund, and other funds as appropriate should include sites and projects from the Enhancement Plan. Funds should be accumulated and applied to these sites and

projects in a logical and timely manner to offset the loss of resources due to approved fill projects.

Existing funds have criteria established by legislative or other regulatory structures. Their priorities cannot be easily rearranged to accommodate the environmental enhancement sites. Neither can these funds be used to accumulate fees from any other compensation system. The Wetlands Acquisition Fund accumulates monetary compensation (for transfer of property interests) associated with state wetlands licenses, and the Fisheries Research and Development Fund accumulates commercial fishing fees. Since the Corps of Engineers has definitely ruled out the use of an environmental enhancement fund to replace the mitigation requirement, the recommendation no longer applies.

5. The Maryland Board of Public Works should consider leasing as an option instead of a one-time fee for filling open water.

The Board of Public Works considers a one-time fee the simplest means of accumulating funds for compensation. Leasing of submerged lands, such as is undertaken in Delaware, would raise the price of compensation and discourage economic development. The state would also be burdened with administration of such a fund.

6. If recommendations three through five are accomplished, the federal environmental review agency should accept compensation to the state for use in recognized mitigation projects as fulfillment of the federal mitigation projects for approved fill in Baltimore Harbor.

Since many of the previous steps proved to be inappropriate, this final step could not be taken. Instead, the Corps of Engineers has agreed to accept the mitigation requirements as fulfilled when an agreed-upon mitigation project has been completed, regardless of who actually performs the work. This leaves the door open for state, local government, or other groups to cooperate in constructing enhancement projects that could be used as mitigation for fill projects. These mitigation projects would have to be designed on a case-by-case basis to fulfill the mitigation needs of each fill project.

Implementation

The use of the Environmental Enhancement Task Force throughout the development of the plan makes the implementation of the plan considerably less complex. The task force representative becomes an advocate for the plan within his/her agency and works together with other task force representatives to develop a coalition in favor of the plan's implementation. At various stages of the development and before the recommendations had been approved by the task force, the plan was reviewed by the Coastal Zone Metropolitan Advisory Board. This group represents citizens, government, and special interest categories from the coastal jurisdictions within the Baltimore Region. Constant public review by groups such as this one and occasional presentations to larger advisory groups such as the Coastal Resources Advisory Committee (which covers the entire coastal area of Maryland) and the Regional Planning Council have added additional depth of support to the plan. These groups give more than adequate public support for the idea. The development community has indicated that any reduction in delay or up-front money needed is welcome.

As stated in the previous section, the two major changes the task force suggested (an up-front fee for mitigation and a state fund to accumulate and apply these funds to enhancement projects) were not accepted. Instead, a letter of understanding was signed by all parties to implement a coordinated approach to using the enhancement projects as mitigation whenever possible. The following agreements were reached in the letter of understanding:

> The Baltimore District Corps of Engineers will evaluate the dredge and fill permit applications of projects in Baltimore Harbor in accordance with applicable federal laws and regulations. If the Corps determines, during the public interest review including the application of section 404 b(1) of the Clean Water Act, that habitat mitigation is necessary due to resources lost, the Corps, in coordination with the applicant and appropriate local, state, and federal agencies, will determine the size and type of mitigation necessary at a location satisfactory to the Corps. The mitigation sites identified in the *Baltimore Harbor Environmental Enhancement Plan* will be considered to the maximum extent possible. Any mitigation required will have appropriate time limits to insure its completion.

> The U.S. Environmental Protection Agency (EPA), U.S. Fish and Wildlife Service (USFWS), and the National Marine Fisheries Service (NMFS) will continue to comment on Corps evaluations of dredge and fill permit applications, regarding compliance with applicable statutory and regulatory criteria and the need for mitigation. If these agencies recommend mitigation (either separately or collectively) to the Corps, the applicant will be informed of potential mitigation sites identified in the *Baltimore Harbor Environmental Enhancement Plan*. Representatives of these agencies will participate on the Environmental Enhancement Task Force to discuss the amount, type and location of mitigation with the Corps and the Maryland Department

of Natural Resources. The EPA, USFWS, or NMFS may inform applicants that they may request a meeting with the Environmental Enhancement Task Force to discuss mitigation alternatives.

The state of Maryland Board of Public Works will continue to evaluate the acceptability of projects requiring licenses to dredge and fill state wetlands on the basis of the public policy set forth in state law, the recommendations of the Department of Natural Resources, and the advice of those commenting on the applications. In order to facilitate implementation of the Enhancement Plan through dredge and fill projects in Baltimore Harbor, the board requests that the Department of Natural Resources work with the Corps and the Environmental Enhancement Task Force to determine the characteristics of the mitigation—if the mitigation is deemed necessary by the Corps and the department. The board will then hear the recommendation of the department and approve or deny the license. If the license is conditioned upon mitigation, the board may require security for performance. The requirement of mitigation does not limit the board's power to attach other reasonable conditions to the issuance of a license. The board may require monetary compensation for the transfer of property interests in addition to requiring mitigation.

The Department of Maryland Natural Resources will continue to evaluate the appropriateness of dredge and fill projects in Baltimore Harbor through application of applicable statutory and regulatory criteria along with public and private interest review provided for under the Wetlands Law. After consultation with federal review agencies and local jurisdictions (or the Baltimore Harbor Environmental Enhancement Task Force), the department will consider the suitability of mitigation and, if warranted to compensate for lost resources, select a candidate site considering those described in the *Baltimore Harbor Environmental Enhancement Plan*. The department will encourage joint preapplication review among federal, state, and local agencies to expedite this process. The department will inform applicants that the Environmental Enhancement Task Force is available to discuss mitigation alternatives either before or after an application is submitted. The department will make a recommendation to the Board of Public Works concerning the dredge or fill project application including mitigation, if necessary.

The jurisdictions of Baltimore City, Baltimore, and Anne Arundel counties will notify state and federal permit agencies of developments planned which would entail dredge or fill activities in Baltimore Harbor, if the jurisdiction receives an application prior to a state or federal permit application. The local jurisdictions also agree to inform an applicant proposing to dredge or fill in Baltimore Harbor of the necessity to comply with state and federal permitting requirements and ask them to consult with the Environmental Enhancement Task Force at the earliest possible stage of the project.

Implementation and its feasibility were of primary concern from the very beginning of the study. Continuing review of alternatives for implementation was under way at every meeting of the Environmental Enhancement Task Force. Without both environmental and economic advantages, the plan would never have had a chance to succeed, but careful development of both aspects gives the plan an excellent chance for continuing implementation.

Conclusion

Although questions continue to surface about whether the Baltimore Harbor Environmental Enhancement Plan will result in more filling in the harbor, there are definite safeguards built into the plan to avoid this. All permit applicants must satisfy the same criteria (that is, reducing adverse impacts, water dependency, etc.) before mitigation or compensation is considered. Priority enhancement projects will be determined by federal, state, and local environmental agencies to coincide with expected fill projects. Coastal Energy Impact Program planning for Baltimore Harbor has prepared a list of expanding shoreline industries that can be surveyed on a regular basis to project expected fill permit applications. Public interest and alternatives will still be determined on a case-by-case basis.

The process used to develop the Baltimore Harbor Environmental Enhancement Plan is applicable to other harbors as well as other planning problems. The key to its success is no different from what is used to solve many planning problems. That key is the mutual agreement of *all* parties that they will work together to bring about the best possible solution. The Regional Planning Council's neutral role and ability to prepare necessary information and draft documents is not unique, but a similar agency may not be available to work on every problem. If a group or agency that has a vested interest must take the lead, then certainly a neutral advisory group should oversee the process. In any case, the advisory group (or a technical subcommittee) should comprise *all* vested interests. Mutual benefits must continually be reinforced to develop a solid working group. Another important consideration is to use consultants to prepare the technical information, reserving the policy issues for the advisory group(s). Public review at milestone or decision points is also important to assure that the process does not get diverted by one or more of the agencies involved. All these elements of success are available to planners in other areas; however, a group having the Regional Planning Council's long history of harbor planning may not be available elsewhere. The commitment to continuing planning and small successes is the necessary element that other situations may lack.

The plan is based on existing planning principles, building on common interests, and recognizing that different parties have different goals and charges. Building mutual trust through positive interaction and persistence will eventually lead to a workable process.

The plan is being used as part of several efforts to improve the mitigation process. The U.S. Army Corps of Engineers has incorporated aspects of the plan into its national requirements. EPA Region III, the National Marine Fisheries Service, and the U.S. Fish and Wildlife Service are applying the technique to the Delaware River near Philadelphia.

Evaluation

The preparation of the Baltimore Harbor Environmental Enhancement Plan was both fascinating and frustrating for all involved. The relationships developed among agencies as well as among citizen groups and those agencies have been an important by-product of the study. Even though the plan has not been fully implemented, the value of these relationships has made the process worthwhile. The key to the success of the process is flexibility. Common occurrences included adding or substituting people in the process, coping with new information and updating these new people, and lengthening or shortening time frames to suit the needs of those people and the available information. Without flexibility on everyone's part, the likelihood of success would never have been as great. With the cooperation of everyone and their respect for each other, the plan is now being implemented and improved.

Additional references

Baltimore Regional Planning Council, 1981. *Environmental Enhancement Task Force Interim Report.*
———, 1981. *Hawkins Point/Marley Neck, Development Opportunities in the Port of Baltimore, Final Report.*
———, 1982. *The Baltimore Harbor Environmental Enhancement Plan.*
———, 1975. *The Baltimore Harbor Plan.*

Ecological Analysts, Inc., 1981. *Environmental Report, Marley Neck Coal Terminal*. Prepared for Soros Associates.

Maryland Department of Natural Resources, Water Resources Administration. *Maryland Water Quality 1980*.

National Conference on Ports and Coastal Management, 1979. *Final Report*. Boston.

Oregon Land Conservation and Development Commission, 1979. *Statewide Planning Goals and Guidelines*. Salem.

U.S. Department of the Army, Corps of Engineers, 1980. *Current Corps Fish and Wildlife Mitigation Policy*.

————, 1984. *Final Regulations for Controlling Certain Activities in Waters of the United States*. Federal Register (49:195) 5 October 1984.

U.S. Department of the Interior, Fish and Wildlife Service, 1980. *Mitigation Policy—Final Draft*.

————, 1980. *Criteria for Reviewing Proposed Fill and Dredge Projects*.

U.S. Department of the Interior, Office of the Secretary, 1979. *Fish Wildlife Coordination Act: Notice of Proposed Rulemaking*.

U.S. Environmental Protection Agency, 1979. *Guidelines for Specification of Disposal Sites for Dredged or Fill Material—Proposed Rules*.

————, 1982. *Chesapeake Bay: Introduction to an Ecosystem*.

————, 1983. *Chesapeake Bay Program: A Profile of Change*.

San Bruno Mountain
Habitat Conservation Plan

Lindell L. Marsh and Robert D. Thornton

Special area management processes may also be applicable to the protection of endangered species habitat. In San Bruno, California, local, state, and federal representatives devised a habitat conservation plan to protect several endangered species of butterfly threatened by a proposed housing development. Under the plan, the landowner will fund future habitat management efforts. The plan is implemented through a conservation agreement that provides detailed assurances to the agencies that the plan will be adhered to and assurances to the private sector that no further mitigation will be required. Congressional recognition of the success of the San Bruno approach has also catalyzed habitat conservation planning efforts in other areas, such as Key Largo, Florida. This chapter describes the public-private partnership that led to the San Bruno plan's adoption and discusses the plan's significance for future planning efforts concerning conflicts over the protection of rare or sensitive resources. The authors of this chapter represented the landowners and developers in the development of the conservation plan.

The adoption of the San Bruno Mountain Habitat Conservation Plan in March 1982 marked what was then thought to be the culmination of a twenty-year war over the development of the last major parcel of privately held open space on the San Francisco Peninsula in California. This engagement focused on several subspecies of butterflies that were either listed or proposed to be listed as endangered under federal and state laws to protect endangered species.

Rather than fight, representatives of the various interests (developers, environmentalists, agencies) had agreed to explore a principled reconciliation of the conflict that would provide for protection of important wildlife and plant resources while permitting limited development on the mountain. This reconciliation process ultimately involved three cities, a county, the California Department of Fish and Game and the Department of Parks and Recreation, the U.S. Fish and Wildlife Service, the major landowner and three major developers, as well as the passage of federal and state legislation. The process produced a detailed habitat conservation plan for the mountain that was to be implemented by an extensive and detailed agreement providing for the long-term preservation of the habitat of the endangered butterflies, as well as a number of other rare or unique wildlife and plant species, in conjunction with the implementation of the county's plan for urban uses within the area. The plan also specified the contractual obligations of each public and private sector participant at an unprecedented level of detail. Most significantly, the San Bruno Mountain Habitat Conservation Plan was recognized in amendments to the Endangered Species Act as a unique method to preserve habitat and foster cooperation between public and private sectors on these issues.

The setting

San Bruno Mountain is located in San Mateo County, California, immediately south of the city of San Francisco. It is surrounded by the cities of Brisbane, Daly City, and South San Francisco. (see figure 6.1) It comprises approximately 3,400 acres of undeveloped land, of which 1,500 acres are privately owned and the rest reserved for open space by public agencies. The mountain is the largest contiguous island of undeveloped property in this portion of the San Francisco Peninsula.

Roughly 95 percent of the mountain is undisturbed open space. The mountain consists of steep hillsides, dominated by brush, small forested areas and grassland, which is the habitat for the Mission Blue butterfly[1] (a federally listed endangered species), and the Callippe Silverspot butterfly[2] (a species that was previously proposed for listing). The mountain provides habitat for a number of other endangered or unique species, including the San Bruno Elfin butterfly, the Bay Checkerspot butterfly,[3] the San Francisco garter snake, and several rare plant species. Because of its open-space character, its location and prominence within the San Francisco metropolitan area, and its unique assemblage of plants and animals, the mountain has attracted extensive environmental interest. It stands as the last vestige of the natural environment in this portion of the Bay Area—an island of open space amid a sea of urbanization.

Events leading to adoption of the plan and agreement

San Bruno Mountain is the only remaining undeveloped property left from the original Spanish land grant of "Canada de Guadalup Visitacion y Rodeo Viejo." By 1884 the mountain was largely owned by the Califor-

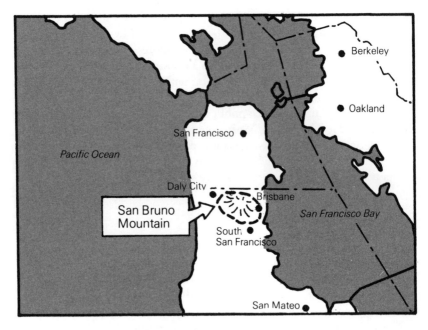

6.1   San Bruno Mountain Regional Location Map

nia pioneer and "robber baron" Charles Crocker. Until recently, cattle grazing has been the primary use of the mountain.

In 1965 the owners proposed to excavate earth from the mountain to provide fill for the San Francisco Airport and a proposed southern crossing of San Francisco Bay. This proposal was extremely controversial and is thought to have caused the formation of the Save the Bay Association and the ultimate creation of the San Francisco Bay Conservation and Development Commission, which regulates dredging and filling within San Francisco Bay. In addition, this proposal triggered the formation of a local citizens' group, the Committee to Save San Bruno Mountain, which has been intensively involved in the conservation of the mountain since that time. Late in the 1960s other development proposals were advanced, but all of them either languished or were effectively thwarted by opposition to development of the mountain.

In 1970 the mountain was purchased by Visitacion Associates, a joint venture of Foremost-McKesson, Inc., and Amfac, Incorporated. In 1975 Visitacion proposed the construction of approximately 8,500 residential units and two million square feet of office and commercial space on various portions of the mountain. An intense political battle ensued.

In early 1976 the San Mateo County board of supervisors, by a 3–2 vote, ended the decade-long dispute over the appropriate level of development on the mountain by adopting a General Plan amendment that allowed the construction of 2,235 residential units, but killing plans for 5,420 housing units in the Saddle Area of San Bruno Mountain (a key aspect of the controversy). The board of supervisors' decision on the General Plan represented a clear victory for the environmental and open-space advocates. Litigation followed but was settled without altering the essential terms of the county's decision. As part of the settlement, Visitacion donated and sold 1,711 acres, consisting of almost the entire main ridgeline of San Bruno Mountain, to the county of San Mateo. In 1979 the state of California began negotiations with Visitacion for the acquisition of the Saddle Area of the mountain for a state park. After extensive negotiations, Visitacion donated and sold an additional 298 acres to the state. In total, Visitacion conveyed over two thousand acres to public entities for open space and park purposes—more than two and one-half times the size of San Francisco's famous Golden Gate Park.

Proposed designation of butterfly's critical habitat

Within two weeks after the last conveyance of park and open-space lands by Visitacion to the state Department of Parks and Recreation and the county of San Mateo, Visitacion received a letter from the U.S. Fish and Wildlife Service advising of the proposal to list the Callippe Silverspot as "endangered" and to establish its "critical habitat" pursuant to the provisions of the Endangered Species Act of 1973.[4] The critical habitat proposal substantially overlapped all of the remaining areas on the mountain designated for development under the county's General Plan. Indeed, in several areas the proposed critical habitat boundary precisely followed the remaining private property on the mountain.

Visitacion executives were in a state of shock. They suspected that the butterfly issue was a further ploy on the part of environmental interests to prevent development. They began to gird themselves for another battle, preparing for a public meeting scheduled for 1 May 1981. A team of experts was assembled and counsel engaged to develop a strategy to force the U.S. Fish and Wildlife Service to withdraw its proposed listing of critical habitat. The other old combatants on San Bruno Mountain issues were also present at the public meeting. They included Edward Bacciocco, county supervisor for the area and the swing vote for the county's controversial General Plan, and Tom Adams, an attorney and primary advocate for the local conservationist group that won the battle over development of the mountain. All seemed ready (but perhaps less willing than usual) for yet another protracted development-preservation struggle.

At the suggestion of Bacciocco, the group assembled to discuss the availability of alternatives to another protracted legal-political battle over the mountain. The Committee to Save San Bruno Mountain (the primary group involved in the open-space battle) agreed to seek a reconciliation of the county's General Plan with the butterflies but acknowledged it was tempting to use the butterflies to score yet another victory over the landowners.

While Visitacion was pleased with the indications of cooperation on the local level, it was extremely concerned that the proposed listing and designation would further polarize the situation in that Visitacion would be required to strenuously oppose the administrative proposals and initiate litigation to protect its position. Accordingly, representatives of Visitacion urged the Fish and Wildlife Service to defer the question of listing and critical habitat designation until a "habitat conservation plan" could be developed. The concern was that once critical habitat was designated, no investor, developer, or bank would be interested in pursuing development or acquisition of the mountain, even though technically such a designation might not necessarily preclude development.

After several meetings with Fish and Wildlife Service personnel, the service indicated that it did not have the authority under the Endangered Species Act to participate in the development of the habitat conservation plan. Rather, the service believed that it must wait for a specific request from another federal agency in order to "consult" on such a plan.[5] Visitacion argued that no federal agency would be involved until long after the completion of more detailed planning—almost certainly invoking an irresolvable conflict between species preservation and development.[6] After further discussions with the service and with members of the congressional subcommittee that authored amendments to the act in 1978 specifically to encourage early consultation as proposed by Visitacion, the service changed its position. During this effort the delicate fabric of cooperation with the environmentalist interests established at the airport meeting was beginning to fray. The environmentalists believed that the Washington meetings were focused on the defeat of the proposed listing rather than on obtaining the agreement of the service to attempt to reconcile the conflict in a principled manner. These fears seemed to be confirmed when the Fish and Wildlife Service postponed the listing of the Callippe Silverspot, even though the service did so with the knowledge that, because the mountain included the habitat of the endangered Mission Blue, it was very unlikely that development could proceed without a resolution of endangered species issues.

Proposed listing by the California Department of Fish and Game

While pursuing discussions with the Fish and Wildlife Service, Visitacion became aware of a proposal by the California Department of Fish and Game to list the Silverspot butterfly as well as two other butterflies found on the mountain as "rare" under the state endangered species law—the equivalent of "endangered" under the federal act. In arguing against these listings, counsel for Visitacion maintained that the state law did not provide for the listing of invertebrates, only for a listing of fish.[7] Nevertheless, the California Fish and Game Commission indicated an intention to list the butterflies as fish, only to have a newly created agency charged with overseeing the proliferation of state regulations determine that butterflies are, indeed, not "fish" and that the proposed regulation was not authorized by California law. This skirmish provided more grist for the media, which appeared to relish anything related to a conflict between residential development and a subspecies of butterfly.

Convening the steering committee

The effort to resolve the endangered species issue was directed by a steering committee that was chaired by the county and composed of representatives of the key interest groups. The steering committee met in both formal and informal sessions—with some of the most important occurring through three- or four-party conference calls and over breakfast. This group provided a forum for the venting of concerns and the development of a basic trust among the key players. The fragility of the group was first threatened by the environmentalists' resentment of perceived lobbying efforts by Visitacion.

The steering committee had no formal members but was attended by representatives of the U.S. Fish and Wildlife Service (Ralph Swanson), the California Department of Fish and Game (Steve Nicola and Larry Eng), the county (Bacciocco, Koenig, Bacciocco's assistant Joan Donovan, the county attorney David Byers, and others), Visitacion and the other landowners and developers, the cities, and the conservationists.

All decisions of the steering committee were by consensus. This did not mean that votes were taken. In fact, the understanding was that while the steering committee served a valuable function in forcing consensus on elements of the plan, each agency would have final authority in their jurisdictional area (for example, the Fish and Wildlife Service on the Endangered Species Act permit, the county regarding its General Plan and the operation of what became the conserved habitat, and the cities within their jurisdictions). Accordingly, the function of the steering committee was similar to that provided by scoping meetings under the National Environmental Policy Act, but with the significant difference that the key participants understood that key decisions would be worked out within the steering committee.

Significant discussions did take place between members of the committee outside of the meetings, with the meetings being used to confirm understandings and to review specific points with the entire committee. In addition, each of the constituencies tended to have their caucuses in order to review the progress of the committee or make strategy for future meetings. The committee continued to meet until after the permit had been issued by the Fish and Wildlife Service and the implementing agreement signed.

Conducting necessary scientific studies

In addition to the ground rule that the resolution of the conflict had to be a principled one (that is, the resolution had to comply with the spirit and letter of the Endangered Species Act), it was agreed by the committee that care must be taken to assure the various constituencies involved that everything was done carefully and above-board and that the result was supported by the best scientific information available. It was therefore agreed that the county would engage and supervise the technical consultants who would conduct the necessary studies. The landowner agreed to pay the county the amounts necessary for this work, but with no right to limit or direct the studies.

For this work the county engaged Thomas Reid, of Thomas Reid and Associates, to supervise and conduct the necessary studies. Reid became one of the most critical players in the entire process. Over the next year Reid had teams of up to fifty field-workers capturing and recapturing butterflies, searching for host plants, scanning historic aerial photographs, and determining strategies for protecting and promoting the populations of butterflies as well as other wildlife and plant species on the mountain. The consulting firm conducted an elaborate analysis of the butterfly populations based on this fieldwork, which was documented in a lengthy biological study.[8] The biological study probably represents the most in-depth study to date of the population of a federally listed insect species.

In addition, and perhaps more important, Reid began to assist the committee in developing an understanding of the biological principles that were key to any resolution of the conflict. For example, the committee slowly came to realize that the initial concern for a single species was misplaced. What needed to be addressed was the habitat provided by the mountain as a whole. The butterflies were only further indicators of the uniqueness of that mountain, which had led to environmental concern for the mountain some twenty years earlier.

This fact became more obvious as the members of the committee began to understand the complex biology of the butterflies. The Mission Blue and Callippe Silverspot butterflies are both grassland species, that is, they require a grassland habitat, but there are a number of significant differences in their habitat needs. The larval food plant of the Mission Blue, Lupine, grows best on rocky outcrops, in poor soils where grass grows poorly, and in areas of recent disturbance. The Callippe Silverspot's larval food plant, Violet, grows best in openings in grassland where it is not overgrown by dense grass or brush. Both species depend on a mixture of high- and low-density habitat within the grassland. The Mission Blue can find its basic requirements within a very small area, but its food plant shifts from year to year. Thus, succeeding generations of the Mission Blue must shift along with food sources. The Callippe food plants, on the other hand, are scattered over a larger area, so that this species is forced to use more of the habitat on a daily basis. In addition, the Callippe is a hilltopping species; males patrol hilltops and females instinctively fly uphill to mate and fly downhill to lay eggs. This fact dictated that hilltops or ridgelines be maintained in the habitat conservation plan.

The complexity of biological needs of these two species alone provides a glimpse of the difficulty of developing a habitat conservation plan that addressed the ecology of the mountain in a holistic fashion. The effort at San Bruno was significantly assisted in this regard by the substantial amounts of open space that had been previously conveyed into public ownership by the major landowner. This fact permitted a substantial amount of attention to be focused on modifying the proposed developments to accommodate the needs of the butterflies and other species of concern.

In the end, although the habitat conservation plan continued to focus on the butterflies, it did so in the context of preserving the ecological vitality of the mountain as a whole. The plan was guided by several key principles—preservation of the ecological values of the mountain, preservation of existing diversity of habitat types, and a reliance on preservation rather than restoration wherever possible—resulting in a plan that is responsive to the needs of the butterflies but also responsive to the biological needs of other species on the mountain.

The availability of high-quality and trustworthy biological information was clearly a key to a resolution of the habitat issues. Throughout the effort on the habitat conservation plan, there was very little disagreement over the adequacy or completeness of the studies. Only a small group of opponents to the completed habitat conservation plan argued that the biological studies were inadequate. These charges were summarily rejected by the courts, however, who pointed to the highly favorable peer review of the biological studies.

Drafting the plan and agreement

Following the completion of the annual studies on the Silverspot and Mission Blue butterflies, the committee turned to the next phase, which was the development of a plan to reconcile habitat conservation with development. A drafting committee was formed of representatives of the county, Fish and Game, the Fish and Wildlife Service, and the private interest groups.

A major conflict developed in the drafting committee regarding the form of the plan. The biological consultant and the developers' representatives presented two opposing drafts. The environmentalists generally advocated a plan that would satisfy the detailed concerns of the biological community, while the developers argued for a plan which would be sufficiently clear to satisfy the concerns of lawyers, lenders, financial institutions, and other interests that ultimately would be expected to provide financing for the development projects on the basis of the assurances provided in the plan. The environmentalists contemplated a detailed plan that would be implemented by a permit that would require the developments to be consistent with the plan. The developers, in contrast, argued for a plan that would also serve as a legal agreement.

The conflict was settled with an interim understanding, brokered by Bacciocco, that the plan would be detailed but with a summary that would be in the nature of a legal agreement. This arrangement evolved into a two-volume plan with an implementing agreement of fifty pages (excluding exhibits and subsidiary agreements).[9] The agreement provides that it constitutes the sole evidence and basis for the interpretation of its terms and provisions, and that the habitat conservation plan is not to be referred to in the interpretation of the agreement except where the provisions make specific reference to the habitat conservation plan. The agreement incorporated, in their totality, the provisions of the habitat conservation plan relating to specific developments. These provisions included maps of each development area, identified areas to be conveyed as conserved habitat and areas to be graded in the course of development, and specified buffering and other requirements.

The technical aspects of the plan were primarily developed by the consultant working with the various individual developers, applying the general principles and biological information derived from the studies. With respect to several key parcels, others became heavily involved, with extensive discussions on a one-to-one basis among the various members of the committee.

Drafting the agreement

As the plan was being completed, the drafting committee turned to the drafting of the agreement. There was a constant tension between the desire to move the process along and the reluctance of the attorneys for the developers to approve drafts for distribution that had not been extensively reviewed by their clients.

The county designated a staff aide to Supervisor Bacciocco to administer the process for review and approval of the agreement, which had begun to bog down. Firm deadlines for the production of documents were established. The administration of the development of the technical documents in this fashion was critical to the success of the effort. Nevertheless, the initial negotiation of the agreement was a long, painful task. The task was made more difficult by the fact that the agreement was precedent-setting in its scope, as discussed in greater detail below.

Interestingly, as the negotiation process bogged down, others with the committee began to participate on an ad hoc basis depending on the issue involved. A representative of the developer and later an environmental consultant were particularly effective in resolving conflicts between the positions of the two attorneys.

Once the thrust of the agreement had been agreed upon by the drafting committee, the almost monumental task of obtaining concurrence from the necessary parties began. Attorneys for the three cities objected to the fact that they had not been included in the discussions at an earlier point. The Fish and Wildlife Service expressed major concerns that were finally resolved only after several extended negotiating sessions in San Francisco, Portland, and Washington, D.C., with as many as three attorneys from the solicitor's office, attorneys from each of the cities and the county, attorneys for the conservationist groups, and attorneys for the landowner developers. These conferences were usually attended by the Fish and Wildlife Service's biologists and county staff as well. In addition, there were less formal consultations with attorneys representing parties in each of the extended constituencies, such as the environmental community and the developers involved, which took place on a continuing basis.

Within the Fish and Wildlife Service the project was managed on several levels. The regional director was primarily responsible for managing the service's interests. He delegated to the service's Sacramento office the task of communicating the service's views on the agreement. The issuance of permits under the Endangered Species Act, however, is the province of the Federal Wildlife Permit Office located in Washington, D.C., and is not under the authority of the regional director. Thus, as a consensus was being developed on the plan within the region, the permit office was not involved. This became a significant problem when the local agencies submitted a formal permit application, and the permit office wanted to reconsider early points of agreement.

The final coordination of the service's position on the precedent-setting agreement fell to the associate solicitor within the Department of the Interior (Washington, D.C.) for fish and wildlife matters. He understood the potentially positive effect of the plan and agreement for wildlife conservation in general and for the mountain in particular. As an experienced hand within the solicitor's office, he also understood that the unique and complex nature of the agreement and the contemplated Endangered Species Act permit would be difficult to process through the multiple layers of the Department of the Interior bureaucracy.

Summary of the plan and agreement

The plan comprehensively resolves the wildlife issues on the mountain. The plan designates sites for development on a small portion of the mountain's open space and establishes a permanent program for funding and managing the habitat on the mountain. The primary features of the plan include the following:

1. *Protection of Open Space* The plan preserves in open space 80 percent of the mountain; all but 2.7 percent of this total is preserved in an undisturbed condition. Approximately 90 percent of the habitat of the Mission Blue and Callippe Silverspot butterflies is protected under the plan.

2. *Diversity of Habitat Protected* An essential feature of the plan is the preservation of the diversity of habitat on the mountain, including hilltops and valleys, north- and south-facing slopes, grasslands, brush, and other habitats. The effort was to protect the butterflies by protecting the diversity of the mountain's ecological community.

3. *Protection During Construction Activities* The implementing agreement includes detailed provisions regulating construction activities in the interest of wildlife on the mountain. The protections include monitoring of compliance with the plan by a "plan operator" under contract to the county, fencing of conserved habitat areas during grading, educational sessions, or "chalk talks," with the construction crews regarding the prohibitions in the plan, performance bond requirements, and liquidated damage provisions.

4. *Funding of Plan Activities* The plan provides a source of permanent funding to carry out conservation activities through assessments on units constructed on the mountain. It is anticipated that the assessments (which will be imposed through recorded covenants and restrictions) will raise approximately $60,000 per year, which is in addition to substantial interim funding provided by the developers. The agreement provides that the permanent funding will be adjusted annually for inflation to insure an inflation-free source of funding. The level of ongoing private support for endangered species conservation is unprecedented.

5. *Ongoing Management of Public and Private Habitat* The plan establishes the county as the ongoing manager of the habitat throughout the mountain and insures a uniformity of management within the various jurisdictional areas on the mountain. One of the key components of the plan is that it subjects both public and private activities within conserved habitat areas to the conservation principles enunciated in the plan. Thus, county and state parklands on the mountain are required to be managed in the interest of habitat conservation to the same extent as privately held habitat.

6. *Assurances to Private Sector* The implementing agreement includes unprecedented provisions that assure the private sector landowners and developers that, except as specifically set forth in the agreement, no further mitigation or compensation will be required in the interest of wildlife or their habitat on the mountain.

7. *Miscellaneous Provisions* The agreement includes a number of other detailed provisions governing amendments to the plan, procedures to address unforeseen circumstances, and detailed enforcement provisions.

Amending the Endangered Species Act

During the spring of 1982 Congress initiated legislation to reauthorize appropriations for the Endangered Species Act. As had been the case previously, this legislation became the focus of efforts by industry and environmental groups to amend the act to address their concerns regarding the administration of the endangered species program. Environmental groups wanted to limit the secretary's decision in preventing the listing of species; industry groups again sought to modify the requirements of section 7 despite their inability to do so in both 1978 and 1979. In this process it became apparent that an opportunity existed for obtaining legislation that would help solve the San Bruno Mountain problem as well as establish a procedure for addressing such problems generally.

Previously, the steering committee had agreed to seek a permit from the Fish and Wildlife Service to "take" individual butterflies pursuant to section 10(a) of the act.[10] This section authorizes the service to issue such permits "for scientific purposes or to enhance the propagation or survival of the affected species." The legislative history of this provision indicated that Congress intended it to apply to traditional research and enhancement activities.[11] It is certainly unlikely that Congress had specifically contemplated that a section 10(a) permit could be issued to "take" endangered species to promote their survival through a complex plan that also sought to resolve a conflict between species preservation and urban development. This did not mean the provision could not be used for that purpose; it simply increased the possibility that the permit would be subsequently challenged in court if for no other reason than the regulatory precedent established by using the act in this fashion.[12] Accordingly, a more express authorization appeared to be highly desirable.

There were several problems associated with approaching Congress on this issue. First, after the adverse conservationist reaction to the developers' efforts in Washington, D.C., in 1980, the environmentalists had agreed not to lobby regarding San Bruno without the consent of the steering committee. Second, the environmentalists' demand that any resolution regarding the mountain be within the spirit and letter of the Endangered Species Act ruled out any amendment establishing special treatment for the mountain. Any amendment would be exceedingly difficult to obtain in any event. The Tennessee Valley Authority, for example, had received an exemption from the Endangered Species Act for the Tellico Dam only after three years of effort and highly questionable legislative maneuverings.[13] Finally, an undertaking to amend the Endangered Species Act could be expensive and was at best a very distant possibility.

Therefore, as a pro bono undertaking, the developers' counsel testified before the House subcommittee and suggested that the act be amended to institutionalize the process utilized at San Bruno. Counsel emphasized that the developers were not seeking a special exemption for the mountain; rather, they wanted a recognition in the statute that conflicts over species preservation and development activities can be addressed and resolved through a collaborative planning process and that the statute's prohibition on taking individual animals might be modified in limited circumstances where the plan provides for the protection of the species or population as a whole. These concepts were endorsed during the subcommittee hearings and in separate discussions with the attorneys representing the environmental community on the reauthorization of the Endangered Species Act.

A proposed amendment to the statute was drafted and circulated to the House and Senate subcommittee staffs, the Fish and Wildlife Service, and environmental representatives. The amendment was significantly revised during the House and Senate consideration of the reauthorization legislation. Ultimately, the amendment was supported by the major environmental groups that were working on the reauthorization legislation.

As the negotiations on the agreement came to a close in the fall of 1982, the amendments to the act were honed to contemplate more specifically the process used at San Bruno Mountain. At this point, the congressional staffs were convinced of the environmental benefits of the habitat conservation plan and the potential application of the process in other settings. Nevertheless, certain staff members continued to express concern about the potential abuse of the amendment in other contexts. Accordingly, they included language in the conference report on the legislation that specifically referenced the key elements of the habitat conservation plan (the extensive biological studies, the preservation of significant amounts of open space, and the funding provisions) as a way of clarifying congressional direction for the future use of the provision.[14] The conference report also included language that emphasized the need to address unforeseen circumstances in any habitat conservation plan. The final version of the 1982 Endangered Species Act amendments included an amendment to section 10 of the act authorizing the issuance of permits for the incidental taking of individuals of an endangered species in the context of the implementation of a habitat conservation plan that promotes the survival of that species.[15]

Completing the environmental documentation and issuance of the federal permit

A joint environmental document required under both the national Environmental Policy Act and the state equivalent was prepared.[16] The complexity and detail of this process deserve a separate discussion. The process became extremely time-consuming, and with the full cooperation of all of the agencies was completed in just over a year from the time when the consultant was engaged to begin preparing the draft statement.

Allaying the concerns of the environmental community

Throughout the process the local environmental group had generally kept several individuals in the national environmental community apprised of the progress of the study. In addition, there was an attempt made to involve another scientist, Richard Arnold, who had conducted the original fieldwork on the butterflies for the Department of Fish and Game and the Fish and Wildlife Service. While Arnold chose not to participate in the steering committee and did not participate extensively in either the environmental review process or the review of the permit, he and an associate in the California Native Plant Society prepared a "white paper" attacking the plan and Reid's underlying studies, as well as the integrity of a number of individuals active in the process, including three eminent entomologists[17] who served in a peer review capacity on the biological studies. The white paper was sent to environmental groups throughout the nation with the request that they oppose the issuance of the permit.

It seemed that all of the careful work devoted to keeping the process straight might be lost to a final polarizing conflict precipitated by this white paper. In response, the biological consultant and counsel to the environmentalists drafted an open letter that rebutted each of the points raised, and with numerous meetings and telephone calls with concerned groups satisfied each of them that the white paper significantly misrepresented the plan and the process underlying it.

The authors of the white paper sued to enjoin development on the mountain, arguing that the habitat conservation plan violated the Endangered Species Act and the National Environmental Policy Act. The substance of their argument was that the Fish and Wildlife Service's environmental assessment was faulty because it was based on allegedly inadequate biological studies. The district court, and the circuit court on appeal, denied their requests for an injunction and granted the motions of the government and landowners for summary judgment.[18] The defeat of the litigation was further testimony to the care that went into the biological studies and the environmental documents. The courts pointed, for example, to the extensive peer review comments that were solicited by the county on the biological studies. While not devoid of criticism, the comments prepared by noted entomologists generally praised the thorough nature of the biological studies.

Key elements of the San Bruno planning process

There are a number of key elements of the San Bruno planning process that are significant for a more generalized application of the approach. In the broadest view, the process is a marked departure from the advocacy/judicial models of land-use decision-making procedures that have been prevalent in the United States. It recognizes the shift that has taken place from primary dependence on the private sector for land-use management decisions to a more pluralistic management system. The following section discusses elements of this process.

Defining the elements of the conflict

Initially, the conflict was focused on the Silverspot butterfly. However, as the underlying philosophy of the significance of endangered species was explored, the committee began to focus on the particular species as an indicator of an endangered or unique habitat that comprised a network of species—an ecosystem. Thus, the focus of the effort moved from the biological requirements of the Silverspot to the requirements of other species, and finally to the entire San Bruno Mountain area and a list of "species of concern," which included three species of butterfly either listed or proposed for listing, an endangered moth and an endangered snake, together with a number of plant species that may be proposed for listing. The steering committee appreciated that this was the last island of privately held open space on the San Francisco Peninsula, and because of the topographic features of the mountain it provided a unique habitat. The focus of the conflict, therefore, became not only the protection of the endangered species, but also the protection of those elements of the habitat that were particularly significant.

Selection of constituency representatives

The representatives for the steering committee were self-selected. Each agency or group that desired to be involved was welcomed. In part, this approach worked because no votes were taken. The decision makers were the individual agencies and, therefore, as mentioned above, the committee was more in the way of an ongoing "scoping" group. It was clear, however, that the county and each of the wildlife agencies involved were committed to establish the committee as the resolving forum.

The failure to require that some of the less central agencies have a representative at the table constituted a major mistake. For example, the

California Department of Parks and Recreation did not send a representative on an ongoing basis. Later, the department's counsel raised a number of insignificant objections to the agreement—then in virtually final form —that could have been easily addressed at an earlier stage. The cities as well tended to defer participation until the later stages of the process when it was difficult to satisfy their concerns without disrupting the agreement as a whole. Finally, additional consideration should have been given to keeping the broader environmental community more informed. This could have anticipated and lessened the eleventh-hour objections to the permit based on very misleading representations in the white paper.

On the other hand, the process was sufficiently unwieldy with the large committee membership that did participate. In the end, consensus represented in the agreement was sufficient to moderate effective opposition to its execution. It is clear, however, that greater consideration should have been given to expanding the representation of other signatory agencies.

Selecting the forum

The selection of the forum was easier with respect to the San Bruno Mountain project than it may be in other cases. The county had local general planning jurisdiction with respect to virtually all of the lands involved and had indicated a strong interest in assisting to solve the conflict. The county provided the center of gravity with respect to the issues involved—the lead agency in an environmental impact statement/report context. The county could host the meetings, administer the process, contract for consulting and technical services, and generally lead the process and carry out any program agreed upon. Finally, because of the county's past decisions with respect to the General Plan, it was a trusted forum by the local environmental groups.

Leadership

With respect to San Bruno, the selection of a leader of the process was not a difficult task. Bacciocco was a supervisor for the county, had been the swing vote on the General Plan, was intelligent and educated and possessed a deep understanding that his role was to be the trusted facilitator, not the advocate. He was also able to enlist the trust of the other agencies in the process.

Bacciocco was not involved in the day-to-day administration of the process. This task was delegated to the director of planning for the county, and later to Bacciocco's assistant. This distance from the process proved to be valuable because it kept Bacciocco from becoming too embroiled in the controversies that flared up from time to time.

The supervisor served a number of functions. He was available to assure that protocols (such as those with respect to Washington communications) were observed. He was available to resolve disputes that were not resolved by the technical-level participants. He was the spokesman for the effort as a whole to agencies and others not involved in the process. For example, when Dick Myshak first took his position as regional director of the U.S. Fish and Wildlife Service, Bacciocco initially met with him and briefed him on the undertaking. Bacciocco was the liaison to the county board of supervisors, and he encouraged and inspired the various camps along the uncharted path that was being followed. For example, at times he met with the different constituencies—the cities, the developers, the conservationists—to allay their fears and assure them of fair and impartial treatment. He soothed tempers. Of most importance, however, was his function as mediator—which he performed superbly.

Bacciocco's commitment to the effort was demonstrated by his personal choice to postpone a serious medical operation in deference to the demands of the process. For all of this, he was honored by conservationists, developers, and others in the community at testimonials and later at the ceremony celebrating the issuance of the Endangered Species Act permit. At this ceremony the director of the U.S. Fish and Wildlife Service presented him with the National Conservation Award, the highest award available to members of the public for contributions to wildlife conservation.

In order to serve this delicate function, it was important that Bacciocco not become an advocate for any point or constituency. His reserve, as suggested above, helped to protect him from being seduced into an advocacy role on particular issues.

Cohesion: keeping the parties at the table

For collaborative planning processes to be successful, it is necessary for all of the essential parties to stay at the bargaining table and to reconcile their positions—overcoming the frustrations and desires to have everything their way. The San Bruno Mountain process included its share of controversies and issues that at the time appeared insurmountable. There were a number of factors that provided sufficient cohesion to keep the parties together and moving toward a solution.

First, the battle between the landowner and the environmentalists over the General Plan was very painful. There was a strong interest in avoiding a similar experience. Further, the environmentalists had won the earlier encounter and to some degree did not need the victory to satisfy the sense of outrage toward development interests that generally characterized the environmental movement during the 1970s. They also felt a degree of commitment to the General Plan, which was adopted in a form they had advocated.

Second, there was an appreciation, which grew as the process succeeded, that the undertaking could be precedent-setting as a collaborative planning process that in fact worked. Toward the end, this probably more than any other factor kept the effort together. In fact, the personal and extraordinary commitment on the part of a number of essential participants at first appeared as a fluke circumstance. As time passes, it appears that the extraordinary commitment on the part of these people reflected almost a hunger for an effective process.

Third, as the parties worked together, their growing trust in one another enhanced the cohesion of the group.

Fourth, for the development constituency, there was virtually no alternative save lengthy litigation and regulatory proceedings—the potential success of which was problematical. The landowner had entered into sales agreements with developers for major parcels. These sales would have been lost, and, of more significance, the landowner was not prepared to plan and develop the lands on its own. Accordingly, the landowner would have been at a severe disadvantage in trying to properly frame the issue for litigation.

Finally, there was sufficient support for the process from the local, state, and federal agencies, supported in several significant respects by elected officials, to provide the momentum that carried along individuals who would have otherwise objected to all but a do-nothing alternative.

In summary, the San Bruno Mountain process was, to an extent, blessed by a combination of factors that helped to bring the effort together. However, the belief that the process would work grew slowly to become one of the most compelling factors in the process.

Administering the process

The administration of the process was a significant problem. The process embarked upon was unique. It was beyond the established regulatory program of a single agency. It involved state and federal issues that were beyond the normal experience of county staffers. There were no procedural guidelines to follow. It required the observance of a number of difficult and, in many cases, unrelated regulatory schemes and in general a great deal of creativity, care, and effort.

The delays and loss of time experienced along the way constituted one of the most frustrating aspects of the process. The number of distinct regulatory requirements and the number of parties involved resulted in delay after delay.

While the county undertook to manage the process, it depended on existing staff who were already working full time on their regular tasks. Accordingly, the process was to an extent neglected and delays occurred. One of the major deficiencies of the process was the lack of an attorney to help mediate legal issues between parties as they arose. In retrospect, the participants should have considered the engagement of an independent consultant to manage the process.

Funding the process

The major affected landowner agreed to fund the technical work with respect to the project through the county so as to avoid any questions of undue influence. The county and each of the other participating agencies bore their own expenses.

Because the landowner was bearing all the costs of the technical work, there was little incentive on the part of these agencies to analyze critically the extent of work actually required—virtually whatever the consultant proposed was funded. About $400,000 of technical work was done, significantly more than the landowner thought necessary and significantly more than is often required by state and federal agencies on similar efforts. This problem would have been more acute if a number of small landowners had been involved.

Protocols

Of significant importance were the protocols developed as part of the process. As mentioned above, the most interesting protocol was the understanding that no contacts would be made with the federal agencies or political figures without the participation of the group as a whole. Other protocols of significance were these understandings:

– that the steering committee would work by consensus without votes
– that the committee meetings would be open to all those with an interest in the undertaking—a self-selection process
– that a smaller group of key participants would meet in the event of inflammatory events in order to try to maintain order

Managing the constituencies

It must be kept in mind that each of the interests involved—landowners/developers, environmentalists, the U.S. Fish and Wildlife Service, and local agencies—comprised a different conglomeration of interests. The landowner/developers were made up of the long-term owner of the land, quarry operations, major developers, small developers, and lot users. Each in turn had directors, officers and participants who were liberal or conservative and in some cases incensed by attempts to protect an insect when such protection conflicted with property rights. The environmentalists were even more varied—no-growthers, open-space advocates, conservationists, reasonable, emotional, local in scope, national in scope. Social agencies had councils and boards made up of advocates for low- and moderate-income housing, environmentalists, etc.

In turn, each agency had its constituency of interests. Some low-level agency representatives were committed to the preservation of habitat wherever it occurred without regard to the need for compromise or the positive environmental aspects of the plan as a whole. Agency representatives at higher levels tended to have a larger policy perspective that recognized the need to reconcile conflicting concerns. At the same time, throughout the process, higher-level officials largely deferred to their staff on technical issues.

The private sector. The private sector interests were probably the easiest to manage. There was a clear incentive to resolve the problem. The major conflicts focused on strategy (litigation versus collaborative planning), the emphasis on political influence, etc. The lack of any precedent for such an effort and the absence of any assurance that a solution was possible made the job of developing a consensus difficult. The respect for Visitacion's president by this constituency and, in turn, his faith in the process were the key ingredients that held this constituency together.

Public agencies. There were two constituencies of particular importance within the public agencies: the local agencies and the U.S. Fish and Wildlife Service. The local agencies comprised the county, which, because of Bacciocco, generally supported the process, and the cities, which ranged from the pro-development city of Daly City to the pro-environmental community of Brisbane. The major problem with the cities was that there was little incentive for them to cooperate. They had very little downside liability or desire for further development.

The U.S. Fish and Wildlife Service presented far more complex problems. Initially, the indication of the Office of Endangered Species was that they were not required or prepared to consult before a federal agency instructed them to do so. They had little experience or desire to become involved in such a potentially time-consuming and contentious project. Further, there was an institutional policy in favor of delegating issues to the lowest rungs of the organization—the area office that tended to be staffed with young, idealistic biologists with perhaps less sense of the broad policy picture.

Further, any attempt to raise the issue to a higher level was viewed as going over the head of the lower echelon or as "political." There was not the kind of organizational understanding in the public sector that was enjoyed by the private sector—the understanding that, as required by its complexity and significance, an issue should be elevated and managed at a higher level in the organization.

Ultimately, the conflicts between the area office biologists, the regional office, and the Washington permit office and endangered species office required careful management. During the early stages the regional director provided this management. Later the Washington endangered species office and the solicitor's office provided a reconciling function.

Public interest groups. The environmentalists were the most difficult constituency to manage. The interests and concerns involved were extremely diffuse, and the organizations were of varied sizes and organizational sophistication. They ranged from local to national. Some had little internal organization. In short, communicating and obtaining consensus from this constituency was an almost impossible task. In the broadest sense, attorney Tom Adams represented this constituency. It fell to him to make sure that these interests were addressed and ultimately satisfied.

Adams did maintain a loose communication with several key individuals in this constituency, but in large part the bulk of this constituency was not familiar with the details of the process or the plan that was ultimately developed. A test of Adams's effectiveness and his understanding of his charge occurred at the time the white paper was issued. As a result of the white paper (and based solely on its assertions), a number of objections were filed to issuance of the Endangered Species Act permit.

Adams and his cocounsel, Ann Broadwell, with the technical support from the biological consultant, drafted a brilliant response, and after numerous meetings and communications (including lengthy sessions with the local chapter of the Sierra Club), they managed to convince the broader constituency of the value and effectiveness of the plan and the process. This episode underscores, however, the lack of faith of this constituency in our governmental institutions and the difficulty of obtaining the necessary consensus for this constituency.

Legal and institutional considerations

Historically, based on Anglo-Saxon precedent, our society has drawn a stormy boundary line between its management of lands by the public and private sectors. Consensual agreements have generally been the province of the private sector, while the public sector acts by regulation. Consensual arrangements between the private and public sector regarding future regulation have been severely circumscribed.

The tacit understanding has been that the private sector is the primary determiner of land use, with the public sector providing necessary support. Over the past fifteen years that relationship has evolved, with the public sector taking more decision-making authority with respect to what were previously considered "externalities," generally those considerations and effects that are not adequately addressed by the private sector in the market economy, including environmental concerns.

With that shift, the need for other foci of assurances with regard to specific projects has grown. San Bruno Mountain is an example where the provision of assurances was a key element of any resolution of the conflict between the protection of the endangered species and urban development. If individuals of a species were to be lost, assurances would have to be provided that the species as a whole would be protected. On the other hand, if the private sector were to make funding commitments or to provide lands, it would have to be assured that no further mitigation or compensation would be required.

The agreement among all the parties became a critical element, therefore, in the overall resolution of the conflict. The agreement is precedent-setting in the content and significance of the long-term assurances that it provides.

Summary

The most striking observation regarding the San Bruno Mountain dispute was the absence of any established procedures to reconcile the conflict between the adopted General Plan of the county and the requirements of the Endangered Species Act. When Visitacion requested early consultation, the endangered species office of the U.S. Fish and Wildlife Service indicated that it had no authority to try to resolve the matter unless requested to consult by another federal agency. Visitacion recognized, however, that another federal agency might not become involved until a serious conflict evolved into an irresolvable crisis. Thus, while the Fish and Wildlife Service was quite willing to adopt a "critical habitat" designation for the area that would put all (including lenders, prospective investors and purchasers, etc.) on notice of the problem, it did not believe that it had the authority to solve the problem and reconcile the conflicting interests.

The provisions authorizing the development of a "habitat conservation plan" and the issuance of an incidental taking permit provide the basis for a process that will emphasize the reconciliation of concerns regarding endangered species with other legitimate concerns of our society. The process envisioned by these provisions stresses cooperation and reconciliation over advocacy and polarization. It does not require compromise, nor is it characterized by a co-opting of any of the participants. It provides the opportunity for a principled reconciliation, with a challenge for all participants to develop an approach that addresses the needs of all participants.

The San Bruno Mountain Habitat Conservation Plan was thought to represent the last stage of a twenty-year battle over the development of the mountain. Unlike earlier disputes concerning the mountain, however, the conflict between species preservation and urban development was settled in a collaborative planning process by an unusual coalition of developers, environmentalists, political leaders, and agency personnel. The process resulted in a precedent-setting plan and agreement that specifically defines the rights and obligations of the landowners, developers, the three cities, the county of San Mateo, the U.S. Fish and Wildlife Service, and the California Department of Fish and Game and the Department of Parks and Recreation.

The essential ingredients that led to the plan's development were the following:

1. The county of San Mateo, and specifically Supervisor Bacciocco, provided a trusted forum for the resolution of the conflict.
2. Bacciocco, Adams, and others exercised sufficient leadership with respect to their constituencies to allow the process to go forward in the face of recurring problems along the way.
3. The biological consultant provided critical technical expertise on the biological issues and was instrumental in convincing the conservationists and wildlife agencies of the environmental merits of the plan.
4. The attorneys for the developers and environmentalists were committed to making the process work.
5. The county of San Mateo and the Fish and Wildlife Service considered the process important enough to devote the staff time and attention that were absolutely critical in ensuring constructive participation by these entities.
6. The major antagonistic parties, the developers and environmentalists, recognized the value of solving the process in this fashion rather than resorting to litigation or to Congress.

Despite the ultimate success of the effort, the process revealed a number of significant obstacles to consensual planning on this scale. First, the legal and regulatory institutions do not adequately recognize the legitimacy of collaborative planning. The process for the development of these plans must become more formalized and integrated into the environmental regulatory process. The development of the San Bruno Mountain plan was both time-consuming and costly. Second, environmental laws must evolve to provide greater assurances to the private sector that the terms of any consensual agreement will be adhered to by the regulatory agency and will not be nullified by subsequent agency regulatory decisions. Third, an orderly procedure needs to be developed to ensure the participation of critical entities. The San Bruno plan was nearly jeopardized at the eleventh hour by the absence of sufficient involvement by the California Department of Parks and Recreation.

Maintaining consensus over time also remains an important obstacle. Recently, for example, many of the interest groups have returned to their previous adversarial positions on related mountain issues because one of the developers discovered that an additional amount of work in grading the conserved habitat area would be necessary to insure against the potential for landslides. This suggestion touched off a furious debate over the sanctity of the plan and was viewed by the environmentalists as a precedent-setting issue. They successfully blocked any amendment to the plan in the short term by convincing one of the participating cities to oppose the amendment (the agreement required amendments outside of a triennial "window" period to be approved unanimously). This same city subsequently adopted a growth-control ordinance that would effectively nullify a major project contemplated by the plan and agreement. The developers responded with litigation against the growth-control ordinance, and the environmental community counterpunched with a local referendum to derail yet another project on the mountain. In the words of one participant in these recent battles, "the era of good feeling is over."

Ironically, the issue that touched off this latest controversy—a minor amendment to the plan to allow for additional geotechnical work in the conserved habitat—was subsequently approved under the amendment procedures of the agreement and after compliance with state and federal environmental review requirements was certified. The reasons for the breakdown in the collaborative planning process are many and varied (change of key players, absence of ongoing consensus process), but the return to the historic conflict on the mountain is largely a testimony to the inability of our regular governmental institutions to resolve these disputes amicably without the kind of special process used for the endangered species issues on the mountain.

Despite these difficulties, the San Bruno process has spawned the subsequent development of four habitat conservation plans.

1. a plan for the Coachella Valley (California fringe-toed lizard)
2. a habitat conservation plan for the 12,000-acre island of North Key Largo, off the coast of southern Florida, to conserve endangered species (American crocodile, North Key Largo wood rat and cotton mouse and the Shaus Swallowtail butterfly), native hardwood hammock forests, and offshore coral reefs (the only living coral reef in the continental United States)
3. a habitat conservation plan for the protection of riparian habitat for the Least Bell's Vireo throughout its southern California range
4. a conservation plan to protect the Bay Checkerspot butterfly and to resolve issues relating to the development of a municipal landfill in the city of San Jose, California

While the Coachella Valley and Bay Checkerspot efforts address only the conservation of a single species, it is anticipated that the North Key Largo plan will regulate all land uses on North Key Largo, hopefully becoming the common guideline for all local, state, and federal agencies asserting land-use regulatory jurisdiction. The Vireo plan is significant in that it offers the hope of a plan that will extend beyond the species to conserve riparian habitat throughout southern California.

The North Key Largo effort, under the aegis of Florida Governor Bob Graham, was funded in part by a special congressional appropriation. The steering committee is chaired by a professor of planning from North Carolina and staffed by an attorney, both of whom enjoy nationwide reputations, thus providing the strongly centralized technical planning capacity that was missing in the San Bruno process.

The Vireo process is chaired by the San Diego Association of Governments, a council of governments under state legislation that provides a portion of the necessary funding. It is by far the most ambitious process due to its broad geographic scope.

These efforts have helped to refine and improve the elements of the habitat conservation planning process. They confirm that the success of the San Bruno experiment was not just the result of chance but is replicable and provides an approach that could revolutionize our planning and decision-making process for wildlife as well as other issues of national concern.

New York's Adirondack Park Agency

Richard Booth

Created in 1971, the Adirondack Park Agency (APA) is a state agency that guides land use in the Adirondack Mountain region of upstate New York. APA approval is also necessary for most major projects in the region on both state-held lands and in privately-owned local areas. This strong mandate has engendered significant local opposition, especially from private landowners who object to the APA's strict land-classification and regulatory system. Nonetheless, the agency's unique status has remained largely unchanged over the years, primarily because of state-wide support for the APA's mission to protect the unique beauty of the area. The APA's experiences have therefore served as a model for other limited-acquisition land-management efforts in the United States.

The Adirondack Park encompasses approximately six million acres in northern New York State. Made up of both state-owned lands and private and other nonstate lands, the park is one of the largest and most significant natural areas in the United States. This chapter discusses the comprehensive regional land-use planning and control framework that New York State has established to govern the use of both the public and nonpublic lands in the Adirondack Park. That framework, centering on the role and duties of the Adirondack Park Agency (APA) and the various provisions of the Adirondack Park Agency Act, clearly constitutes one of the outstanding land-use planning and control efforts undertaken to date in the United States.

The Adirondack Park—A Description

Size and location

The Adirondack Park occupies a great deal of the huge bulge of New York State that juts north from the Mohawk Valley toward Canada and lies east of Lake Ontario and west of New York's border with Vermont. (see figure 7.1.) Covering some 9,375 square miles,[1] the park is approximately the same size as the state of Vermont and constitutes nearly 20

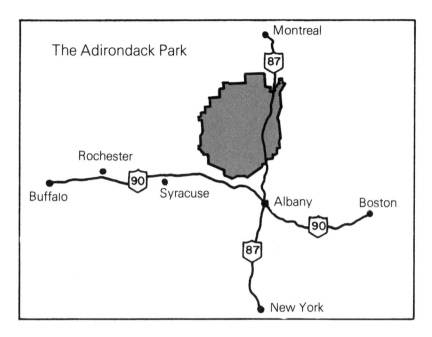

7.1   Adirondack Park Regional Location Map

percent of the land area of New York State.[2] As a map of the United States indicates, the park lies in close proximity to the large metropolitan areas of the eastern seaboard and the major population centers of eastern Canada. A park of such enormous proportions located in the country's second most populous state makes the Adirondack Park a resource of truly national significance. Indeed, it constitutes one of the nation's premier natural resources. To emphasize that significance, we may note that the four largest national parks located in the lower forty-eight states (Yellowstone, Glacier, Grand Canyon, and Everglades) would all fit together inside the Adirondack Park, with considerable room to spare.

Status and ownership

New York State's Environmental Conservation Law defines the outer perimeter boundaries of the park as it exists today. New York initially created the park in 1892 and has substantially enlarged it since that time.[3] Today the Environmental Conservation Law prevents the park's boundaries from being decreased except by enactments of two successive, regular sessions of the state legislature.

While it is a state park defined in state law, the Adirondack Park is truly a special type of park in the sense that it is made up of both public and private lands. In that sense it is similar to some other recent efforts to manage areas that include both public and private lands—for example, certain national recreation areas (see chapter 9) and the Pinelands region of New Jersey (see chapter 8). At the present time approximately 2.3 million acres of the park (about 38 percent) are owned by the state of New York.[4] The remaining 62 percent (3.7 million acres) consists of lands owned by tens of thousands of individuals, corporations, institutions such as universities and youth camps, and municipalities. A large percentage of these nonstate lands is owned by citizens residing outside the park and by corporations.[5] The park contains two entire counties, parts of ten other counties, and 107 municipalities.

A land-ownership map of the Adirondacks indicates a number of outstanding features. First, state-owned lands and nonstate-owned lands are intermingled to a very significant degree so that there is a very direct, intimate, and vastly important relationship between these two major categories of land ownership.[6] Second, state lands occur in parcels of various sizes, ranging from just a few acres to more than 225,000 acres.[7] Third, the nonpublic lands of the park consist of parcels ranging from thousands of small house lots to tracts owned by paper companies, other corporations, and various private individuals that are tens of thousands of acres in size.[8]

Natural Resources

The natural resources of the Adirondack Park are diverse, abundant, and truly outstanding. It contains parts or all of the headwaters of five major water basins. These include the Lake George–Lake Champlain Basin, the St. Lawrence River, the Black River, the Mohawk River, and the Hudson River.[9] In these five major watershed areas exist some 2,800 lakes and ponds and more than 30,000 miles of free-flowing rivers and streams.[10] More than 1,200 miles of Adirondack rivers have been designated under New York State's Wild, Scenic, and Recreational Rivers System Act,[11] and more than 500,000 acres of freshwater wetlands exist in the park.

Great forests stretching across thousands of square miles cover the vast majority of the park's rugged terrain. The best-known portion of the park is the Adirondack high peaks area, located in the park's northeastern part. There more than forty peaks rise to elevations above 4,000 feet, including the highest point in New York State, Mt. Marcy (elevation 5,344 feet). These ancient mountains provide extensive opportunities for hiking and other recreational purposes.

The park's biological resources are diverse and valuable. The wild and open spaces of the park and its diverse water resources support some fifty species of mammals, 220 species of birds, thirty species of reptiles and amphibians, and sixty-six species of fish. The plant resources of the park are equally varied, with some thirty tree species native to the park. Wildflowers, shrubs, and other plants exist in great abundance and variety.

The park's varied and enormous landscape is famous for its beauty and its open-space quality. Ranging from quiet, rural landscapes dotted with small farms to the tops of its wildest peaks, from a quiet stream in an Adirondack village to its wildest river, the park offers diversity, extraordinary opportunities for solitude, and simply room for countless people to enjoy the outdoors.

Population

The Adirondack Park has a permanent population of approximately 125,000 persons, who live primarily in the many small villages and hamlets that are scattered throughout the park. These community centers range in size from just a few houses to incorporated villages of 3,000–7,000 inhabitants. In addition to the permanent residents, the park supports two other major populations. First, there is a large seasonal population of about 90,000, which lives in second homes in the park, primarily during the summer months. Second, a much larger transient population uses the park for a wide variety of tourist and recreational pursuits.[12] This transient population is much larger in the summer months than during the rest of the year, but it is a significant factor in portions of the park (for example, the Lake Placid and Old Forge areas) during the winter months.

Use of the park's resources

Nearly all state lands in the Adirondack Park are part of the New York State Forest Preserve. Since 1895 an extraordinary clause of the New York State Constitution has protected the Forest Preserve as forever wild lands. This mandate (now set forth in article XIV of the state constitution)[13] requires New York State to maintain these lands in a wild forest condition. It has no legal parallel in the laws of this nation. These lands are not subject to management, manipulation, or resource extraction (for example, New York allows no timber to be taken from these millions of acres). Consequently, most state lands in the Adirondacks are used for a variety of nonintensive recreational uses (for example, hiking, camping, hunting, fishing, and boating). In parts of the Forest Preserve the state maintains a million acres of designated wilderness areas.[14] In other parts of the Forest Preserve the state has provided intensive-use areas as campgrounds (which have always raised interesting questions as to their consistency with article XIV and the applicability of that constitutional provision to them) and, pursuant to amendments to the state constitution, ski areas.[16] A small percentage of the state lands in the Adirondacks is not considered part of the Forest Preserve; these other lands are used for a variety of other governmental uses, including the state highway system.

The nonstate-owned lands in the Adirondack Park are used for a wide variety of human uses. These include residential, commercial, industrial, recreational, and public uses. For example, thousands of permanent and seasonal homes, numerous types of tourist accommodations, extensive forestry and mining activities, private camps and institutions, hunting and fishing clubs, and farms exist throughout the park. The communities in the park consist of the entire spectrum of uses typically found in small, rural centers. The wide variety of uses on the park's private lands complements the park's state-owned Forest Preserve lands.

Economy

Tourism, forestry, mining, agriculture, and public service (that is, government employment) form the basic economic activities of the region. Of these, tourism is clearly the major industry, providing thousands of jobs in the summer months and many (although far fewer) jobs during the winter. Many types of outdoor recreation activities occur on both state and nonstate lands in the park. Because of its proximity to major population centers, the Adirondacks offer an enormous range of recreational activities for millions of people. Camping, picnicking, hiking, hunting, fishing, swimming, water skiing, downhill and cross-country skiing, boating, canoeing, ice skating, snowmobiling, snowshoeing, and golfing are among the popular recreational pursuits that many thousands of persons enjoy every year.[17]

Resource extraction industries constitute an important part of the park's economy (as they have traditionally). Forestry forms the economic base for much of the region. Large forest products companies own hundreds of thousands of acres of the Adirondacks and actively manage their forests for forestry purposes.[18] The Adirondacks also contain significant deposits of various minerals. Mining is economically important in certain areas of the park.

Agricultural activities exist primarily in the Lake Champlain Valley on the eastern fringe of the park, and there are some valuable agricultural lands in other parts of the Adirondacks. A short growing season limits agricultural activities in the park. In addition, the terrain of the park and its generally poor soils are not highly conducive for agriculture.

Notwithstanding the existence of certain economically viable activities, the overall economic picture in the park, particularly for many of its permanent residents, is bleak. The park suffers from high unemployment and inflated welfare rolls. Economic prosperity in the region is apparently most closely tied to the well-being of the tourist industry, and the seasonal fluctuations of that industry aggravate these problems.[19] New industries traditionally have not located in the Adirondacks because of the distance from markets, poor transportation, and the lack of a skilled work force. These fairly dismal factors are long term and do not appear to be the result of New York's land-use program in the park.[20]

History—development of a regional framework

The history of the Adirondack Park is long and notable. Samuel de Champlain was probably the first European to see the Adirondacks. In 1609 he discovered the large lake that now bears his name. For nearly two centuries French- and English-speaking peoples and Indian tribes used the Lake Champlain–Lake George corridor as major battlefields in the wars that determined the eventual English control of most of the North American continent.[21] That same corridor played a major role in the American Revolution and the War of 1812.[22]

The large westward migration of the American people in the late eighteenth century and nineteenth century largely bypassed the Adirondacks.[23] However, mining and forestry interests discovered valuable resources in the region. Throughout the 1800s resource development companies raced to acquire and exploit as many of those resources as they possibly could. Logging activities in particular devastated much of the region. Toward the end of the nineteenth century the Adirondacks became a popular retreat for many of this country's wealthiest families and for many avid hunters and fishermen. Their love of the Adirondacks and their desire to protect the area's natural qualities became a powerful force in the eventual effort by New York State to guarantee the area's future protection.

As a result of widespread and growing interest in protecting the resources of the Adirondacks for future generations, particularly from the widely destructive activities of the forest industry, New York State began a long and remarkable course of action in the 1880s that led eventually to the comprehensive regional land-use planning and control framework that exists today in the park. State lawmakers defined the Adirondacks as a state park in 1892 (a much smaller park than exists today). In 1894, dissatisfied with statutory protections adopted in the 1880s for state lands in the Adirondacks, the citizens of New York State passed a constitutional amendment that required the Forest Preserve be forever protected as wild forest lands. It took effect in 1895.

By the middle of the 1960s it was clear that in spite of the protection of the Forest Preserve by the state constitution, the overall protection of the Adirondack Park was largely a fiction. Many New Yorkers shared a growing awareness of the absence of an overall framework to protect the entire park. Local governments in the sparsely populated park were neither interested in nor capable of using their local land-use powers to protect the region's natural resource base and open-space character. In fact, at that time few Adirondack local governments had comprehensive land-use controls of any kind.[24] Increasingly, large subdivision developments threatened significant areas of the park, and the anticipated completion of Interstate 87, the Adirondack Northway, linking New York City and Albany to Montreal (which finally occurred in 1967) was expected to increase pressure dramatically on many of the park's resources. Furthermore, it was clear the state's Forest Preserve lands would be increasingly threatened by development of nearby private lands.

In the absence of a satisfactory solution for handling increasing pressures on the resources of the park, in the 1960s various interests began to look for a more comprehensive solution for the Adirondacks. In 1968 Laurence Rockefeller, a noted conservationist and brother of New York's governor, Nelson Rockefeller, released a report recommending that approximately one-third of the Adirondack Park as it then existed be incorporated into a new national park. This proposal, it was suggested, would insure long-term protection of the vitally important central region of the park. Interestingly, virtually every major interest group in New York State strongly opposed that proposal. Conservationists, industrialists, Adirondack local governments, Adirondack residents, and the New York State government joined hands in forcefully opposing a role by the National Park Service in the Adirondacks.[25]

In 1968, as a result of the popular rejection of the national park proposal, Governor Rockefeller created the Temporary Study Commission on the Future of the Adirondacks. For two years this blue-ribbon commission and a small but talented staff studied a broad spectrum of questions regarding the region's future. In 1970 the commission issued 181 detailed, extensively documented recommendations.[26] Its leading recommendation was that the state of New York create a new state agency to be responsible for comprehensive land-use planning and control for both public and private lands in the Adirondacks. Its dozens of other recommendations included such things as the establishment of a wild, scenic, and recreational rivers system for the park, the use of conservation easements to protect lands in the park, and a more aggressive and directed state land-acquisition program.

The recommendations of the Temporary Study Commission had a major impact on the thinking of the state's political leaders. In 1971 the New York State Legislature passed the Adirondack Park Agency Act, creating the Adirondack Park Agency (APA) and requiring it to prepare a comprehensive management plan for the park's state lands and a land-use and development plan for the nonstate lands in the Adirondacks.[27] The APA came into existence in September 1971.

It did not take much time for the APA to become a visible and important entity in New York State government. In the summer of 1972 the agency completed the Adirondack Park State Land Master Plan, heavily based on recommendations of the Temporary Study Commission. After public hearings it was sent to Governor Rockefeller for his signature, and it took effect in August 1972.

In the second half of 1972 the APA and its staff mounted an intense and remarkable effort to complete a proposed plan for the park's nonstate lands. They were successful in doing so. In January 1973 the APA held a series of dramatic, emotional, and heavily attended public hearings on a draft land-use and development plan for those lands.[28] While creating a great deal of controversy and opposition in the park, the plan appeared to most concerned political constituencies to present a viable means for insuring long-term protection of many of the park's resources. After further agency deliberations, the APA sent a revised plan to the legislature in March 1973. The legislature made numerous amendments in the APA's plan but retained the substantive land-use control mechanisms proposed by the agency. It amended the Adirondack Park Agency Act by adopting the Adirondack Park Land Use Development Plan, and Governor Rockefeller signed the amended statute in May 1973. The so-called "Private Land Plan" took effect on 1 August 1973.[29]

The history of the Adirondack Park since August 1973 has been one of controversy and progress. New York State has successfully established and undertaken the most comprehensive regional land-use planning and control effort yet attempted in the United States. It has done so in the face of major opposition within the Adirondacks and from certain segments of the state legislature.[30] The Adirondack Park Agency Act has withstood the political challenges and the major legal challenges that have threatened it at various times.

In 1932 the Winter Olympics at Lake Placid focused national and international attention on the Adirondack Park. The 1980 Winter Olympics at Lake Placid again focused a great deal of attention on this splendid area and posed the threat of significant environmental degradation. By that time, however, New York State could argue that it had found a responsible solution for reasonably balancing the need to protect the natural environment with the desires for economic growth and development.

Adirondack Park Agency

Over the past fifteen years the Adirondack Park Agency has been the focal point of many major policy decisions respecting the park and of the controversy that has surrounded New York State's land-use efforts there. Located in the executive department and directly responsible to New York's governor, the APA and its professional staff merit special attention in this discussion.

The APA's membership reflects a careful balancing in the APA Act of major Adirondack interests. It has eleven voting members. Three of those eleven are state officials appointed by the governor—the secretary of state, the commissioner of environmental conservation, and the commissioner of commerce.[31] These officials provide direct representation on the APA for the state's major interests in the park. The eight remaining members are private citizens, appointed by the governor with the advice and consent of the state senate. They serve staggered four-year terms so that the APA is somewhat insulated from the appointment power of any currently sitting governor. These appointed members reflect the strong interest of New York's citizens in the park. Of these eight citizen-members, five are required by law to be full-time residents of the park, and three are required to be New York residents living outside the park. No more than five of the eight appointed members may come from the same political party, and no two of the in-park members may be residents of the same county. These various requirements provide an agency that is, at least in theory, sensitive to the major interests at stake in the Adirondacks.[32]

Except for its chairman, the APA's members do not serve on a full-time basis. The three state officials have other, major duties, and each may appoint one or more designees to carry out his duties on the APA. While the chairman now receives a substantial, full-time salary, the other seven citizen-members are paid on a per diem basis of $100 a day up to a maximum of $5,000 per year. Service on the agency requires a great deal of work by the eleven members. It is, therefore, not a rich political plum, but agency members do enjoy a fair amount of political visibility.[33]

The APA has its own professional staff. That staff has always been small in comparison with the staffs of other New York State agencies and certainly modest in light of the agency's extensive responsibilities. It now contains approximately forty individuals, including resource specialists, lawyers, planners, and technicians.[34] Notwithstanding its small size, the APA staff has often proved to be an effective operator in the politically charged atmosphere in which the APA has operated since its inception. Furthermore, the fact that it has had its own staff has helped the APA preserve its own identity, priorities, and purpose.

The regional land-use planning and control framework

The regional land-use planning and control framework in the Adirondack Park consists of several major elements: the structure for controlling use of state lands in the park, including most importantly article XIV of the state constitution and the Adirondack Park State Land Master Plan; the provisions of the APA Act relating to the control of land uses on the park's nonstate lands, including most importantly, the Adirondack Park Land Use and Development Plan, a regional project review system, and the respective roles of the APA and Adirondack local governments regarding the use of nonstate lands; and several other significant elements. This section discusses each of these.

Controlling the use of state lands in the park

A. Article XIV. Article XIV of the state constitution is the legal center-piece respecting the use of state lands in the park. With the exception of a minor percentage of state lands (some of which, like state highways, have been specifically exempted from article XIV), article XIV's extremely strong provisions apply to the enormous tracts of land New York owns in the park.[36] The critical constitutional language is as follows: "The lands of the state, now owned or hereafter acquired, constituting the forest preserve as now fixed by law, shall be forever kept as wild forest lands. They shall not be leased, sold or exchanged, or be taken by any corporation, public or private, nor shall the timber thereon be sold, removed or destroyed." This general mandate prohibits management of the Forest Preserve for resource extraction purposes or disposition of any part of it. The several exceptions to that mandate set forth in article XIV (for example, for the construction and maintenance of state highways and of certain ski areas on the Forest Preserve) do not alter the essential meaning and purpose of the strong protection it affords Forest Preserve lands in the park. Having been initially set forth in the state constitution of 1895, this powerful legal mechanism has shaped many of New York's decisions about the Adirondack Park.[37]

   B. *The Adirondack park state land master plan.* The Adirondack Park State Land Master Plan[38] establishes an overall system of standards and controls for managing the approximately 2.3 million acres of state lands in the park. As mentioned previously, most state lands in the Adirondacks are protected by article XIV of the New York State constitution and required by that constitutional provision to remain forever wild. The State Land Master Plan does not alter that constitutional mandate, but rather attempts to classify the park's state lands into categories that reflect both current uses of those lands and desired principles to guide future uses. The State Land Master Plan incorporates the APA's assessment of four primary elements: *physical characteristics* of land and water resources, including soils, slopes, elevations, and the types and qualities of water bodies; *biological characteristics,* including the locations of fragile ecosystems and important wildlife habitat; certain *"intangible considerations,"* such as remoteness, degrees of wildness available in different areas, ruggedness of the terrain, and density of forest cover; and the existence of *established facilities* on state land, such as campgrounds, highways, and ski areas.

   Prepared by the APA in consultation with the New York State Department of Environmental Conservation, the plan divides state lands into nine land-use categories. The state land plan delineates these nine land-use categories by map and defines in text their essential characteristics and the uses compatible with each category. The nine land-use classifications are as follows:

1. wilderness areas: fifteen areas, covering a total of approximately 1,000,000 acres
2. primitive areas: nineteen areas, covering a total of approximately 65,000 acres
3. canoe areas: one area covering approximately 18,000 acres
4. wild forest: fifteen major areas and many smaller ones, covering a total of approximately 1,200,000 acres
5. intensive use areas

6. wild, scenic, and recreational river corridors
7. travel corridors
8. state administrative areas
9. historic areas

Ranging in size from approximately 15,000 acres (with a required minimum of 10,000 acres) to more than 225,000 acres, wilderness areas constitute the most restrictively controlled areas of state lands. Permitted uses focus on outdoor recreational activities through which humans leave only minimal impacts on the natural resource base. Intensive human uses and nearly all nonemergency motorized or mechanical equipment uses are barred. The definition of wilderness areas in the Adirondacks and delineation of uses compatible with their resources closely parallel the standards established for the Federal Wilderness System.[39] Given the sparcity of wilderness resources in the eastern United States, these designated wilderness areas are an exceptionally important resource.

Restrictions for primitive and canoe areas are very similar to those for wilderness areas. While some of the primitive areas may in the future become wilderness areas through removal of existing nonconforming uses (such as an existing road or structure), some will not because they are too small.[40] The one canoe area now designated in the park is designed to protect a unique area of small ponds and lakes.

Wild forest areas include about half the state lands in the park. They are available for some recreational uses that are more intensive than those allowed in wilderness areas. These include limited motorized activities, such as snowmobiling on designated trails.

Wild, scenic and recreational river corridors are those areas of state land that have received special designation under the state's Wild, Scenic and Recreational Rivers System Act. That statute is designed to protect the free-flowing character and natural qualities of specified rivers. In addition to these areas on state lands, the statute designates major river segments on nonstate lands.

The other land-use areas set forth in the State Land Master Plan serve a variety of special purposes. Intensive use areas include campgrounds, boat launch sites, beaches, and ski areas. Administrative areas contain a variety of state buildings used by various state agencies. Travel corridors encompass the state highway system in the park and immediately adjacent lands and a major railroad right-of-way, which the state purchased. There are two key historic areas in the park. Others may be added. These several categories occupy a small percentage of state lands in the park.

The New York State Department of Environmental Conservation (DEC) is responsible for managing most state lands in the park, including the Forest Preserve.[41] DEC has several major tasks pursuant to the State Land Master Plan: first, to make sure that the uses occurring in various areas comply with the plan; second, to remove uses that do not conform to the plan, including such things as roads, fire towers, and ranger stations in certain areas; and third, to prepare unit management plans. DEC has done well with its first task and quite well with the second. Unfortunately, it has not until very recently made much progress on the third task because of lack of commitment, as well as budget and personnel restrictions.[42]

The APA is responsible for reviewing the State Land Master Plan and determining whether it should propose any changes in it. It is also responsible for classifying new state land acquisitions. The agency must consult with DEC respecting any amendments it proposes and must submit proposed revisions, after public hearing, to the governor for approval. The APA adopted a set of fairly important amendments in 1979, but those amendments did not change the basic structure or content of the State Land Master Plan.

Controlling the use of nonstate lands under the APA act

A. *Adirondack Park Land Use and Development Plan.* The Adirondack Park Land Use and Development Plan, as adopted by the legislature and set forth in the Adirondack Park Agency Act, contains the major land-use restrictions for the park's nonstate lands. Because it regulates private lands, it has been far more controversial than the State Land Master Plan insofar as Adirondack residents are concerned.

The Land Use and Development Plan was based in large part on Ian McHarg's ecological approach to land use planning.[43] Two major considerations dominated the plan's preparation: first, that development of the park's nonstate lands should occur where natural resources can best sustain it and where existing development already exists; second, that development should be limited in remote areas, in areas where resources are sensitive, and in areas where provision of local government services is difficult.[44] In developing the plan, the APA created a series of development constraint overlays to reflect the physical and biological resource base of the park's lands—for example, soils, slopes, key wildlife habitat—and the scenic, recreational, open-space, and historic qualities of the park. The APA used that resource information and its assessment of the existing land uses and facilities existing in the park in creating a land-use classification system. In doing so, it had to fulfill the purposes of the APA Act to insure the protection of the park's resources and the wise use and development of those resources and to reflect statewide and local interests in protecting and using the park. Those statutory purposes required a very difficult balancing act.

The plan divides nonstate lands into six land-use areas. The Adirondack Park Land Use and Development Plan Map delineates these six land-use areas. The map uses boundaries that are primarily roads, political boundary lines, water bodies, and similar indicators that can be easily identified on the ground. The six land-use areas are as follows:

1. Hamlets: the park's settled communities, including both incorporated villages and the region's other small population centers
2. Moderate-intensity-use areas: largely residential areas, many of which are located along the shores of lakes and rivers
3. Low-intensity-use areas: largely residential areas but less densely developed than moderate-intensity-use areas
4. Rural-use areas: largely open space areas, covering some 37 percent of the park's nonstate lands
5. Resource management areas: open space areas where resources are remote or particularly sensitive to development, encompassing more than 50 percent of the park's nonstate lands
6. Industrial-use areas: areas encompassing the park's major industrial centers, including mines and large paper production facilities, and a few potential industrial sites

The Land Use and Development Plan establishes a series of guidelines that control the use of those areas. Its text describes the general character and purpose of each land-use area and establishes lists of compatible uses for each area. There is a good deal of flexibility in the use lists; the plan does not attempt to segregate different *types* of uses to nearly as great a degree as local land-use ordinances typically do. The plan also sets shoreline restrictions for each land-use area. These include such standards as building setbacks, minimum lot widths, minimum septic facility setbacks, and vegetation-cutting restrictions. Furthermore, the plan sets development considerations that are to be used in reviewing new development proposals in the park.

The most important restrictions established by the Land Use and Development Plan are the "overall intensity guidelines," which set density restrictions for development on nonstate lands. These density controls are the most critical "teeth" in the land-use plan and the center of much of the controversy that surrounds the APA.[45] The overall intensity guidelines vary in the different land-use areas. The plan sets no guidelines for hamlet areas because density in those areas is considered a matter of local concern, and it sets none for industrial-use areas where they would be inappropriate. For the other four land-use areas, the density guidelines are as follows:

— Moderate-intensity use: 500 principal buildings per square mile
— Low-intensity use: 200 principal buildings per square mile
— Rural use: 75 principal buildings per square mile
— Resource management: 15 principal buildings per square mile

The sliding scale of density limitations indicates the state's major concern that development be carefully controlled in the more remote and fragile resource regions of the park.

Because the overall intensity guidelines are expressed in terms of buildings per square mile (640 acres), many persons typically think of them as lot size requirements (moderate intensity—1.3 acres per building, low intensity—3.2 acres; rural use—8.5 acres; and resource management— 42.7 acres).[46] Actually, instead of being lot size requirements, they are intended to encourage developers to place buildings in the areas where the existing natural resource base can support them, leaving undeveloped other areas with sensitive resources such as steep slopes, wetlands, and shallow soils. They are applied to each individual piece of land on which a proposed regional project (see discussion below) is to be located; in that way, no landowner is allowed to use up his neighbor's allowable building density. Based on the premise that controlling building density is critical to protecting the natural and open-space character of the park, the density guidelines regulate land development in the park, encourage that development to occur in areas where it will be most compatible with the park's resources, and discourage development of fragile and remote areas.

While the two regional plans serve very different purposes and are based on very different legal underpinnings, the Land Use and Development Plan for nonstate lands and the State Land Master Plan have some similarities and interrelate in several ways. Both are heavily oriented toward the goal of resource protection (although article XIV of the state constitution establishes a far stronger basis for protecting state lands than does the APA Act for nonstate lands). To that end both utilize a regional scale land classification scheme. Because the State Land Master Plan was heavily based on work done by the Temporary Study Commission and prepared prior to the Land Use and Development Plan, it influenced aspects of the "private land plan." The Land Use and Development Plan did not greatly influence the State Land Master Plan, even though they were prepared by the same people and at approximately the same time.[47]

Some of the specific land-classification decisions made by the APA for nonstate lands incorporated various considerations from the State Land

Master Plan. Given the purpose of protecting designated wilderness areas on state lands in order to preserve naturally functioning ecosystems and to minimize human impact on those systems, the APA classified a number of privately owned areas as resource management in order to protect the natural resources of wilderness areas. This occurred, for example, where drainage from private lands would flow into a designated wilderness area. Furthermore, for wilderness, primitive, canoe and wild forest areas, the State Land Master Plan attempted to encourage use of those lands for open-space recreational purposes consistent with article XIV of the state constitution. The APA was conscious in designating private lands adjoining these state land areas of maintaining the ambiance of a rural landscape consistent with the interests of the recreational user on state lands. Accordingly, private lands were frequently classified rural use or resource management in part because of their relationship to important recreational values that could be found on nearby state lands. This was particularly true around a number of major entrances to state land, where recreational users would be particularly aware of the character of surrounding lands. From a somewhat different perspective, the APA was conscious of the probable need for compatible commercial development near some of the intensive-use areas on state lands—for example, around ski areas—and classified a number of areas into rural use, low-intensity use, and moderate-intensity use for these reasons. In some of these cases the APA even expanded hamlet classifications because of the presence of nearby intensive-use areas beyond what those classifications would otherwise have been.

The two plans are also related at a more general level. The classification decisions respecting private lands incorporated a number of broad concerns that related to the existence of state lands. These included, for example, aesthetic concerns, protection of the park's open-space character, and the remoteness of certain private lands and the difficulty or impossibility of ever providing services to them (often because of state-nonstate land configurations).[48] In addition, the implementation provisions of the APA Act relating to the Land Use and Development Plan incorporate a number of concerns relative to state lands. The development considerations and the project review system (see next subsection) exhibit concern about the impacts of developing private lands on nearby state lands—for example, most new development activities within one-eighth mile of certain critical state land classifications are defined as regional projects and require a permit under the APA Act.[49] Finally, and perhaps most important, it was the state's tremendous landholdings in the park, the intermingled nature of state and nonstate lands, and concern that misuse of nonstate lands could harm the qualities of the Forest Preserve that provided a great deal of the impetus for New York State to undertake comprehensive land planning in the Adirondack Park.[50] That concern permeated both plans.

The relationships between the two plans do not mask their essential differences. The State Land Master Plan is oriented primarily toward stringent protection and nonintensive use of the forever wild lands of the Forest Preserve. The Land Use Development Plan attempts to balance protection and development of nonstate lands in the park. Those are very different goals.

B. *Regional Project Review System.* Except for the act's shoreline restrictions, which apply as a matter of law to all development in the park, the substantive land-use controls of the Land Use and Development Plan become operable only through the regional project review system established by the APA Act for new regional projects in the park. No project defined by the APA Act as a regional project may proceed unless the project sponsor obtains a permit under the act. Those activities that are not large enough or critical enough to meet the thresholds established in the act's lists of regional projects are not regulated by the act and do not require a regional project permit under the statute.

The APA Act defines regional projects for each of the six land-use areas. The lists of projects vary considerably in the different land-use areas. For example, many more activities are subject to review as regional projects in rural-use and resource management areas than in hamlet areas. The lists vary accordingly for moderate-intensity-use and low-intensity-use areas. These differences in the treatment of the various land-use areas reflect the state's greater interest in the less-developed areas of the park and the very great interest of local residents and local governments in the park's settled areas.[51]

The act also divides regional projects into two categories: Class A and Class B regional projects. Generally speaking, Class A regional projects are larger or raise more serious resource impact considerations than Class B projects. Class A regional projects require permits from the Adirondack Park Agency. Class B regional projects require permits from the agency until the applicable local government has its local land-use controls prepared and approved by the agency. Once that approval is obtained (see following subsection), the local government takes over review of Class B regional projects from the APA.

The Class A and Class B project lists set forth in the APA Act are different for the various land-use areas. Many more activities are Class A regional projects in resource management areas than in hamlet areas, with appropriate variations for the other areas. For example, in resource management areas any two-lot subdivision is a Class A project, whereas a subdivision in a hamlet area usually must be at least one hundred lots to be a Class A project. Furthermore, any group camp is a Class A project in a resource management area but only a Class B project in a moderate-intensity-use area. Again, these differences in treatment under the act reflect the differing interests of the state, local residents, and local governments in the park.

The act defines one or more categories of critical environmental areas in each of the land-use areas except industrial-use areas. In these designated critical areas the act makes nearly all development proposals (including individual dwellings), other than agriculture and forestry activities, regional projects requiring permits. Again, a sliding scale exists among the several land-use areas. In hamlet areas the act treats only freshwater wetlands as critical environmental areas. In resource management areas, critical areas include wetlands, areas of 2,500 feet in elevation or more, areas within one-eighth mile of certain categories of state land, areas within 300 feet of state and federal highways and certain designated county roads, and areas within one-quarter mile of rivers being studied for possible inclusion in the state's Wild, Scenic, and Recreational Rivers System. The concept of critical environmental areas within the several land-use areas allows special consideration for certain types of resources by enlarging the scope of regional projects for those areas.

The APA Act establishes requirements for the agency's review of regional projects. In many respects that system is typical of other project review systems, with provision made for applications, public notice, public hearings, issuance of decisions on applications, and the establishment of permit conditions. Two special, although not unique, characteristics of that review process are a stipulation that the APA may not disapprove a project application without a public hearing and a requirement that the agency must make a decision on a permit application within a specified period of time or the project application is deemed approved by operation of law.[52]

Equally as important as the process established for review of regional projects, the act also establishes the standards that a project applicant must meet for a project application to be approved. Those standards are generally as follows:

1. A project must be compatible with the Land Use and Development Plan and with the land-use area in which it is to be located.
2. It must satisfy the act's shoreline restrictions.
3. It must meet the overall intensity guidelines. (These controls are often

the single toughest specific requirements established by the act.)
4. Finally, the project must not have an undue adverse impact on either the park's resources or the ability of the public to provide services required for the project. This consideration of "undue adverse impact" must take into account the social, economic, or other benefits the project may generate. The standards, therefore, require a balanced consideration of the pros and cons of a proposed project, the essence of any sound environmental review system.

Because the project review system is the essential mechanism that brings the substantive controls of the Land Use and Development Plan into operation, the review of projects is a major feature of the APA Act. The agency's operations and those of local governments with APA-approved local land-use programs must necessarily focus a good deal of their energies on the review of regional projects.

C. *Land-Use Planning and Control Roles of the Adirondack Park Agency and Adirondack Local Governments Under the* APA *Act.* The APA Act establishes a number of responsibilities for the APA and local governments. The roles of each are critical to the overall implementation of the act. This subsection outlines those responsibilities.

(1) APA *Responsibilities.* The APA has many responsibilities for implementing the APA Act with respect to the park's nonstate lands. The APA's key implementation responsibility is the project review system established by the APA Act. Shortly after the act took effect in August 1973, the APA committed most of its staff resources to getting the project review system under way. The act thrust extensive project review jurisdiction and responsibility on the agency's shoulders, and the implementation of the act's regulatory system, with its many detailed provisions respecting applications, review periods, notices, public hearings, and decisions on permits, became and has remained a major challenge for the agency. It issues an average of three hundred permits each year, out of a total load of four hundred applications per year, and handles numerous requests for determinations of APA jurisdiction.[53] Its staff has to handle the full range of administrative, project sponsor consultation, project review, resource analysis, public involvement, investigation, and enforcement activities common to any full-scale regulatory process. In addition to its normal project review responsibilities, it has to handle requests for variances to the Land Use and Development Plan's provisions (for example, variances are commonly requested from shoreline restrictions).

The APA also has responsibility for maintaining and reviewing, and in some instances revising, the Land Use and Development Plan Map. This map, adopted initially by the legislature, may be revised by the agency up to certain limits (amendments in excess of those limits require decisions by the legislature, an event that has not occurred since the map was first adopted). The APA may initiate map amendment requests on its own initiative, at the request of landowners, or at the request of local governments. Many of the map amendment requests to the agency come from local governments as they attempt to prepare their local land-use plans under the APA Act. The agency receives approximately forty-eight map amendment requests each year. It approves about thirty-eight of them, covering an average of 6,800 acres in a year.[54]

Except for its project review system, no task of the agency has absorbed as much of its talents and energies as its local planning efforts. Under the act the APA is responsible for helping local governments prepare local land-use plans and for reviewing those local plans to see whether they comply with the provisions of the act. As part of this responsibility the APA has overseen New York's special efforts to provide funding to assist Adirondack local governments in carrying out their planning responsibilities. The APA has totally approved a relatively low number of local land-use plans, and those local governments have taken over review of Class B regional projects under the act. Most of the remaining local governments in the park are engaged in an active local planning effort with the agency.[55]

Where a local government's land-use program is approved by the APA and a local government assumes jurisdiction over Class B regional projects, the APA still retains significant influence in that municipality. The APA maintains jurisdiction over all Class A regional projects there. It receives notice of all Class B projects proposed to that local government, has a right to participate as a party in the review proceedings, and has standing to challenge the local government's decisions on Class B projects in court. Furthermore, the APA has authority to reverse the issuance of a variance by the local government that involves the provisions of the Land Use and Development Plan. Finally, the agency has authority to institute a court proceeding to revoke its approval of a local land-use program and to reassert its jurisdiction over Class B regional projects in that municipality.

The APA is responsible for overall enforcement of the regulatory aspects of the APA Act. The act provides civil penalties for those who violate its provisions, and the agency has authority to refer cases to the state's attorney general for initiation of enforcement actions. (The attorney general may also start enforcement actions on his own initiative.) Given the enormous size of the park and the APA's always small staff, enforcement has been a time-consuming and very substantial challenge.

(2) *Local Government Responsibilities.* There is little doubt that the major thrust of the APA Act has been to interject the state of New York into many land-use decisions that traditionally had been the province of local governments (and still are for New York local governments outside the Adirondacks).[56] That aspect of the APA Act has not been popular within the park. Nevertheless, the major state government role established by the act and the unpopularity of that role in the Adirondacks do not obscure the fact that local governments have a significant role to play in the implementation of the APA Act. The two most important roles of local governments involve the preparation of local land-use programs under the provisions of the APA Act and their eventual assumption of part of the regional project review system established by the act when their local land-use programs are approved by the agency.

With respect to the first of these roles, the Adirondack Park Land Use and Development Plan is clearly a regional land-use plan that contemplates further specific plans prepared at the local level in conformance with the APA Act's overall provisions.[57] The act does not require local governments to prepare local plans for APA approval, but they cannot recover review of Class B regional projects from the APA unless they do so. The act establishes requirements for the APA's approval of local land-use plans (which are to include zoning and subdivision controls and sanitary code provisions). In general, in order to receive APA approval, a local land-use plan must 1) be compatible with the general provisions of the Land Use and Development Plan; 2) reasonably apply the overall intensity guidelines and the compatible uses lists of the plan; 3) incorporate the act's shoreline restrictions; 4) require review of Class B regional projects in a manner reasonably parallel to the APA's project review decision-making process; and 5) contain adequate authority and provision for the local program's administration and enforcement.

The APA Act establishes fairly tough guidelines for local governments' preparation of local land-use programs. However, there is flexibility inherent in deciding how the regional land-use controls should apply in a particular jurisdiction (for example, local governments have some freedom in how they meet the overall intensity guidelines of the plan), and the act recognizes that the local land-use planning process may lead to some amendments to the Land Use and Development Plan Map. Accordingly, the local planning process offers local governments a significant opportunity to shape the state's regional land-use controls to meet their local needs.

The second major role of local governments under the APA Act can take shape only after the APA approves a local land-use program. That approval transfers project review jurisdiction over Class B regional projects under the APA Act from the agency to that local government. This gives a local government a major role in making critical decisions about activities that use the resources of the park. The fact that the APA retains jurisdiction over Class A regional projects in that municipality does not diminish the significance of the role the act contemplates for local governments.

Unfortunately, from the point of view of the act's original design, not many local governments have been able to obtain APA approval of their local land-use programs. This has resulted from the fact that many small Adirondack local governments cannot fully complete the necessary planning effort the act requires or because certain local governments simply have not experienced the development pressures that would justify that effort. In other cases, continued political opposition to the agency has led some local governments to avoid entering into the necessary cooperative planning effort with the agency.[58]

Other elements of the land use planning and control framework

In addition to the elements of the regional framework in the park respecting state lands and the control of uses on nonstate lands under the APA Act, there are several additional factors that merit attention. This section addresses the most significant ones.

A. Long-range planning. The first of these additional elements is an aspect of the APA Act that bridges both state and nonstate land concerns and relates to the overall purpose of the APA Act—namely, the APA's responsibility for long-range planning about the park's future.[59] Long-range planning and development of state policy for the future must necessarily go far beyond the content and implementation of the two regional land-use plans that now exist.[60] Among the long-range issues demanding future solutions are the impact of real property taxes on the state's efforts to maintain the open-space and natural qualities of the park, the overuse of Adirondack lakes, the overdevelopment of Adirondack shorelines, and the development of nonregulatory mechanisms to supplement the APA Act's regulatory structure (including possibly conservation easements and preferential taxation mechanisms).

The agency has struggled with its long-range planning responsibilities. In its early years the enormous task of bringing its regulatory and local planning assistance programs into full effect seriously strained its ability to look toward the future. However, in spite of continued limitations, it has achieved a number of successes in recent years. Among its more significant long-range planning and policy efforts have been preparation of a major report on the strategies necessary to protect the park's open-space qualities,[61] preparation of significant amendments to the State Land Master Plan (signed by Governor Hugh Carey in 1979), leadership for an interagency and citizens' effort to help insure that proposed highway projects fit reasonably well into the Adirondack environment, and an extensive investigation of forest clear-cutting in the park.[62] While doubt remains about the effectiveness of the APA's long-range planning efforts,[63] it has begun to establish a track record that offers some hope for its having a major role in shaping New York State's future policies and actions in the Adirondacks.

B. *Local government review board.* The Adirondack Park Local Government Review Board is an institutional element of some importance in the structure created by the APA Act. The 1973 amendments to the APA Act established the review board as a mechanism to help Adirondack local governments advise the APA and monitor its actions. The board consists of one member from each of the twelve Adirondack counties, and it receives its operating funds from those counties, not New York State. It has been a visible and vocal component of the Adirondack framework and has spent a great deal of recent years as a bitter critic of the APA, openly calling for the abolition of the agency on a number of occasions.[64] The review board, therefore, has not been a terribly constructive actor. However, with its ability to provide an independent assessment of the APA's performance, the review board has had a visible role in New York's regional land-use efforts in the Adirondacks.

C. *Wetlands and river management.* The New York State Freshwater Wetlands Act[65] is part of New York's two-pronged effort to protect wetlands: tidal wetlands in the state's tidal areas[66] and freshwater wetlands throughout the state. The state's wetlands acts are essentially regulatory in nature, setting up an extensive permit-issuing program for each type of wetland. The adoption of the Adirondack Park Land Use and Development Plan in 1973 predated the Freshwater Wetlands Act by two years. In the Adirondacks the important environmental contributions made by wetlands justified making virtually any development involving a freshwater wetland a Class A regional project requiring a permit from the APA (except wetlands in industrial-use areas). When the Freshwater Wetlands Act became law in 1975, the state legislature recognized the special role already being played by the APA respecting wetlands in the park. While the New York State Department of Environmental Conservation is the state agency responsible for overall implementation of that act throughout the rest of the state (with a strong role provided for local governments), the APA is responsible for its implementation in the park. Adirondack local governments have an opportunity under the wetlands statute to gain some jurisdiction over activities in wetlands (notwithstanding the Class A regional project lists of the APA Act). Furthermore, again in recognition of the special role wetlands play in the Adirondack environment, the Freshwater Wetlands Act regulates far smaller wetlands in the park than it generally does elsewhere.

The state's Wild, Scenic, and Recreational Rivers System Act is another important ingredient in New York's Adirondack framework. That statute attempts to protect the free-flowing character of designated rivers and the natural character of the land corridors adjoining those rivers.[67] New York State has designated more than 1,200 miles of rivers in its Wild, Scenic, and Recreational Rivers System.[68] Most of these are in the Adirondacks. In the park the New York State Department of Environmental Conservation is responsible for implementing the rivers act for those segments of rivers on state lands. The APA administers the statute for all segments of these rivers not on state lands. Its responsibilities primarily involve implementation of an additional set of land-use restrictions that pertain to river corridors. These restrictions, which are set forth in APA regulations and apply in addition to the requirements of the APA Act, make specific provisions, for example, for building setbacks, use restrictions, lot widths, and vegetation-cutting limitations along shorelines.[69]

D. General local land-use authority. An important element of the state's land-use planning and control framework is the general land-use authority of local governments. Notwithstanding the major role the APA Act establishes for the state government respecting land-use matters, Adirondack local governments retain their land-use powers under the various enabling statutes that pertain generally to New York local governments.[70] Therefore, while the APA Act provides an important layer of state authority on top of traditional local controls, the act does not remove the power of those local governments to adopt and implement such local land-use controls as they wish. This is not a contradiction. It means simply that in the Adirondacks persons wishing to undertake development activities have to meet two sets of requirements—those adopted by the local government and those adopted by the state. When the local government's land-use controls are brought into conformance with the provisions of the APA Act and approved by the APA, that local government takes over certain jurisdiction under the act. However, APA approval of those local controls is not necessary for them to be completely valid and enforceable.

The result of the APA Act's lack of preemptive force respecting local land-use control is a dual system of control in many communities—that is, a local system and the system established by the APA Act. In respect to those activities regulated by the act, persons wishing to undertake those developments must meet both state and local controls. In addition, local land-use controls cover many activities that fall below the thresholds of review established by the APA Act. Local regulation of these uses can be a very positive factor in the park's land-use framework.

   E. *Other state agency responsibilities.* In addition to the APA's major land-use control powers, three state agencies—the Department of Environmental Conservation (DEC), the Department of Health, and the Public Service Commission—play major roles that affect many land-use decisions in the park. DEC is New York's major environmental agency. DEC's regulatory responsibilities cover many activities that also are subject to APA, local government, or Department of Health jurisdiction. These activities include, for example, regulatory authority over landfill projects,[71] discharge of pollutants pursuant to the state's various pollution laws,[72] alterations to the state's rivers and streams,[73] and acquisition of water for public water supplies.[74] The Department of Health, acting as the state's major health agency, regulates many activities that are subject to the jurisdiction of one or more of the other major agencies in the land-use field.[75] These powers include approving water supply systems for many kinds of facilities, sewage disposal facilities, and realty subdivisions. Obviously, APA, DEC and the department of health's various jurisdictions overlap a good deal, and they hve gone to considerable lengths to resolve potential conflicts among the agencies through various administrative arrangements.[76] The Public Service Commission makes decisions respecting significant transmission lines in the park. Because a number of transmission lines already exist in the park and several new ones have been proposed in recent years, the Public Service Commission has the opportunity to play a significant role on certain major Adirondack issues.[77]

   F. *Land acquisition.* The last major element meriting mention here is the state's land acquisition program. Pursuant to the Environmental Quality Bond Act of 1972, DEC has bought and is continuing to buy a significant number of properties to add to the Forest Preserve.[78] Between 1972 and 1982, DEC made 167 acquisitions, totaling 67,776 acres, for the Forest Preserve.[79] These acquisitions range in size from just a few acres to several parcels that are thousands of acres. Land acquisitions, particularly large ones, can have significant land-use impacts because they remove certain existing private uses (for example, when lands are bought, any buildings are usually demolished) and bring to the fore a different type of use—that is, passive, public recreation use. While state lands generally require few, if any, local government services, land acquisitions may significantly alter local taxes by removing valuable properties from the tax rolls (although New York makes significant payments in lieu of taxes on Forest Preserve lands in the park).[80] Acquisitions may also reduce the land available in certain areas for important economic uses such as forestry or agriculture, and they may prevent development of key areas such as specific shorelines. Notwithstanding a variety of potential impacts, in terms of protecting the park's resource base by enlarging the Forest Preserve over the course of many decades, the state's land-acquisition program has been an enormously positive factor.[81] The magnitude and major impact of that acquisition program are evident in the fact that since the 1890s the state's Forest Preserve lands in the park have grown from about 551,000 acres to approximately 2.3 million acres today.

Strengths and weaknesses in the Adirondack framework

The existing regional land-use framework in the Adirondacks has a number of obvious strengths. At the same time it has some significant weaknesses. This section addresses the most important of each.

Strengths

The existence of the APA as a strong land-use agency and as the central institutional actor in the Adirondack framework is one of the most critical elements of that framework. The APA has often been controversial among Adirondack local interests, in the state legislature, and even at times among environmentalists. In spite of that controversy it has established itself as a small but central institutional and political factor in the Adirondack context.

The APA is highly visible in the state government as it exercises its various powers. Those powers are significant. The APA holds both important planning and policy-making powers and major regulatory powers. It is politically accountable in that it reports directly to the governor, but it also retains a significant degree of political independence because of the staggered four-year terms of its members. The agency's membership incorporates and balances major state and local interests in the park by means of the different categories of members. Finally, the agency maintains its own interdisciplinary staff, instead of having to rely on other entities for staff resources. The agency's control of its own staff resources has meant it could set and meet its priorities for various tasks and could successfully develop and defend its positions on the large number of issues that constantly arise in the politically charged atmosphere in which the agency has always functioned.

A second major strength in the Adirondack framework is that both regional plans incorporate a strong resource protection philosophy that recognizes that the natural resource base of the Adirondack Park is unique and enormously valuable. Article XIV of the state constitution mandates that philosophy for virtually all state lands in the park. With respect to the park's nonstate lands, the state of New York has clearly adopted the position that protection of the resources on those lands merits state intervention and guidance. However, particularly with respect to the park's nonstate lands, the state's resource protection philosophy is not a blind statement of "bar the gate and don't let anything harm the animals." The APA Act recognizes that protecting the resources of the Adirondacks requires a careful balancing of natural and human needs. In the long run, the resource protection philosophy of the APA Act may succeed dramatically because it stresses that while the natural resource base must be protected, the strategies created to accomplish that goal must at the same time be compatible with sustaining the human environment that exists in the park. The Adirondack Park is a truly special park because in it man and the environment may be able to achieve a sustainable balance over the long term. It is that balance which the APA Act strives to maintain and enhance. Indeed it is the basic mandate of the APA Act to achieve "optimum overall conservation . . . and use" of the park's resources.

A third major strength is the powerful political and legal sanction and support that both regional plans enjoy. Article XIV of the state constitution forms the essential legal basis for the State Land Master Plan. For more than nine decades the voters of New York State have demonstrated time and again that in spite of many arguments and forces to the contrary, they will insist that the Forest Preserve in the Adirondacks Park remain forever wild. From that mandate flows the extraordinarily strong protections for wilderness, canoe, primitive, and wild forest areas in the State Land Master Plan. That mandate has been strongly supported by the courts.[82] The Land Use and Development Plan for nonstate lands in the park is set forth in the APA Act. The APA clearly had a major role in creating the land-use controls, but they exist today with the formal imprint of approval by the state legislature. Any major changes in the land-use controls applicable to nonstate lands now will require a positive vote of both houses of the state legislature and approval by the governor (or, if the governor should disapprove, a vote of two-thirds of the state legislature to override his veto). Where challenged in court, the land-use control system for nonstate lands has fared remarkably well.[83] With the significant political and legal support both regional plans apparently enjoy across the entire state, it is difficult to imagine the state's leaders will willingly accept major changes in the APA framework.

A fourth major strength is the regional project review system established by the act. The Adirondack Park Land Use and Development Plan necessarily attempts to achieve broad, regional land-use goals. Its specific provisions were designed with regional, parkwide concerns in mind. The case-by-case project review system brings those regional controls to life in the context of decisions regarding individual projects. It permits an individual balancing of environmental concerns in light of the regional goals of the APA Act and the social and economic benefits that a proposed project will generate. Whether those project review decisions are made by the APA or by an Adirondack local government, the project review system permits the flexibility necessary to make a broad regional land-use plan work.[84]

A fifth strength stems from the fact that in the Adirondacks the state of New York moved to create a strong regional land-use planning and control framework before the resources of the park were seriously jeopardized by overdevelopment. Clearly, the APA did not have the opportunity to plan from scratch for an untouched environment, but it always had the enormous advantage of being able to make major land-use policy choices before land-use alterations irrevocably altered the most significant characteristics of the park.[85]

Finally in terms of strengths, the state of New York's regional land-use efforts in the Adirondacks have enjoyed strong, capable leadership. The Temporary Study Commission on the Future of the Adirondacks was both farsighted and highly capable, as reflected in its excellent reports on the park and recommendations regarding its future. All of the APA's four chairmen have been strong leaders. Each pursued somewhat different goals and provided different assets to the agency, but each helped maintain the APA's identity and sense of mission.[86] Equally important, the APA has been fortunate to have a number of very capable and politically skillful commissioners, and it has been able to maintain a talented staff. At a broader level, from the days of the Temporary Study Commission to the present, the state's executive and legislative leaders have been willing to make the most important decisions in favor of protecting the Adirondacks.

Weaknesses

The existence of a number of significant strengths in New York's land-use planning and control framework for the Adirondack Park does not mean that the state faces no difficulties in the mechanisms it has created for preserving this large, unique area. This subsection discusses several of the most significant limitations and difficulties in that existing framework.

The shorelines of the Adirondack Park's lakes, ponds, rivers, and streams are among its most sensitive, aesthetically important, and economically valuable resources. Unfortunately, while the APA Act establishes a number of strong land-use controls respecting nonstate lands (compared to other controls of private lands in the United States, the APA's regulation of private lands certainly is an example of very stringent government controls),[87] the shoreline restrictions of the APA Act are not nearly strong enough to protect these resources adequately. While the APA Act establishes specific shoreline restrictions, including building setbacks, minimum lot widths, septic facility setbacks, and other controls, those controls do not sufficiently protect of the shoreline resources of the park. It is clear that those restrictions are for the most part similar to what a typical (and generally inadequate) zoning ordinance or other local land-use control mechanism would require for rural areas. As such, they stand out as probably the single most identifiable weakness in the Land Use and Development Plan.

The weakness of the shoreline restrictions of the statute, compared, for example, to the overall intensity guidelines that regulate building density, is particularly serious because of the fact that in preparing the Land Use and Development Plan Map, the APA zoned many of the shorelines of lakes and ponds into the land-use classifications that allow fairly intense levels of development. For example, the devised map places the shorelines of many Adirondack lakes in the most developed classifications: hamlet, moderate-intensity-use, and low-intensity-use classifications. In part, these delineations reflect the fact that much of the human activity that occurred in the Adirondacks historically happened in and around the park's water bodies, as well as the high economic value and demand for shoreline properties.[88] Furthermore, the statute exempts from regulation as Class A or B regional projects many small subdivisions along Adirondack shorelines. These several factors in combination mean that the APA Act's protection of these critically important resources is far less comprehensive and environmentally sensitive than much of the rest of the framework created for the park.

A second liability in the existing Adirondack framework arises from the continuing opposition of Adirondack local governments to the APA and from the fact that few Adirondack local governments have been able to undertake and complete the land-use planning process envisioned by the statute. As discussed previously, the APA Act intends that state and local governments should share responsibility for implementing the regional project review system once local governments have their local controls approved by the APA. To date, relatively few local governments have been able to obtain that approval, and it is an open question whether the lack of significant involvement by Adirondack local governments to date in implementing the regional project review system indicates a significant weakness in the structure of the Adirondack Park statute. It is possible that the APA could continue to administer the entire regional project review system in most Adirondack local governments on an essentially permanent basis. However, it is also possible that the long-term continuation of that type of state role and the absence of significant local participation may indicate that some of the underlying political assumptions about the APA Act were in fact inaccurate and require reassessment. That reassessment, if undertaken, would necessitate an inquiry into several broader questions about the structure of a state land-use planning and control effort in the park—for example, what role the APA should play if many local governments will not become significantly involved in helping to implement the APA Act.

A third difficulty arises from the fact that whereas the Adirondack Park Agency has significant jurisdiction to approve or disapprove development undertaken by private individuals or corporations or by Adirondack municipalities, it has somewhat confused and limited jurisdiction vis-à-vis government projects undertaken by the state of New York in the Adirondack Park. Under the APA Act, new state projects in the park, other than those undertaken by DEC under the State Land Master Plan, are subject to the APA's review. Pursuant to that authority, the APA may determine whether or not a proposed state project is consistent with the purposes of the Adirondack Park Land Use and Development Plan and protection of the park's resources. However, the agency's conclusion regarding the desirability or nondesirability of a particular project proposed by a state agency is only advisory in nature. The APA does not have the authority under the APA Act to prevent an incompatible state project from being undertaken by the responsible agency. This situation has limited the ability of the APA to insure that development by state agencies in the Adirondacks is consistent with the general intent of the APA Act. For example, several years ago the New York State Department of Corrections decided to proceed with the establishment of a state prison at a site in the park that involved rehabilitation of a number of existing buildings in spite of the APA's conclusion that this project should not be undertaken.[89]

Not only is the APA's jurisdiction under the APA Act limited with respect to state agency projects, but the rationale for that limitation is not at all clear, given the provision of two other state statutes the APA administers. Under its jurisdiction pursuant to both the New York State Freshwater Wetlands Act and the New York State Wild, Scenic, and Recreational Rivers System Act, state agency projects are not exempted from the APA's regulatory authority to approve or disapprove projects in the areas covered by those statutes. Therefore, to the degree the APA Act reflects a decision by the government of New York State not to allow the APA to have regulatory jurisdiction over the activities of other state agencies, that rationale breaks down in the face of the APA's existing jurisdiction under two other land-use statutes. From a broader political perspective it is likely that the double standard New York State has established in the Adirondacks between development on the one hand by private citizens, corporations, or by Adirondack communities, and on the other hand by the state of New York itself will become an issue of significant concern and will reflect poorly on New York State's overall efforts in the Adirondack Park.

A fourth significant limitation in the Adirondack framework relates to the failure of the New York State Department of Environmental Conservation to undertake and complete unit management plans for the various major pieces of state land in the Adirondacks.[90] As discussed previously, the Adirondack Park State Land Master Plan classifies the park's state lands into a series of land-use areas, and the APA Act requires DEC to prepare unit management plans for those areas. These unit management plans will be necessary for DEC to make specific decisions respecting the use of various resources on state lands in the Adirondacks. These decisions would cover, for example, trail access, parking control, development of trails and lean-tos, and needs for other types of facilities necessary to control public use of the Forest Preserve. Unfortunately, while New York State has made great strides in the implementation of the Land Use and Development Plan pertaining to the activities of private interests and municipalities, for years following the plan's adoption in 1972 the state did not undertake in any significant fashion the unit management planning process. Some unit management plans are now appearing, but the process is years from completion. With fourteen years having gone by since the Adirondack Park State Land Master Plan was initially adopted, and with tremendously increased use of the Adirondacks evident over that time, it is clear that the failure of New York State to complete this planning process is a significant drawback.

A fifth limitation in the existing framework involves the difficulty experienced by the APA in stepping outside of its immediate responsibilities for implementing the APA Act and developing and setting policy for long-term issues in the Adirondacks. It is clear that the two regional land-use plans adopted for the park reflect far-reaching decisions, and the APA deserves major credit for having been able to develop them. However, the future of the Adirondacks will require New York State to come to grips with a large number of issues that fall at the present time beyond the parameters of those two regional plans. Because the APA has been very busy with the day-to-day implementation of the APA Act, it has often had neither the time nor the resources to enable it to look at long-range issues. While the agency's role in recent years on such long-range issues as forest clear-cutting and the protection of open space offers encouragement, it is likely the APA will continue to struggle to find the resources, time, and philosophical commitment necessary to deal with the broad issues that will shape the park's future.

The sixth and final limitation discussed here derives from the fact that the existing framework does not deal adequately with the cumulative impact of development in the park.[91] The Land Use and Development Plan is clearly a strong statement regarding what may and should occur in the park in the future. However, the plan allows and in fact encourages a significant level of development of the park's resources. In implementing that plan, the APA reviews and approves hundreds of regional projects each year, and local governments may eventually take over review of many of these projects from the APA. Given the structure of the regional project review system, the APA and local governments can realistically review these projects only on a case-by-case basis, with little appreciation for the cumulative impact of projects across the whole park or any significant portion of it. Local governments, in particular, are not likely to be willing or capable of considering the cumulative impact of regional projects on the park. In addition to the development authorized pursuant to the regional project review system, many development activities fall below the thresholds established for review under the APA Act. Local governments review some of this small-scale development activity under their various local controls, but much of it occurs without any type of government review at all.

The conclusion seems obvious. Even if development activities in the park occur in such a manner that every new activity is completely consistent with the purposes of the APA Act (which of course is an ideal that probably cannot be even remotely approached), those activities will inevitably and significantly alter the park. Accordingly, it is likely that over the next half-century the cumulative, incremental alteration of the park is likely to be far more significant than most people concerned about its future now appreciate.

This section has discussed significant strengths and weaknesses in the existing regional land-use planning and control framework. Neither listing is exhaustive, but each of these items is important. We now turn from a consideration of the present structure to a view of the future.

The future

The success of New York's Adirondack experiment in regional land-use planning and control stems from the state's willingness over many years to make hard choices about the Adirondacks in a manner that achieves a viable balance between the natural environment and human activities. Maintenance of that balance in the future will necessitate further choices on many difficult issues.

Existing land-use planning and control structure

The existing regional land-use framework in the park has been, is, and will continue to be controversial, primarily because the APA Act imposes strong land-use controls on private lands. One of the major issues New York must face, therefore, is whether it will retain that basic structure.

Taking all things into account, it is reasonable to expect that the structure New York has created to guide land-use decisions in the Adirondack Park will remain for the foreseeable future in essentially its present form. That structure has proven sound in the face of various legal and political challenges, and there appears to be ample evidence that New York's citizens are willing to retain its basic ingredients. However, issues, challenges, and controversy inevitably will remain a part of the Adirondack scene.

Recent years have seen repeated proposals for amending article XIV in various ways.[92] These have included suggestions that citizens be permitted to gather deadwood on the Forest Preserve for home-heating purposes,[93] that parts of the Forest Preserve be opened to various management schemes in order to increase wildlife production (most particularly, production of white-tailed deer) or to allow timber extraction,[94] and that Forest Preserve lands be exchanged for other lands in order to accomplish various purposes (for example, to allow a mining company to mine a mineral deposit on lands that are now part of the Forest Preserve).[95] Each of these and other proposals about the Forest Preserve has its own constituencies, and it is likely that significant political battles regarding the basic forever wild mandate of article XIV will occur within the next decade. Because article XIV is the critical element on which all the rest of the Adirondack framework rests, the future of that framework will depend on the outcome of those struggles.

The APA will remain controversial. Its policy and policy-implementing decisions will do much to shape the future of the Park. As a small agency and one that involves the careful balancing of numerous important interests, we can expect that appointments by the governor to the APA will continue to be particularly crucial. In 1981 the state legislature voted to upset the current balance of membership on the APA by enlarging the number of in-park residents on the agency. Although Governor Carey vetoed that bill, similar battles about the APA's membership will certainly occur again.

Vitally important to the continuation of the APA as a significant policy-making and policy-implementing agency will be its ability to maintain an adequate political and fiscal foothold in the state government. In recent years New York's agencies have been under increasing economic pressure. The APA will have to compete for funding and staff resources with many other powerful government interests. While its record to date in holding its own has been generally excellent, it is likely future battles will be more difficult.

Challenges will continue to arise from each of the weaknesses previously identified in the current regional land-use structure—that is, weak shoreline restrictions, lack of local government participation, lack of APA regulatory jurisdiction over state projects, lack of completed unit management plans under the State Land Master Plan, the difficulties the APA has had in undertaking long-range planning on park issues, and the inability of the current system to assess adequately the cumulative impact of development in the park. None of these weaknesses is likely to be fatal to the current structure in the park, but in all likelihood each of them is likely to prove difficult to manage over the long term. Reasonable solutions to each should be feasible, although not necessarily easy to accomplish because of political opposition from one interest group or another, depending on the issue at stake. Solutions might include, for example, strengthening the act's shoreline restrictions, amending the APA Act to make state projects subject to the APA's permit authority, and providing DEC some modest resources specifically tailored for doing unit management plans for state lands.

*Threats to the Adirondacks outside the
existing land-use control framework*

Compared to virtually any other effort to protect a sensitive land resource area, New York's efforts to establish a comprehensive regional land-use planning and control framework are indeed impressive.[96] Unfortunately, some of the most severe threats to the natural resource base of the park fall significantly, or even completely, outside the land-use framework New York has established.

The most serious current threat to the resources of the Adirondack Park is the devastating impact of acid precipitation.[97] Some of the remotest parts of the park, where society's direct impacts are least evident, are under serious attack by industry-generated pollution brought by the prevailing winds from the Midwest and Canada. Hundreds of Adirondack lakes and ponds are losing or have already lost their capacity to support biological systems. Some scientists are expressing increasing concern about impacts on forest resources and other parts of the ecosystem. Of course, neither the sources of this pollution nor the solutions to the problems presented by acid precipitation are in any way subject to the existing land-use framework established for the park. State, interstate, national, and international efforts will be necessary to create workable solutions to the problems caused by acid precipitation. There is tremendous irony in the fact that despite its decades of concern and action respecting the Adirondack Park, New York State stands largely helpless in the face of this tremendous onslaught.

This is a complex, wealthy industrial society. Its demands for natural resources are expanding and in many respects appear insatiable. It is likely that the future will bring much greater demands for wood products, energy (including hydropower), minerals, and water resources from the Adirondacks.[98] It is equally likely that society's recreational demands in the Adirondacks will increase dramatically.[99] While the Adirondack land-use framework establishes controls on certain development activities that may result from those increased resource and recreational demands, it is very important to recognize that the existing framework clearly cannot control the increase in those demands, since they will arise essentially independently of New York's land-use decisions respecting the park.

There is ample evidence that resource and recreational demands on the park are now increasing. The APA has adopted stronger regulations dealing with clear-cutting activities (over which it has regional project review jurisdiction once the clear-cutting activity exceeds twenty-five acres) in anticipation of greater clear-cutting of private forest lands in the park.[100]

Recent years have seen renewed and increased interest in the possibility of using Adirondack wood, both from private and state lands, for energy purposes, and developing Adirondack waters for hydropower.[101] It is not a very difficult jump to imagine proposals for supplying Adirondack water to millions of people in southeastern New York.[102] With respect to recreation, parts of the Forest Preserve are under mounting pressures, leading to serious management problems and deterioration of natural resources through too-intensive human use.[103] Increasingly, heavy use of the park's water bodies for recreation is apparent.

In many instances increasing resource and recreational demands will result in development activities that lead to assertion of regional project review jurisdiction under the APA Act or jurisdiction under some other state statute that applies in the Adirondacks. For example, the APA Act and the state's Environmental Conservation Law taken together regulate new impoundments of water, and the APA Act regulates significant forest clear-cutting activities and development of many tourist accommodation facilities. As natural resource demands rise, however, there will be strong pressures to alter the controls imposed by the existing land-use planning and control framework to allow those demands to be satisfied regardless of the existing framework New York has created.

In fact, political pressures to alter significantly the existing controls in order to allow the extraction, development, and use of natural resources are already clearly evident. The APA's initial effort in 1981 to clarify its regulations respecting forest clear-cutting were met by enormous opposition from the forest products industry.[104] Much of the industry's attack on the agency focused on the basic question of government control—that is, the propriety of the APA's having jurisdiction over those activities. While the agency has now adopted a compromise set of regulations that for the moment appears to have satisfied both the forest products industry and environmentalists,[105] the industry's attack on the basic assertion of jurisdiction by the APA under its enabling statute foreshadows future and perhaps more powerful and successful attacks that may void agency jurisdiction. Furthermore, as mentioned previously, recent years have brought a steady stream of proposals to alter the prohibitions of article XIV of the state constitution in order to allow timber and wildlife management of the Forest Preserve and collection of deadwood for home-heating purposes.

Other political demands for change are evident. There is renewed interest in damming certain Adirondack rivers for hydroelectric purposes in spite of various state prohibitions at the present time. Furthermore, in the area of mineral resource acquisition, several years ago the state legislature took the first step toward a constitutional amendment that would allow New York State to give a mining company a piece of Forest Preserve land on which the company believes there is a valuable mineral deposit in exchange for other land and for part of the mining company's proceeds from the mineral deposit. While that particular effort was eventually stopped, such a precedent might create a willing attitude on the state's part to change or bend all the existing rules in the face of natural resource demands.

Even if the existing framework is not altered to allow resource and recreational demands to proceed, in some cases that framework does not now control important resource development and utilization activities. As noted previously, the APA Act establishes only limited jurisdiction for the state over forestry activities. While it regulates the development of sawmill facilities and the like, only in the case of significant clear-cutting does the act give the state control over the taking of timber products from the park. It is clear, therefore, that a dramatic upswing in efforts to remove wood products from private lands in the Adirondacks for timber or energy purposes could proceed largely without review and approval under the land-use planning and control framework New York has established.

A present and potentially serious demand on the resources of the park arises from the recently increased interest in developing hydroelectric power. In spite of New York's efforts to the contrary, it appears that hydro development may occur on Adirondack rivers pursuant to federal law outside the control framework New York has established. Article XIV of the state constitution allows some impoundment on Forest Preserve land for water supply purposes, but it does not allow impoundments for purposes of producing hydropower.[106] Furthermore, the Wild, Scenic, and Recreational Rivers System Act prohibits new impoundments on designated rivers, and the APA Act and article 15 of the Environmental Conservation Law regulate impoundments on other streams.[107] Nevertheless, the Federal Energy Regulatory Commission (FERC) apparently may override the prohibitions and controls imposed by state law and issue licenses for hydro facilities under federal law.[108]

Given the current intention of the Reagan administration to encourage the exploitation of natural resources, this development is a significant threat to the structure the state has created. New York has contemplated various strategies to try to offset the authority of FERC to end-run the provisions of state law. One possible strategy includes having New York's wild, scenic, and recreational rivers designated under the Federal Wild and Scenic Rivers Act, because FERC may not issue such licenses on rivers designated under that federal statute.[109] The state government, however, has not yet found any effective strategy to that end. Accordingly, New York's APA Act, its Wild, Scenic, and Recreational Rivers System Act, and, most important, the strong forever wild protection afforded by article XIV of the state constitution may be unable by themselves to control federally approved hydro development of the park's rivers.

Similarly, increased recreational demands on many of the park's resources are not now the subject of effective controls under the existing framework. For example, that framework offers no effective means for controlling extensive use of lakes and ponds for motorboat use. Furthermore, intensive outdoor recreational use of private lands, even in critical environmental areas (for example, for use of off-road motor vehicles in wetlands), is not subject to any significant controls under that framework. Dramatically rising levels of many kinds of recreational use may occur entirely outside the land-use planning and control framework established for the Adirondack Park, and those activities may pose impacts on the park that New York has not yet confronted.

Economic equity and vitality

Inevitably, economic considerations will continue to surround New York's land-use planning and control efforts in the Adirondacks. The state has imposed strong regulatory controls in an historically depressed region. A significant portion of the constant tension between the APA, on the one hand, and local citizens and local governments, on the other, has stemmed from the common (although not documented) belief that the strong land-use controls set forth in the APA Act have seriously harmed the area's economy.[110] While it is clear that the park's economic problems predated the APA Act by many years[111] and that all of New York has suffered in recent years from the nation's economic problems, concerns about the equity of any financial impacts the regional land-use planning and control framework may impose and about the future economic vitality of the park merit serious attention. If in fact the Adirondack Park is to be a unique park in which people can coexist with the natural environment, there must be concern for both the natural and human environments.

Ever since the APA Act was adopted in 1971, residents of the Adirondacks have argued that the act negatively affects the real property tax base of Adirondack local governments and local school districts, and that the state should determine the extent of those impacts and help eliminate them.[112] It is appropriate to criticize New York State for its efforts in the Adirondacks, because it has never closely assessed the impacts of the regional land-use planning and control framework on the real property tax base of local taxing jurisdictions in the park, in spite of a specific commitment in the 1973 amendments to the APA Act that the state government would in fact complete such an assessment.[113] At a minimum New York should assess comprehensively the impacts of the APA Act on the ability of local governments to raise revenues. If those impacts are found to be significant, strategies for alleviating them will require attention.

Whatever the real property tax situation for Adirondack local governments may be, real property tax reform appears necessary to deal more equitably with the burdens the APA Act places on certain landowners. By any measure the act imposes stringent land-use controls, particularly in its resource management classification. Because New York State has not developed any clear picture of the real property tax implications of the APA Act, and because real estate taxes among different landowners in resource management areas across the park presumably vary significantly, it is not possible to be very precise about the impacts of the APA Act on individual landowners. Nevertheless, it seems inevitable that the act's most stringent restrictions have placed a number of landowners in a very difficult posture: their land is very strictly regulated, but their real property taxes do not necessarily reflect the extent to which those restrictions have limited the potential use of their property. This author is not suggesting in any way that all resource management land in the Adirondacks is being overassessed in light of the restrictions placed on those areas by the APA Act. However, real property tax assessment in New York is widely known to have serious problems in terms of accuracy and fairness, and the Adirondacks have long experienced their share of those problems.[114] Accordingly, serious inequities are likely to exist. We should expect, therefore, that New York State will have to try to identify and resolve equitably any major difficulties that its land-use planning and control framework has created or significantly influenced.

If New York determines there are significant real property tax inequities caused by the APA Act, it will be necessary to explore alternatives to alleviate those inequities. One example of a potential strategy is to restructure the real property tax system in the park. Such a system could recognize the nature of the real property tax implications of the APA Act, the statewide interest in protecting the park's natural and open-space character, and the state's responsibility for helping meet those burdens. Such a system could require lower taxes on heavily restricted property and authorize necessary payments by the state to Adirondack local governments to offset losses in needed tax revenues.

The need for real property tax reform and other fiscal reforms in the Adirondacks is evident, even if one simply ignores the equity issues respecting financial impacts on Adirondack local governments and landowners. New York State has attempted to protect the open space and natural quality of the Adirondack Park through an almost exclusively regulatory program. That regulatory program is obviously critical (in this author's opinion) to the future of the Adirondacks, but it relies entirely on the power of the government to say "no" to certain types of development. Many states have experimented in a variety of ways with real property taxation mechanisms to protect important natural resources.[115] However, New York State has done relatively little in this area.[116]

It has been clear since the Temporary Study Commission Report in 1970 that New York's efforts to protect the park should also include incentive mechanisms that encourage good land-use practices. However, the state does not now offer any incentives specifically designed to encourage landowners to maintain the integrity of the park. A real property tax structure that rewards private decisions to maintain Adirondack land in a natural condition without harming the fiscal viability of Adirondack local governments is an obvious, potential strategy. Such a strategy might go a long way, for example, toward encouraging the maintenance of a viable forest products industry in the park. Furthermore, many interest groups long sought legislation that would encourage a conservation easement program that allows landowners to benefit from their decisions to maintain their lands in a natural state while selling or giving up their rights to develop those lands. New York State finally adopted conservation easement legislation in 1983 and 1984. This program could achieve significant positive benefits in the Adirondacks, but it is much too early to determine what the overall effects will be.[117]

New York State has been more than tardy in failing to recognize that encouraging landowners to protect their lands in the park will make its overall effort there far more feasible and perhaps even reasonably popular. The state needs to move beyond a strictly regulatory structure as a means for protecting this unique area. It needs to create and actively implement positive mechanisms that supplement and enhance the important regulatory structure it has created in the Adirondacks.

New York's efforts respecting the economic future of the Adirondacks should extend beyond real property tax reform and the development of various incentive mechanisms to encourage private activities that are consistent with protecting the park's resources. Most important, the state should more forcefully attempt to identify those economic activities that could help build a strong economy in the park while at the same time being compatible with protection of the park's natural resource base, and to devise strategies to maintain and enhance those activities. While the

APA cannot become an economic development agency for the Adirondacks and remain capable of carrying out its other responsibilities, the Land Use and Development Plan reflects a strong step in the right direction — encouraging those human uses of the land that are indeed compatible with the natural resources base of the park.

New York has undertaken an exceedingly ambitious goal in attempting to maintain a six-million-acre park that has significantly more than half of its land owned by private interests and devoted to a wide range of uses. The goal of maintaining such an enormous park of both public and private lands is achievable in the long term only if there exist economically viable uses for private lands that are compatible with the park's resources. Without the existence of a sufficient economic base for private lands in the park, two negative outcomes seem inevitable: first, resistance to New York's land-use planning and control framework will inevitably rise; second, with the passage of time that opposition will be likely to gain an increasingly sympathetic hearing for protests that the entire structure is inequitable and that drastic changes in that structure are needed.

It is certainly an open question whether New York State will focus adequate resources on figuring out how to encourage economic activity compatible with the park's natural resource base. It is an even larger question whether the state can effectively help to bring about such a viable balance. However, one very clear lesson emerges from the past fifteen years about the Adirondack experiment: that is, with effort New York State can do much to help achieve that balance. With respect to tourism, the most significant positive economic force in the park over the long term, the regional land-use planning and control framework established by the APA Act provides a basic and important ingredient of any overall strategy to maintain and enhance that industry, that is, sustaining the natural resource base on which it depends. Similarly, protecting that natural resource base is a vitally important step for insuring that the forest products and agricultural industries remain positive economic forces for the long term. The point is not that the economic problems faced in the Adirondacks are less than serious, that Adirondack residents are blind to the actual economic advantages of the APA Act, or that New York State can easily promote feasible economic strategies respecting the park's private lands. The point is that New York's actions to date in establishing the regional land-use planning and control framework for the Adirondacks appear very consistent with eventually achieving the balance between the natural and human environments necessary to make the Adirondack Park a truly unique human experiment.

The vision of the Adirondacks as a park

For more than ninety years New York has defined the Adirondack Park as a legal entity. It acted in the last two decades of the nineteenth century to protect state-owned lands in the park and took major steps in the eighth decade of this century to protect both state and nonstate lands. Despite these long-term important actions, the state's vision of the Adirondacks as a park remains unclear. The future will require the state to grapple with that vision and to make better sense of it with respect to the enormously varied decisions the state must make about the Adirondacks.

Indeed, if one looks at the various actions of the state of New York in the park, one becomes acutely aware of many discrepancies in the policies it makes and actions it takes. For example:

– New York's Department of Environmental Conservation and the Adirondack Park Agency have strongly opposed amending article XIV in order to allow management of the Forest Preserve for various resource development purposes. At the same time, significant elements of the state legislature seem determined to pass such "management" amendments into law.[118]
– On one hand, the laws of New York authorize and mandate the expenditure of state money to add significant and sensitive resource lands to the Forest Preserve. On the other, the state has spent money authorized in 1972 for Forest Preserve acquisition very slowly and typically without any overall sense of how that money could be used to improve the Forest Preserve.[119]
– The Adirondack Park Agency has established an enviable record in implementing one of the most powerful and controversial environmental land-use plans established in this country. However, in spite of that record, the APA has not taken serious account of the threats evident to the quality of Adirondack shorelines, and it has even proposed legislation that would seriously aggravate the development pressures that now burden the fragile and valuable resources of Adirondack shorelines.[120]
– On the one hand, the APA Act and Adirondack Park State Land Master Plan establish a series of policies regarding state agency actions in the park. On the other, other state agencies largely ignore those policies when it suits their other interests.[121]
– While the APA Act and other state environmental laws express serious and specific concern about environmental quality issues in the Adirondacks, until 1982 the state Department of Health funded indiscriminate

aerial pesticide spraying programs in the park.[122]

- The APA has long recognized the severe threat acid precipitation presents for Adirondack resources and has attempted to be an effective leader in drawing attention to that problem. However, New York State aggravated the impacts of acid precipitation by encouraging conversion of New York power plants to coal, and by largely ignoring in its State Energy Master Plan those steps the state itself could take to reduce the enormous devastation occurring in parts of the park. Only recently has it taken steps to reverse these trends through the adoption of legislation that will curtail sources of acid rain pollution located in New York State.[123]

- While the State's Public Service Commission has done a generally good job of reviewing new transmission line proposals in a manner sensitive to the resources of the park, it has failed to exercise significant leadership in reducing the blight imposed by many existing lines in the Adirondacks.[124]

- The state department of transportation has made some notable advances in designing road improvement projects in a manner that is sensitive to the protection of the park's resources and the need for travelers to be both safe and appreciative of the natural beauty that surrounds them in the park. However, the transportation department also has continued to encourage the placement of advertising signs along state highways in a manner that detracts from travelers' aesthetic appreciation of these same resources.[125]

- On the one hand, New York State has established a dynamic, innovative land-use planning and control framework for the Adirondack Park and protected this enormous area while many other environmental resource areas have suffered serious degradation. On the other hand, New York State has seriously failed by almost all measures to interpret the park in a way meaningful to residents and visitors respecting its history, natural history, resources, and opportunities. Given New York's high-visibility attention to promoting tourism in the state (as in the "I Love New York" campaign), the state has done very little to focus people's attention on the extraordinary qualities of the park through such means as information centers, park interpretation programs, publications, and tasteful roadside markers. Only in 1986 has the state finally committed itself to constructing two appropriate visitor education centers in the park.[126]

Inevitably a six-million-acre park that incorporates both public and private lands will involve some policy conflicts. However, it is incumbent on New York State to attempt to define much more clearly than it has to date the overall character of the Adirondack Park. The two regional plans New York adopted in the early 1970s are powerful and important elements of New York's definition of the future of the park. Nevertheless the state's definition of the park should go beyond just the matters of land-use concern dealt with in those two regional plans.

New York's attempts to create a clear definition of the Adirondack Park and its future should involve a willingness to ask and answer the most fundamental questions about the park. For example:

- whether subjecting nearly 20 percent of the state to a comprehensive, stringent land-use planning and control framework is in the long-term interests of the people who live in New York State, including those residing in the park;
- what this private-public park in fact is and should be, what purposes it can serve, and what the full range of political, social, environmental, and economic strategies must be in order for it to fulfill those purposes;
- whether a public land–private land park is viable in the long term for protecting and enhancing the natural environment and the human environment that exists within it;
- whether New York (or perhaps even the federal government) should attempt to increase dramatically the percentage of public lands in the park and if so, to what end, to what degree, and at what cost.

Many long-time supporters of the concept of an Adirondack Park and of the state's existing land-use framework are confident that New Yorkers will answer such questions in favor of maintaining a splendid park in the Adirondacks. However, that confidence does not obscure the need for asking and answering those many questions more clearly than the state has done to date.

Summary

The Adirondack Park exists today as an outstanding natural resource area of statewide and national significance. New York's land-use planning and control framework for the park is both innovative and strong. In spite of its strengths, however, that framework is not without its flaws, and the park faces a number of significant long-term threats.

The greatest challenge in the Adirondack Park is mirrored in the somewhat anomalous language of the basic purposes of the APA Act—that is, "to insure optimum overall conservation, protection, preservation, development and use of the . . . resources of the Adirondack Park." Achieving and maintaining a viable balance between conservation and use will be difficult, stimulating, and continually controversial. New York State's inherent political complexities, the fact that any strategy for the park will affect various powerful interest groups, both public and private, in different ways, and the inevitable conflicts between what are believed to be short-term needs and long-term goals will insure a lively discussion of Adirondack issues for a long time to come.

The existing framework in the park reflects a lengthy evolution over many decades. That framework was not the product of hasty thinking in the first blush of the environmental decade of the 1970s, but rather the product of a long series of decisions and compromises made over many years. Evolution is a pertinent phenomenon for both the natural environment and the human institutions of the park. Because of the park's size, the quality and diversity of its resources, and political, social, economic, and environmental questions that any efforts to manage it inevitably raise, we should not expect that the currently existing Adirondack framework is immutably cast. The Adirondack Park of today is a product of the vision of the state's leaders, beginning a century ago, and the insistence of a statewide constituency that the future of the Adirondacks is a matter for the entire state to determine. Both that vision and that constituency have remained vibrant and powerful, and it is likely that the actions of today will be as influential a hundred years from now as the decisions from the 1880s and 1890s have been to date.

In the end only a few basic conclusions are apparent. The Adirondack Park represents a legacy from the past, a responsibility for the present, and a vision of the future. People and mountains (and the other elements of the natural world) can coexist there if people make wise choices. Conflicts and opportunities will inevitably arise from those choices, necessitating many further choices. Much has been done to protect both the natural and human resources of the Adirondacks, and much remains to be done. The dream of an enormous, unique, diversified, and beautiful park available to all the citizens of a busy society is both an accomplished reality and an unfulfilled goal.

New Jersey Pinelands Commission

Daniel S. Carol

The Pinelands Commission was established in 1978 to protect and preserve the land and water resources of the New Jersey Pinelands area. Composed of fifteen local, state, and federal representatives, the commission relies on local planning and regulation to implement its recommendations for types and intensities of land use in the region. Because of its power to assume control of land development in recalcitrant localities, the Pinelands Commission has been able to elicit significant local involvement in a relatively short time. Like the Adirondack Park Agency, the Pinelands Commission provides important lessons in large-scale resource management.

The Pinelands Region of New Jersey is managed by a unique combination of federal funding and oversight, state legislative authority, and local planning and regulation subject to state review. The key focal point of this management structure is the New Jersey Pinelands Commission, established in 1978 as the first demonstration of a new "national reserve" concept. The concept was initially proposed by Charles Little of the Congressional Research Service as a method for preserving recreational landscapes in urban areas. Under the notion of "Green Line Boundaries," existing land-use activities such as farming or housing can be retained by employing a flexible management structure rather than imposing the stricter regulations of the national park system. An added advantage to this approach is that larger urban greenways can be designated, because the areas are not to be acquired in fee simple (which would normally be an expensive undertaking near urban areas).

Thus, unlike the National Recreation Areas (such as Gateway NRA in the New York City region), the Pinelands Region is in mixed ownership: private, state, and federal. The Pinelands Commission has developed a comprehensive management plan to guide development for the region, which is being implemented and will be described in detail below. The commission's experiences may later serve as a model for other limited acquisition and comprehensive management programs throughout the United States.

Special area identification

New Jersey's Pine Barrens is a 1,600-square-mile region lying in the Atlantic Coastal Plain, which has been formed in the last 170 million years through deposition and erosion of sedimentary materials. These unconsolidated layers of sands, clays, and marls support an extensive surface and groundwater system, which contains an estimated 17–30 trillion gallons of water (larger than the entire water supply of New York City). Although the quality of this extensive resource remains unusually high, the uppermost soil of the region tends to be chemically inert with a low adsorptive capacity, making it incapable of filtering out wastes.[1] Some of the most important acquifer systems are recharged in heavily developed and industrial regions west of the Pinelands region. Therefore, there is a significant threat of contamination to the water resource.

The Pinelands region is located only thirty miles from Philadelphia and fifty miles from New York City, yet it has retained features of near-wilderness. Because of this, the Pinelands represent an unusually valuable open-space resource and the largest such area left unprotected and unmanaged in the Northeast. A map of the Pinelands area appears in figure 8.1.

The gently sloping topography of the Pinelands, characteristic of the Coastal Plain, is generally made up of low, dense forests of scrub pine and oak, hardwood swamps, pitch pine lowlands, bogs, and marshes. The region contains unique areas of pygmy forest (dwarf pine and oak), 850 species of plants, over 350 species of birds, mammals, reptiles, and amphibians, as well as an extensive overlap range where species of 109 southern plants and 14 northern plants reach their respective geographic limits.

The sandy, acid soils are generally unsuitable for most agricultural activities, and this is one of the reasons for the historically low density of population and development in this region. An exception, however, is the suitability of the soils to cranberry and blueberry production, in which New Jersey ranks third and second in total national production, respectively.

Recognition of the special values and ecological fragility of the Pinelands region has developed slowly over the years. During the eighteenth and nineteenth centuries the area was the site of forestry activities, bog iron production, and glassmaking. As these activities lost importance, the growth of the Philadelphia and New York urban areas led to new development pressures. In the late nineteenth century Philadelphia tried to gain access to the region's Cohansey Aquifer to use as a drinking water source.[2]

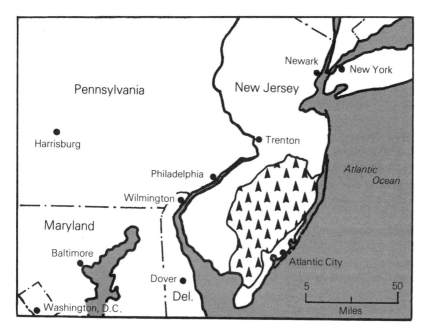

8.1   New Jersey Pinelands Regional Location Map

The most radical development proposal (made by the Pinelands Regional Planning Board in 1964) called for the creation of an international airport and a city of 250,000 within the Pinelands region to serve the growing eastern "megalopolis." In all, there have been over 500 unsuccessful development proposals for the Pinelands region,[3] a reflection of both the high level of development activity surrounding the Pinelands and the region's surprising resistance to outside intrusion.[4]

The publication of John McPhee's descriptive account of the environment and residents of the Pine Barrens in 1968, combined with the environmental consciousness of the late 1960s, were two major factors in changing the statewide perception of the Pinelands. In 1970, New Jersey created a Department of Environmental Protection on Earth Day (22 April), and new wetlands protection legislation was passed by the legislature. Special recognition was paid to the Pinelands in 1971, when the New Jersey legislature created the Pinelands Environmental Council to prepare a master plan for the 320,000 acres of the Pinelands region.

The council was composed of fifteen members, who were to represent the interests of local and county governments, conservation and sportsmen's groups, blueberry and cranberry growers, and the state. The purposes of the council were protection of water and other natural resources of the Pinelands; conservation of scientific, education, scenic, and recreational values of the region; encouragement of compatible land uses that would improve the area's overall environmental and economic position; and preservation and promotion of agricultural interests.[5] However, the council had no actual powers to enforce compliance with its plans or to prevent projects or permit issuances that it found incompatible with proper development of the Pinelands. This failing was well-recognized by framers of the Pinelands Commission.[6]

A quickening pace of development helped strengthen the perception that the special values of the Pinelands were being threatened. The western end of the region was becoming part of the Philadelphia-Camden suburban area, and the number of retirement communities grew dramatically (especially in Ocean County) in the 1970s. Total population in the Pinelands region jumped 35 percent between 1970 and 1974.[7] The passage of the Atlantic City gambling referendum in 1976 was also expected to increase growth pressures in the eastern portion of the Pinelands.

Increased recognition of the vital importance of adequate water supplies in the Northeast region (following several droughts in the 1960s) also served to focus attention on the water resources of the Pinelands. New Jersey's Department of Environmental Protection (DEP) issued nondegradation water quality standards in 1976, which specifically designated parts of the Pinelands region as critical areas for sewerage purposes. This designation established as policy that:

> The Pine Barrens constitute a unique and particularly fragile ecosystem compared with other coastal pine areas both within and outside the state. In light of the vulnerable character of the area, the Department shall not, in the performance of its statutory duties, approve any activity which alone or in combination with other activities, will cause degradation in the existing water quality characteristics.

More important, DEP's designation of the Pinelands region as critical areas for sewerage purposes meant that the state could effectively prohibit the issuance of building permits by localities, pending its own review and approval of proposed sewerage facilities. These water-quality regulations also made it clear that proper management of the Pinelands region would have to include the entire groundwater system to be successful. This understanding would later become important in setting the scope of boundaries for the Pinelands National Reserve.

National reserve designation

In 1975 the Department of the Interior's Bureau of Outdoor Recreation prepared a national significance assessment of the Pinelands region. The report noted that the Pinelands met key criteria both as a natural area (outstanding geologic formations, critical habitat, relict flora) and as a natural recreation area (open space, easy accessibility to users, basic recreational values).[8]

A second series of reports by Interior's Heritage Conservation and Recreation Service again recognized the Pinelands as a "special environmental area."[9] The reports identified the Pinelands as a potential greenline park[10] or national reserve area, which they defined characteristically as "sites of unusual size or complexity often with a large amount of privately owned land and multi-jurisdictional control."[11]

As proposed in the *National Urban Recreational Study,* the national reserve approach would consist of:

1. commitments by local, regional, and state agencies to integrated preservation strategies for designated areas
2. federal review of areas and plans with potential for inclusion in the federal reserve system
3. congressional authorization of federal financial and technical support for development of conservation strategies, with emphasis on alternatives to fee-simple acquisition where possible
4. maximum use of all existing federal planning, grant, loan, license, and permit programs to support conservation goals for congressionally designated areas[12]

Because fee-simple acquisition was specifically discouraged, the national reserve program was distinguished from the national recreation area program (see chapter 9), which was discussed separately in the Interior study. Therefore, the management of national reserves was generally designed to:

1. maximize private, local, and state initiative in the protection and management of such areas
2. give national recognition and technical and planning assistance to the protection of such areas
3. manage and protect these special environments to keep as much land as possible in private ownership and maintain their economic viability
4. use a variety of acquisition, taxation, and regulatory devices carefully handcrafted to guide multi-objective management of each particular area

5. assure that all federal, state, and local programs are administered further, or at least consistent with, the land-use objectives of the area[13]

Following these reports, a number of proposals were introduced in the U.S. Congress in 1977 and 1978 to protect the Pinelands region. The most limited approaches emphasized fee-simple acquisition of modestly sized areas for inclusion in the National Wildlife Refuge System while retaining the present management structure (fee-simple acquisition of the entire Pinelands area was prohibitively expensive, costing near $1 billion). At the other end of the scale, the National Reserves Systems Act proposed the establishment of a local-state-federal partnership, similar in style to the Coastal Zone Management Act of 1972, "to provide a means by which critical areas could be managed as living landscapes, wherein private ownership, existing communities, and traditional land uses would be maintained even as their outstanding public values were protected, without relying on outright purchase."[14] The act specifically designated the Pinelands as a prototype National Reserve Planning Area.

The act as it was finally passed (section 502 of the National Parks and Recreation Act of 1978) fell somewhat in between the above, establishing a national interest in the unique resources of the Pinelands and granting federal funds for the planning and management of the region on the state level. The act did not establish a national reserve system, though it is fairly clear that the Pinelands was seen as a prototype for such a system: "there is a demonstrated need to protect, preserve and enhance the land and water resources of the Pinelands area through a new program which combines the capabilities and resources of the local, State and Federal governments and the private sector and provides an alternative to large-scale direct acquisition and management in cases where such acquisition and management is appropriate."[15] The act required the state of New Jersey to establish a fifteen-member planning entity (composed of seven gubernatorial appointees, seven members appointed by the Pinelands counties, and one representative of the U.S. secretary of the interior) and to prepare a comprehensive management plan within eighteen months after federal funds were first made available. Section 502 also specified certain issues and elements to be addressed in the plan and the conditions for plan approval by the secretary of the interior. The act authorized $26 million for these purposes, $3 million for planning and the remainder for land acquisition (the monies to come either from the U.S. Treasury's general fund or Outer Continental Shelf leasing revenues).

New Jersey responded quickly to the federal legislation. Three months following its passage, on 7 February 1979, then-Governor Brendan Byrne issued an executive order placing a temporary moratorium on further building in the Pinelands and establishing a fifteen-member Pinelands Commission.[16] This moratorium was followed by state passage of the New Jersey Pinelands Protection Act on 28 June 1979, which statutorily established the Pinelands Commission as the planning entity required by the federal act (and abolished the Pinelands Environmental Council).[17]

Though both acts agree on the fundamental resources of the Pinelands worth protecting, there are some minor discrepancies between the final boundaries of the Pinelands region designated in the federal and state laws. The federal act establishes the Pinelands National Reserve, an area of approximately 1,100,000 acres. The state-designated area is somewhat smaller, but includes a larger portion of Atlantic County, New Jersey. The state law also divides the Pinelands into a preservation area and a protection area, requiring more stringent development controls in the preservation area.

As set up, the boundaries of the federal and state Pinelands regions were considerably larger than the area, traditionally identified as the "Pines," planned for by the advisory Pinelands Environmental Council. This is an undeveloped area of approximately 350,000 acres in Burlington and Ocean counties, north of the Mullica River. This core region corresponds with the preservation area in the New Jersey legislation.

The main reasoning behind the inclusion of the additional 700,000 acres (the protection area) in the Pinelands National Reserve is to provide management scope large enough to protect the surface and groundwater resources of the Pinelands. Two of the region's most important aquifers, (the Cohansey and Kirkwood) are highly susceptible to pollution, because the predominant soil materials have low retention capacity for water and nutrients. This leaching tendency has important implications for managing land use and water quality for the region. To preserve the high quality of the groundwater resources, the impacts of residential and agricultural land uses must be closely controlled over the *entire* hydrological system. Pesticides from agriculture, on-site disposal of wastewater, and improper disposal of hazardous wastes all present real threats to the integrity of the water resources in the Pinelands. The porous soils and characteristically low pH of the Pinelands make water quality and dependent flora and fauna especially susceptible to the system stresses associated with land development. Therefore, the designation of both a core and surrounding area is designed to adequately achieve the management goals for this special region.

Existing policies and authorities

Important to the success of an agency affecting many jurisdictions is the coordination of its activities with other agencies whose actions influence regional development. With the repeal of the enabling legislation for the Pinelands Environmental Council in 1979, the Pinelands Commission became the only agency empowered to plan for and regulate the entire 1,000,000-acre Pinelands region. However, there are a number of important local, state, and federal programs that continue to affect development and resource management within the region. The most important programs and policies are reviewed below.

About one-quarter of the Pinelands region falls under the jurisdiction of New Jersey's Coastal Management Program (NJCMP), which is largely funded by the U.S. Office of Coastal Zone Management through the Coastal Zone Management Act of 1972. The State's Coastal Management Program is based on the Coastal Area Facility Review Act,[18] which requires permits for housing subdivisions of more than twenty-four units and most other commercial and industrial facilities. In those areas where New Jersey's Coastal Zone and Pinelands jurisdictions overlap, permit applicants and developers must satisfy both authorities under policies jointly developed by the Division of Coastal Resources and the Pinelands Commission. New Jersey's Coastal Management authority also provides protection for that area within the federal Pinelands Reserve boundary but outside the authority of the state's Pinelands planning area.

A second important state agency affecting Pinelands development is the Casino Control Commission. New Jersey voters passed a referendum in 1976 to allow casino gambling in Atlantic City. In 1977 the state legislature passed the Casino Control Act, which established the Casino Control Commission to regulate casino gambling and licensing. The commission also was given authority to determine how casinos must reinvest a portion of their gross revenues in the Atlantic City area. Although Atlantic City itself lies outside of the Pinelands boundaries, its close proximity to the region means that casino-generated growth will undoubtedly "spill over" into the Pinelands. The eleven casinos that are operating have generated about 30,000 new jobs, and many of these new employees have sought to locate homes in the Pinelands area. Both the Pinelands Commission (through its policies on housing and development intensity) and the New Jersey Coastal Management Program (through its regulation of wetlands and all major developments in the coastal zone) have indirect control over this development and consult with the Casino Control Commission on reinvestment decisions to ease transportation and housing pressures. However, the Casino Control Commission retains final authority to decide on reinvestment policies and the rate of casino development, which will have enormous impacts on the Pinelands environment.

New Jersey has several statewide plans that address concerns of the Pinelands Commission. The 1980 State Development Guide Plan contains New Jersey's overall policies on growth and development. The plan designates the Pinelands region largely for open-space purposes, and defers to the Pinelands Commission and the DEP for more specific management within its general guidelines. Similarly, the state transportation and energy master plans impose no specific requirements on the use of the Pinelands and are generally in accord with the more detailed policies of the coastal program.[19] The Statewide Comprehensive Outdoor Recreation Plan (1980) endorses the land-acquisition plans of the federal and state Pinelands legislation. The Pinelands program also is consistent with New Jersey's State Heritage Program (including historic preservation, natural area, and wild and scenic rivers programs), which aims to identify and protect the state's important natural and cultural resources.

Probably the most important statewide plan relating to the Pinelands' environment is the New Jersey Water Supply Master Plan (1982). The plan notes, "it would never be feasible or desirable to remove a large percentage of this water (of the Coastal Plain Formations) because of the long-term effects on ground water levels, well yields, stream flows, and in some areas, saltwater encroachment. . . . Their [the Formations] vulnerability to contamination from surface activity, their relationship to surface water flows, and potential for saltwater encroachment due to overdrafting all present limitations on the use of this supply."[20] The plan also identifies economic, environmental, and institutional problems with transporting groundwater from undeveloped coastal aquifer areas to water-short localities in the northern part of the state. This policy on water diversions from the Pinelands is further defined by a 1981 state law that prohibits transportation of water beyond ten miles of the Pinelands preserve.[21]

The New Jersey Department of Environmental Protection (DEP) administers a wide range of environmental management laws. Most relevant to the concerns of the Pinelands Commission is DEP's designation of critical areas for sewerage purposes within the Pinelands and the efforts of DEP's Solid Waste Administration. The latter is important because the Pinelands region is both a prime site for illegal dumping of hazardous wastes (because of its sparsely populated roads located close to urban industrial areas) and is highly susceptible to groundwater pollution by rapid leaching of these wastes through the soil. It is state policy that solid waste management will be performed primarily at the county level, and that sensitive aquifer recharge areas will not be used for waste disposal. Studies conducted by the Delaware Valley Regional Planning Commission and others have identified no feasible sites for waste disposal in the Pinelands. However, extensive enforcement efforts by the Solid Waste Administration and the Public Utilities Board (which regulates carriers) will be necessary to preserve water quality in the region.

In addition to the commission, there are also a number of local and regional planning authorities that have jurisdiction in parts of the Pinelands region. The Delaware Valley Regional Planning Commission has authority for regional planning (such as "208" areawide wastewater planning) in the tricounty area in New Jersey fronting Philadelphia, which includes Camden, Gloucester, and Burlington counties. The South Jersey Resource Conservation and Development Council is another advisory body that deals with environmental issues. Finally, the Delaware River Basin Commission (DRBC), established by compact between the states of New Jersey, Pennsylvania, and New York, has regulatory powers to allocate wastewater loads and monitor groundwater uses in the basin. The DRBC's authority stretches over the Maurice River watershed within the Pinelands. Other local authorities relevant to the Pinelands region include municipal utility, sewerage, or other special purpose units of local governments, county "208" plans, and local soil conservation districts that review projects disturbing land surface areas in excess of 5,000 square feet. New Jersey counties also administer septic tank and solid waste disposal planning and regulation.

Finally, several federal activities are also important to Pinelands regional management. The federal government manages two wildlife refuges (Brigantine and Barnegat) and operates three military installations within the Pinelands (Fort Dix, McGuire Air Force Base, and Lakehurst Naval Air Engineering Center). Ensuring that federal activities are consistent with the protection of the Pinelands is dependent largely on cooperation between involved agencies. For federal installations within New Jersey's coastal management boundaries, these activities are required under section 307 of the Coastal Zone Management Act to be consistent "to the maximum extent practicable" with the state coastal management program.

The state of New Jersey has been delegated most federal permit powers for air and water quality programs, although the Army Corps of Engineers administers direct regulation in the Pinelands region through the Clean Water Act's section 404 Wetlands Protection program. In addition, there are a number of federal grants and assistance programs in agriculture, coastal areas and wetlands, endangered species protection, and historic and natural landmarks.

Probably the most important program from the perspective of the Pinelands Commission is the Environmental Protection Agency's review authority under the Safe Drinking Water Act. The commission has recommended that the EPA designate the Cohansey and Kirkwood formations lying beneath the Pinelands as a sole source aquifer under section 1424(e) of the Safe Drinking Water Act.[22] An area containing an aquifer may be designated as a sole source if the EPA Administrator determines that if contaminated there would be a significant hazard to public health. Such designation would provide an added level of protection over the ground-water resources of the Pinelands, because no federal financial assistance may be given for any project in the area that may contaminate that water source unless provision under law is made to assure that such project's plan or design will not contaminate the aquifer. As of February 1985, however, the Cohansey aquifer remained undesignated.

Commission's efforts to identify appropriate development levels

Growth pressures and attendant environmental stress were the primary reason for federal and state legislation designed to protect the unique environment of the Pinelands. Therefore, while the region may be able to support, in theory, fairly high levels of residential development without environmental and water quality degradation (though even this is questionable due to the soil problems noted earlier), the final mandate of the commission is to determine those levels of use that will not impair the natural environment and existing open-space character of the Pinelands. Establishing this basic capacity is the challenge for management under the national reserve concept: to permit compatible new development while retaining the special value of the land and water resources.

Many important goals for managing the Pinelands were already set by the dual state-federal mandates. These included:

1. natural resources protection through coordination of applicable state and federal laws, while retaining a mix of ownership types as an alternative to large-scale public lands acquisition;
2. cultural resources protection through the establishment of a list of designated Pinelands historic sites and federal funds for acquisition of selected resources;
3. recreational and educational values protection by local implementation of recreation planning, designation of several river corridors as

wild or scenic, and the use of federal and state funds for selective acquisition of recreation lands;

4. protection of agriculture and other historic economic activities;
5. encouragement of appropriate patterns of compatible development in or adjacent to areas already used for such purposes in order to accommodate regional growth influences in an orderly way while protecting the Pinelands environment.

It is important to note that the state-enabling legislation establishes two sets of goals for the preservation and protection areas. Most stringent goals are for the preservation (inner core) area. Thus, goal number five above, to encourage appropriate development patterns, is only applicable to the protection area. In no way can it be said, for either area, however, that the commission is explicitly charged to *balance* development and preservation in the Pinelands.

To identify appropriate development levels in harmony with these protective goals, the commission assessed both the region's current growth factors and its natural resource carrying capacity. The commission first evaluated a number of human use parameters and regional growth factors for the Pinelands. The Pinelands is not at all a homogeneous area, but actually consists of several developing regions of differing characteristics. Burlington, Camden, and Gloucester counties fall within the suburban development ring of the Philadelphia region, and western townships of the tricounty area have already experienced significant growth. However, since part of the developable land outside the Pinelands boundaries is prime agricultural farmland, there is some question as to where growth would have the least negative effects. The Comprehensive Management Plan notes, "since the Pinelands Commission has no leverage over the land use policies of non-Pinelands municipalities, the effects (on the agricultural area outside the Pinelands in Gloucester County) could be worse, taken as a whole, than those of carefully controlled and clustered growth within selected parts of the Pinelands."[23]

Although Cumberland County has experienced little development pressure, there has been a large growth of retirement communities in Ocean County over the last twenty years. Since the mid-1960s, for example, 80 percent of New Jersey's new retirement communities—representing more than 23,000 units—have been constructed and occupied in the county, making Ocean County the fastest growth county in New Jersey. Though economic recession may slow the rate of growth, the basic conditions feeding this growth (changing demographics, reasonably priced land, local acceptance) appear to remain.

Probably the largest single growth issue for the Pinelands, however, is the effects of casino development in Atlantic City and Atlantic and Cape May counties. Through 1985, some eleven hotel-casinos were fully opened and operating in Atlantic City. Since each licensed casino must be accompanied by a minimum 500-unit hotel, the level of employment generated by each hotel-casino has been estimated at approximately 3,000 jobs.[24] Projections for full-scale "casino build-out" for Atlantic City in 1995 range as high as twenty-six casinos. Whatever the figure, the magnitude and nature of casino-related growth in housing demand and traffic in the Pinelands regions will be significant.

Managing these regional growth factors would be difficult without an understanding of the natural resource carrying capacity of the area. Carrying capacity was originally developed as an ecological concept to describe the population levels that could be sustained by a particular environment without deterioration. The concept's first applied use was in rangeland management. Since then, planners have enlarged the term's definition to include many variables inherent in man-made systems. Certain assumptions underlie the use of this concept in planning:

1. There are limits to the amount of growth and development the natural environment can absorb without threatening public health, welfare, and safety through environmental degradation.
2. Critical population thresholds can be identified beyond which continuation of growth or development at greater densities will trigger the deterioration of important natural resources.
3. The natural capacity of a resource to absorb growth is not fixed but can be altered by human intervention.
4. The determination of the limit of capacity of a given system is, finally, a matter of judgment.[25]

The Pinelands Commission undertook, as part of its legislatively defined planning efforts, a natural resource assessment to compile a data base and define management issues. This assessment also served to provide information needed for the preparation of land capability maps for the region.

Additional studies helped to define the types of activities that could be tolerated within particular subregions in the Pinelands. Ecologically critical areas were designated under seventeen standard criteria such as pristine water quality, unique habitat, etc. The commission staff also examined the history of land use in the Pinelands to determine if there were presently incompatible land uses that needed to be eliminated. Conversely, it was found that certain uses, particularly those related to cranberry cultivation, have actually helped preserve the existing system.[26]

An example of this approach is in the commission's fire management program. The Pinelands contain some of the most hazardous wildland fuel types, as well as a number of regionally important plant species adapted to the fire hazards. Total prohibition of wildfire would over time change the characteristic Pinelands landscape. As a result, the fire management program attempts to strike a balance by using controlled burning techniques to preserve the natural landscape and to protect public safety and property.

Development limitations were identified in terms of soils, surface and groundwater hydrology, unique vegetative or aquatic communities, wildlife habitat, and air quality. These biophysical capacities provided the basis for determining allowable uses within the land-use classification system employed by the commission. The need for additional research was also identified for the following areas:

1. hydrologic characteristics of the Pinelands and the effects of groundwater withdrawals
2. tolerance of characteristic Pinelands plants and animals to changes in their surroundings
3. location and significance of Pinelands cultural resources
4. cumulative impacts of human use on Pinelands natural resources

However, despite these gaps in biophysical data, there was enough evidence of present and future stress on the Pinelands natural systems to prompt construction of a management plan.

Management program

The Pinelands Commission Comprehensive Management Plan contains the essential elements of the region's management program and details how the commission's program relates to other applicable authorities. Many of the elements are in direct response to the federal and state mandates; however, some parts of the program are solely creations of the commission.

The major elements of the management program are very similar to those employed by the Adirondack Park Agency in New York State. These include a land-classification system and a local planning program linking state-level oversight with local regulation and control. Unlike the Adirondack program, however, there is no substantial distinction between state-owned and private lands for management purposes. It will be recalled that state-owned lands are managed separately by the New York Department of Environmental Conservation with the advice of only the Adirondack Park Agency.

A. Land classification

The classification process used by the commission represents a systematic attempt to balance the environmental goals of the Pinelands legislation with the economic needs of the region's residents. Critical natural resources (such as wetlands, aquifer recharge areas, unique resources requiring protection) were inventoried to establish the areas most representative of Pinelands vegetation. These mapped expressions of "essential character" were then compared to maps identifying areas already subject to or appropriate for development. For those areas exhibiting both characteristic Pinelands features and development potential, the commission used a number of factors to decide whether to classify the area as low-density development district (and therefore be responsive to the preservation elements of the Pinelands legislation) or as a regional growth area (and be responsive to future economic needs of local areas). These factors included municipal and county recommendations, existing levels of development, location of sewerage collection systems, availability of transportation alternatives, compatibility with adjacent uses and areas, and land suitability for development. The final result is that the entire Pinelands region is classified into one of seven distinct management areas.

Each management area permits certain types of uses and activities within its borders while prohibiting other kinds of uses:

1. The *preservation area district* (337,000 acres) is the heart of the Pinelands environment and is an area of significant environmental and economic values that are especially vulnerable to development. Resource-related uses (agriculture, forestry, etc.) and limited residential development are permitted.
2. *Agricultural production areas* (79,000 acres) are areas of active agricultural use, together with adjacent areas of prime and unique agricultural soils or soils of statewide significance. Agricultural uses and related development (including residential) will be permitted. Additional agricultural production areas may also be designated at the option of Pinelands municipalities.
3. *Forest areas* (420,000 acres) are undisturbed, forested portions of the protection area that support characteristic Pinelands plant and animal species. These areas are an essential element of the Pinelands environ-

ment and are very sensitive to random and uncontrolled development. Resource-related uses and low-density residential development are permitted.

4. *Rural development areas* (145,000 acres) represent a balance of environmental and development values that is intermediate between the pristine forest areas and existing growth areas. These areas are somewhat fragmented by existing development and serve a dual purpose as buffers and reserves for future development. Moderate-density development is permitted.

5. *Regional growth areas* (119,000 acres) are areas of existing growth or lands immediately adjacent thereto that are capable of accommodating regional growth influences while protecting the essential character and environment of the Pinelands. Moderately high residential development and commercial and industrial development are permitted.

6. *Military and federal installation areas* (48,000 acres) include Fort Dix, McGuire Air Force Base, Lakehurst Naval Air Station, and an FAA Technical Center. Uses under this classification are consistent with national defense and federal requirements as determined by memoranda of agreement with the commission.

7. *Pinelands villages and towns* are traditional communities primarily outside of regional growth areas. Municipalities will be permitted to determine future land uses that are compatible with the existing character of the town.

Development densities for these seven areas are contained in the New Jersey Annotated Code. Densities vary with the type of development (residential versus other uses) and the person developing (persons with historic and cultural links to the Pinelands can usually develop at higher densities). Generally speaking, then, densities allowed are highest in regional growth areas (up to 3.5 dwelling units per acre) and lowest in the preservation and forest areas.

The use of the land-classification system is ultimately designed to accommodate compatible land uses in a manner consistent with the protection of natural resources. However, a differentiation of requirements, no matter how rationally it is applied, is going to engender some error or conflict. This is because some communities may be designated for and receive significant growth, while other areas may be subject to severe development limitations under their particular classification.

The commission's program deals with this problem in two major ways. First, local governments were consulted in the original delineation process, and their continued involvement is ensured by the local planning process described below. Under this process, management area boundaries may be refined or adjusted in municipal master plans and land-use ordinances provided that the commission determines that the goals and objectives of the Pinelands plan will be implemented by the proposed municipal master plan and boundary changes.

The second way that the commission ensures the overall equity of its management area classification is through programs designed to compensate (at least partially) those individuals whose development opportunities are limited under the plan's operation. This is primarily accomplished through a program providing for the transfer of development rights.

B. Development Credit Program

The Pinelands Development Credit Program is designed to provide a mechanism for landowners in the preservation area district and the agricultural production areas to participate in any increased development values that are realized in the designated growth areas. The program is supplemental to the regulatory elements of the Comprehensive Management Plan and provides an alternative use to property owners in these management areas. This option does not apply to property in the forest areas (which renders the forest area the "strictest").

The Development Credit Program is typical of other transfer of development rights (TDR) programs in that it hopes to discourage growth in the identified preservation zone and direct growth toward existing development, traditional village settings, and regional growth areas designated by the commission. Credits are allocated by formula to vacant landowners within the preservation and agricultural areas (the "sending" area) and sold in the open market for use in the regional growth areas (the "receiving" areas). Sellers of development credits are prevented from developing their land in the future by the placement of a deed restriction on their property. Purchasers of each credit become entitled to build four additional dwelling units above normal density limitations in the receiving area according to formulas contained in revised municipal zoning ordinances. Curiously, owners of wetlands in sending areas receive only one-fifth to one-tenth the credits allocated to owners of upland areas. (The implementation of the development credit program is discussed later in the chapter.)

C. Individual management programs

The commission administers or coordinates sixteen separate management programs for the environmental and cultural resources of the

Pinelands. Programs involving wetlands, vegetation, fish and wildlife, surface and groundwater resources, air quality, scenic resources, and cultural resources, all have a resource protection focus. The other programs deal with development issues and are briefly explained below.

- *Fire management.* The intent of this program is to balance the protection requirements of the public with the important role fire plays in maintaining the characteristic Pinelands vegetation. As such, controlled burning techniques will be encouraged under the supervision of the New Jersey Bureau of Forest Fire Management.
- *Forestry.* Again the intent of the program is to balance the preservation of the Pinelands environment with the mandate to maintain the "opportunities for traditional lifestyles that are related to and compatible with the overall ecological values of the Pinelands." The commission will work with the State Bureau of Forest Management to develop forestry management plans, practices, and incentives (such as tax incentives) to ensure that forestry practices are consistent with long-term maintenance of the resource.
- *Waste management.* It is commission policy to prohibit new landfill siting in the region except where no other alternatives are available. Landfill expansion is also discouraged as an inferior alternative to development of high-technology waste disposal systems. Because of the overall soil condition, disposal of hazardous chemical wastes, septic wastes, and liquid sludge is specifically prohibited. Waste management responsibilities are shared between the commission and the Department of Environmental Protection.
- *Resource extraction.* Primary extractive industries in the Pinelands are sand, gravel, and clay mining. The commission is concerned with the potentially disruptive effects of such activity and has recommended stronger state legislation to require mining operations to submit land-use and mitigation plans along with their registration application. The commission is also exploring methods to reuse sand and gravel mining pits with the help of the U.S. Department of the Interior.
- *Recreation.* The commission's recreation program is managed in tandem with the Department of Environmental Protection and is intended both to protect the natural resources of the region and to provide diverse recreational activities compatible with this first goal. Major components of this program include establishment of a state wild and scenic rivers program, expansion of the trail system, increased interpretive and access programs, and certain limitations on boating (10 hp maximum).

- *Housing.* One of the basic purposes of the Pinelands legislation was to guide the development of residential housing in an environmentally sensitive manner. Regional growth areas designated by the commission are the intended receptacles for the majority of new growth, and it is commission policy to ensure that adequate infrastructure exists to support this new development.

  Another important commission policy is the establishment of minimum standards for low- and middle-income housing units to be included in any new residential development. "The program is designed to enable municipalities to use any number of mechanisms to address these low-income housing opportunities. For example, a requirement could be applied to individual developments or donations of suitable land or money to a public agency for the purpose of providing a variety of housing types. . . . " This policy mirrors the affordable housing regulations set forth under the Coastal Area Facility Review Act for the state's coastal zone.[27]

  Finally, as noted earlier, the commission has made a number of recommendations as to how the Casino Control Commission will reinvest the 2 percent of casino profits it collects. These recommendations are primarily to ensure housing location in regional growth areas *specifically designated* around Atlantic City, as well as appropriate investment in low-income housing opportunity.

- *Capital improvements.* Commission policy on capital improvements is essentially geared toward the provision of adequate public services in regional growth areas and the prohibition of capital improvements that may stimulate or facilitate growth in those areas the commission has intended for low-density use.

- *Agriculture.* The commission's agricultural program is designed to preserve agricultural land by the land-classification system noted above and through the scheme of supplementary transfer of development rights. Additionally, the special agricultural production area designation is specifically designed to include those production areas not originally designated (individual farmers or landowners can also request inclusion into agriculture production areas by petitioning the relevant municipality). The commission also recommends a number of management practices and legislative changes designed to minimize the impact of agriculture on regional water quality and to create tax and financial programs more supportive of agriculture in the state.

D. Acquisition program

The commission's land-acquisition program is responsive to its federal legislative mandate to apply "a variety of land and water protection and management techniques, including but not limited to, . . . acquisition of conservation easements and other interest in land, public access agreements with private landowners, purchase of land for resale or lease-back, fee acquisition of public recreation sites and ecologically sensitive areas, transfer of development rights, (and) dedication of private lands for recreation or conservation purposes. . . ." The commission has stated that it will choose a flexible approach to acquisition by selecting the strategy that will most suitably meet the objectives for the parcel in question.

Acquisition criteria were developed for assessing each parcel and include:

— the presence of critical ecological factors, including threatened or endangered plants and animals, characteristic Pinelands aquatic communities, wildlife concentrations, wildlife diversity, breeding areas, and unique natural features
— the presence of prehistoric or historic resources
— scenic value
— a balanced representation of natural Pinelands features
— management requirements
— contribution to the balance of recreational opportunities
— size
— contribution to the maintenance of contiguous landscape or corridors
— location
— threat to resource (development pressure)
— adequacy of land-use controls
— significant public interest

Financing for the program is expected from three major sources: $23 million authorized under the federal Pinelands legislation, $25 million from the federal Land and Water Conservation Fund, and $33 million from the state's Green Acres Bond Program. Acquisition is expected to be a long-term, phased program (especially given the tight budget situation at the federal level) and will be a coordinated activity between the commission and the Office of Pinelands Acquisition within the Department of Environmental Protection.

Another way the commission intends to be more equitable in the implementation of the Pinelands protection strategy is through a payment in lieu of taxes scheme tied to the acquisition program. This program is intended to lower the burden on counties and municipalities whose tax base is eroded as private land falls into state (and thus tax-exempt) hands.

Though similar programs exist in New Jersey under the Green Acres and other programs, the commission strongly recommended an in lieu of tax scheme that would "provide full tax equivalency payment to local governments on a long-term basis to compensate for the loss of taxes on properties acquired pursuant to the Comprehensive Management Plan." This recommendation explicitly recognizes that current in lieu of tax programs provide for only "a distinctly limited stream of replacement revenues and no long-term solution to erosion of the local tax base." (The Green Acres program, for example, provides payments based on the taxes paid during the year prior to acquisition but then provides payments at a declining rate for a fixed thirteen-year period.)

The commission's position is clearly an attempt to distribute the costs of protecting the Pinelands to all state residents, rather than allowing the financial burden of protection to fall upon the unlucky few who reside in affected areas. It is also a strong political concession to an area already beset by coastal and other regulatory programs and increasingly hostile to the costs of such government intrusion.

E. Implementation structure

Implementation of the Comprehensive Management Plan rests on four major requirements. These are:

1. that state agency actions are to be consistent with the plan
2. that federal land management agencies and facilities will enter into appropriate memoranda of agreement with the commission
3. that implementation of the plan outside the state Pinelands area but within the designated national reserve will be accomplished through the New Jersey Coastal Management Program
4. that municipal and county plans and ordinances will be revised to conform to the Comprehensive Management Plan

The success under each of these components will be the subject of the next section. However, it is useful to review number four in some detail before undertaking this analysis.

According to the Pinelands Commission, "because of the structure of planning and zoning authority in New Jersey, municipal governments exert the most direct influence over land uses within their jurisdiction." As such, the Comprehensive Plan "envision[s] that local governments will be the principal management entities for implementing the plan."

The implementation structure is essentially similar to that of the Adirondack Park Agency (and therefore subject to the same types of political and implementative difficulties inherent in this type of system). All municipalities and counties within the commission's jurisdiction are required to revise their master plans and ordinances to conform to the Comprehensive Management Plan. In the words of the commission, this conformance process "provides an opportunity for local officials to translate the objectives and standards of the regional plan into their land use ordinances in a way that is sensitive to unique local conditions. *It also provides a mechanism to reassess and redefine the Pinelands plan in light of the varied local interpretations*" (emphasis added). Each locality must strictly meet the Pinelands Commission's minimum-density provisions in the designated growth areas and the density limitations in the other areas. Localities can, however, meet these density requirements by deciding upon their own particular distribution of land uses. This process is facilitated by allowing protection area municipalities to cluster development, provided that contiguous open-space land is set aside and other requirements are met.

The Pinelands process is different from the Adirondack Park Agency's in that local approval constitutes full authority over minor and major developments (while the APA retains authority over major developments). However, the Pinelands Commission is the sole reviewing authority for all public sector development, and "call up" for review of any local land-use decision that may fail to meet Pinelands plan standards. Also unlike the APA, the Pinelands Commission has the full power to take over all planning functions for localities failing to achieve conformance.

Implementation experience

On 8 February 1979 then-Governor Byrne issued an executive order creating the Pinelands Commission and instituting development controls while the commission began preparing a comprehensive management scheme for the Pinelands region. Pursuant to the federal Pinelands legislation, the commission had eighteen months to prepare the management program (until 8 August 1980) for submission to the secretary of the interior. Following New Jersey's submission of the plan, the Interior secretary would then approve, disapprove, or recommend changes to the plan (under criteria provided in section 502[g][2] of the act) within ninety days. In a real sense, the race for the Pinelands was on.

Governor Byrne's order placed restrictions on building in the Pinelands and established a temporary development review board to review building applications until the full commission was established. This action was challenged in court by the New Jersey Builders Association, which argued that Governor Byrne had exceeded his constitutional authority. However, passage of the State Pinelands Protection Act rendered this case moot by continuing the interim review process under the powers of the newly created Pinelands Commission.

Resentment by builders and other groups did not end with the creation of the commission in June 1979. The interim controls were designed to protect rampant development activity during the plan preparation period, an important concern for any new attempt to manage growth and development. Part of the resentment derived from the fact that the interim controls were popularly termed a moratorium, when in fact there were a number of exemptions available to allow continued development. As specified by the state Pinelands law, any development could be approved by the commission as long as there was not "substantial impairment" of Pinelands resources and if the project was consistent with the purposes of the state act. Additionally, the act contained a hardship exemption for projects affected by the moratorium. The commission established several hardship categories that would permit a project if the applicant had:

1. spent a "substantial" amount of money on physical improvements for a project that had received local approval prior to imposition of the moratorium
2. borrowed money to finance such a project that could not be repaid unless the project proceeded
3. bought a lot prior to the moratorium to build a house for personal use, and construction delay was costing the applicant a "significant" amount of money
4. health or safety problems that required him to build on property bought before the moratorium

Even with these exemptions, many developers complained of the commission's strict standards and slow reviewing process, despite the fact that the temporary development review board had issued substantially more denials in its four-month existence than the Pinelands Commission generally has.

It is important to realize that the creation of the Pinelands Commission added yet another layer of state control in an area historically resistant to outside intervention. A general feeling persisted among many long-time residents that they had succeeded in protecting the environment for generations without outside help. The commission's own consultants warned of a "general mistrust of government . . . in light of what residents see as shortcomings in the State's management of property it now owns."[28] In addition, there was grave resentment at the perceived lost opportunities in selling private land since land prices were expected to fall under the commission's program.

Local residents also felt that their region was overregulated (probably for good reason). First, the Pinelands program required that localities rewrite their local plans to conform to the Comprehensive Management Plan, despite the fact that localities had just completed this task in response to a 1975 Municipal Land Use Law.[29] Second, the Coastal Area Facility Review Act already required a permit for any major development (public facilities, housing projects of more than twenty-four units, etc.) in a large area designated within the Pinelands region. Finally, part of the Pinelands region (Mullica River area) was proposed for designation as an estuarine sanctuary under the federal coastal zone management program. However, this action was derailed at the last moment by New Jersey congressional representatives responsive to local residents' complaints of overregulation and overprotection.

Another measure of local resentment was exhibited by the poor early showing of the Pinelands Municipal Council. The council was set up under the state act to comment and advise upon commission actions, especially as to the contents of the Comprehensive Management Plan. Few of the fifty-two municipalities chose to be represented at the council's first meeting, and by February 1980 only eighteen were attending. (This participation problem has continued, as the council failed to meet at all in 1983–84.) However, it is important to note the logistical difficulty in bringing together fifty-two mayors or their representatives on any regular basis. The commission has since tried to compensate for the failure of the Pinelands Municipal Council by creating a subcommittee to visit localities and elicit local participation in commission policy-making.

The commission also weathered attempts to soften or abolish its mandate during state senate hearings in early 1980 (though proposals of this sort still continue to be made). This resistance period mirrors earlier experiences of the Adirondack Park Agency, though the level of opposition to the Pinelands Commission appears to have been slightly less intense.

These problems were undoubtedly exacerbated by the extreme time constraints surrounding the tasks expected of the commission (eighteen months to hire a staff, do the plan, and review local developments). The commission was also accused of possessing a "fortress mentality" in dealing with the public and certain state agencies. This can probably be excused somewhat by the small staff levels of the commission's first few months, but it is also due to the staff's strong commitment to the goals of its program. This attitude is reflected in the words of the commission's executive director, Terrence Moore: "We do hurt people. There's no way to get away from that. If you're in the business of protecting land, you have to say no to some people. . . ."[30]

A. Local planning

The Pinelands Commission received its first major appropriation from the federal government in November 1979: $12 million, of which $800,000 was for planning and the remainder for land acquisition. Following public hearing and comments, the management plan was adopted for the core preservation area in August 1980, and for the balance of the National Reserve in November. Governor Byrne then approved the plan on 14 January 1981.

The commission also had to satisfy the interior department (under criteria set forth in section [g][2]) that the plan was adequate to meet the intent of the federal legislation. A federal environmental impact statement (EIS) was written for the plan, comparing the commission's proposal with other alternative management approaches. The EIS noted that

- The net change in land values under the commission's plan would not be significant.
- It was unclear how much land development and water withdrawal the ecosystem could sustain.
- Some Pinelands natural resources *would* be compromised through the plan's substantial accommodation of growth and development demands generated by casino gambling in Atlantic City.
- The federal Pinelands legislation *did not* guarantee any level of federal cooperation from other agencies.

With the EIS process complete and with Governor Byrne's approval, Interior Secretary Cecil Andrus approved the plan for the federal government on 16 January 1981. The first round of consultant work, land classification, standard-setting, and the selection of development control techniques was complete.

With the plan in hand, the Pinelands Commission began disbursing monies to local governments to update their plans and ordinances to "conform" to the plan. (The first $300,000 went out in January 1981, and $300,000 more was disbursed in August 1981). Disbursement amounts were based on town size, as well as the extent of plan revision necessary. The commission established a conformance subcommittee composed of the seven county representatives on the commission to help localities through this process.

As might be expected from the level of local opposition, this process has moved slower than expected. By November 1981, thirty-eight of the fifty-six Pinelands localities had signed contracts to receive conformance planning monies. Some localities, most notably Atlantic County, made little or no effort to conform to the commission's plan. As a result, the one-year conformance deadline had to be extended six months from January 1982 to July 1982.

Yet, as of 5 February, thirty-five of the fifty-two Pinelands municipalities had received plan certification (twenty-one contingent upon minor plan amendments) by completing a natural resources inventory and through revising local ordinances to achieve "conformance" to the Comprehensive Management Plan. Four of the seven Pinelands counties were also in conformance and had received commission certification.

Though plan approvals are not nearly as good a measure of program success as "on-the-ground" land-use change (see next section), the Pinelands Commission has so far succeeded in eliciting a substantial amount of local planning output. The conformance rate compares favorably with that of the Adirondack Park Agency and the Oregon Land Use System (SB 100), which have taken considerably longer to achieve even comparable percentages of local plan approval (see table 8.1).

This apparent success is due to two major reasons. First, local towns in New Jersey have engaged in planning and zoning before, so that the commission has not had to overcome institutional resistance and inexperi-

Table 8.1   Local government conformance

---

1. Pinelands Commission (program began 1/14/81)
   A. As of September 1982, 14 of 59 localities are in conformance
   B. As of January 1983, 35 of 59 localities are in conformance
   C. As of February 1985, 42 of 59 localities are in conformance

2. Adirondack Park Agency (program began 1973)
   A. As of 1979, 7 of 106 localities have received Class B project review powers
   B. As of 1983, 14 of 106 localities have received Class B project review powers*

3. Oregon Land Use Act—SB 100 (program began 1974)
   A. As of January 1976, no local governments are acknowledged**
   B. As of October 1980, 90 of 277 local governments are acknowledged
   C. As of February 1983, 171 of 277 localities are acknowledged

---

*A considerable amount of local government planning (ordinance creation, master planning) has occurred in this rural area.
**In Oregon, acknowledgment means that the state's Land Conservation and Development Commission has reviewed and approved the local plan. The LCDC, like the Adirondack Park Agency, *does not* have the power to take over local planning functions from recalcitrant local governments.
Sources: Pinelands commission, Adirondack Park Agency, and Land Conservation and Development Commission, conformance updates.

ence faced in the Adirondacks and in Oregon's rural areas. Localities' efforts have been guided along with technical support from the commission, particularly through providing natural resources data and maps. Second, the commission has the definite power to take over planning functions from recalcitrant localities, as compared to the Adirondack Park Agency, which retains only the power to review new developments in local areas until local plans are approved. The positive power to initiate new ordinances, zoning, etc., is absent from APA's mandate. The threat of state takeover has compelled many Pinelands localities to go along with the program, rather than risk losing all control over their destinies.[31]

B. Development review

Under the Pinelands plan the following types of development are excluded from regulation: (1) improvements, expansions, or reconstruction to existing single-family dwellings or their accessory structures; (2) improvements, expansion, construction, or reconstruction of structures used exclusively for agricultural or horticultural purposes; (3) repair of existing utilities or installation of utilities to serve existing or approved development; and (4) clearing of less than 1,500 square feet of land that is not located in a wetland or within 200 feet of a scenic corridor.

In the first year of the plan (or until local conformance is attained), development in the state-defined core preservation area could not occur without commission review and approval. In the protection area beyond the core area of 300,000 acres, local governments without commission certification continued to control development. However, developers were (and are) required to obtain certificates of filing from the commission as a condition for local approval (in order to alert the commission to projects that may require full review and "call up.")

After the plan was in effect for one year, development could not take place in any uncertified locality in either the preservation or protection areas without commission approval. The passing of this local conformance deadline (there was one six-month extension) implied a total abdication of land-use powers from uncertified localities to the commission. However, the commission generally allowed permit decisions to continue to be made in those protection area localities that appeared to be moving toward conformance with plan requirements.

Once a municipality has achieved conformance, it assumes primary responsibility for reviewing proposed development projects. However, developers are still required to obtain certificates of filing from the Pinelands Commission, and localities cannot approve developments absent this certificate. The certificates serve as the tool by which the commission can exercise its powers to review any project in the Pinelands it suspects may violate plan standards (whether the relevant locality is in conformance or not). However, to January 1983, only 15 of 434 projects receiving local approval had been formally reviewed by the commission. This represents 3.5 percent of the total projects approved by Pinelands towns.[32]

Since the plan took effect in January 1981, a majority of development projects have been directly reviewed by the commission. Through December 1984, all eighty-six public development projects proposed in the region have been approved. Most significant, however, is the commission's apparent success in preventing construction in the inner preservation area. All but 93 of the 11,639 new home construction waivers (from plan standards) have been or will be constructed in the protection area (and most of these homes are contained in the plan-designated regional growth areas).

Finally, as provided in the Pinelands Protection Act, the commission has issued several hundred letters of interpretation to interested parties. These interpretations are binding on the commission and have helped clarify plan requirements in advance of formal project applications. The interpretations have also helped enhance the predictability of the review process.

C. Direct land acquisition

The commission's acquisition program has moved steadily along, with $14 million in federal monies appropriated so far for this purpose. Direct acquisition activities are actually carried out by the Office of Pinelands Acquisition (within the Department of Environmental Protection), though the identification of potential acquisition sites within the preservation area is contained in the commission's plan. (The plan's target is for 100,000 new acres for state parks, forests, and wildlife management areas.) As of January 1983, 22,578 acres had actually been purchased for these purposes.

Under the state's Green Acres Program, payments to municipalities in lieu of taxes will be made for thirteen years to help mitigate the loss of taxable land (caused by acquisition activities). The commission is also urging the state legislature to adopt a full tax equivalency program to further reduce fiscal stress on affected Pinelands communities beyond the time period provided for in the Green Acres program.

D. Solid waste management

The commission has kept its promise to monitor solid waste disposal practices within the Pinelands. In 1981, 520,000 tons of solid waste were buried at forty-three landfills in the Pinelands. The commission has set a goal to end the use of landfills within the Pinelands by 1990, to be replaced by the use of recycling practices and waste incinerators.

The proposed expansion of the Big Hill landfill in Burlington County was opposed by the commission, which filed suit to require landfill operators to first comply with the Comprehensive Management Plan's landfill regulations before seeking DEP permission to expand operations. DEP joined the commission's suit to prevent further expansion activities, which resulted in court revocation of Big Hill's operating license in July 1982. These activities have been a rare source of good public relations for the Pinelands Commission.

E. Development credit program

Both as a growth-directing tool and as a mechanism for equitably distributing the costs and benefits of land preservation, the commission's development credit program remains in its infancy. One county (Burlington) has established a Conservation Easement and Development Credit Exchange Board to buy development credits from landholders in the restricted preservation area. Funds for the county's credit purchases come from a bond issue approved by county voters in 1977. Credits purchased by the county are planned to be sold at auction to developers who can use the credits to increase the density of their developments in Pinelands regional growth areas. Conservation easements are placed on those properties whose owners sell their development credits.

Over three years several sales of development credits took place in Burlington County (totaling 10.25 acres). There was also one reported private exchange of credits outside of Burlington County.[33] A wider exchange of credits may be expected once all municipalities have achieved plan conformance.

As a management tool, the attractiveness of the transferable development rights (TDR) concept must be balanced against four major recurring problems identified by Banach and Canavan (see chapter 11):

1. TDR programs may be too complex to understand, explain or administer.
2. TDR programs may not succeed in rural areas having a weak development market (compounded by recession).
3. A lack of developer participation may arise because of inadequate density options.
4. Density options may result in development *not* compatible with existing residential communities and outstrip the carrying capacity of public services.

The Pinelands Commission's development credits program receives a mixed review under the above criteria. A landowner's guidance pamphlet on the program amply demonstrates number 1 above, for the credit

Table 8.2   Examples of credit allocations

A. Preservation area
   19.5-acre
   upland $= 1 \text{ credit} \times \dfrac{19.5 \text{ acres}}{39 \text{ acres}} = .5 \text{ credit}$
   19.5-acre parcel

B. Agricultural area
   19.5-acre
   upland $= 2 \text{ credits} \times \dfrac{19.5 \text{ acres}}{39 \text{ acres}} = 1 \text{ credit}$
   19.5-acre parcel

C. Preservation area
   78-acre
   upland $= 1 \text{ credit} \times \dfrac{78 \text{ acres}}{39 \text{ acres}} = 2 \text{ credits}$
   39-acre $+$
   wetland $= .2 \text{ credit} \times \dfrac{39 \text{ acres}}{39 \text{ acres}} = .2 \text{ credit}$
   _____
   117-acre parcel   2.2 credits rounded to 2.25 credits*

D. Agricultural area
   78-acre
   upland $= 2 \text{ credits} \times \dfrac{78 \text{ acres}}{39 \text{ acres}} = 4 \text{ credits}$
   19.5-acre $+$
   wetland (farmed) $= 2 \text{ credits} \times \dfrac{19.5 \text{ acres}}{39 \text{ acres}} = 1 \text{ credit}$
   39-acre $+$
   wetland $= .2 \text{ credit} \times \dfrac{39 \text{ acres}}{39 \text{ acres}} = .2 \text{ credit}$
   _____
   136.5-acre parcel   5.2 credits rounded to 5.25 credits*

Source: Pinelands Development Credits, N.J. Pinelands Commission (1982)
*Since each quarter of a credit allows for 1 additional home to be constructed in a regional growth area, credit allocations are rounded to the nearest quarter.

allocation formula is probably quite hard to understand for the average landowner (see table 8.2). As to number 2, the development restrictions imposed by the commission, coupled with the growth in the Atlantic City area, have created a strong demand for housing (the one reported private sale of credits at $20,000/credit was well within the commission's prediction of a fair credit price). The continued shortage of housing predicted for the Atlantic City area should overcome the effects of recession and provide a strong development market.

The commission has also claimed to have identified an ample amount of receiving area for development at increased density (number 3 above). This appears to be true, for development has been targeted successfully to regional growth areas designated in the plan. One such area, Egg Harbor Township adjacent to Atlantic City, has already felt strong growth pressures. The parallel concern is that areas like Egg Harbor may end up receiving more residential growth than they can handle (and thus confirm Banach's number 4). The problem is complicated further because Pinelands "municipalities" are actually entire townships, so the costs of providing municipal services could be raised significantly by directing growth over an area larger than the average-sized town. Medford Township, on the Philadelphia side of the Pinelands, has joined Egg Harbor Township in expressing fear in this regard.[34]

Finally, the commission has proposed the creation of a Development Credit Bank to strengthen the program. The bank would purchase credits from landowners with financial hardships at the cost of $10,000 per credit. The bank would not serve as a major buyer of credits but be designed to grant short-term relief to Pinelands landowners until the private market for credits expands. The state bank would also guarantee operating loans to Pinelands area farmers. The New Jersey state senate and assembly approved legislation authorizing $6.5 million for this purpose in June 1985.

F. Economic and distributional effects of the program

There are two major distributional issues under the program. First, how the plan affects the fiscal capacities and economic opportunities of Pinelands municipalities, and second, how the plan interrelates with the growth pressures from casino gambling in Atlantic City.

Under the state Pinelands Act, the Pinelands Commission is required to "detail the cost[s] of implementing the management plan" (sec. 13:18A-8[g]). The Coalition for the Sensible Preservation of the Pinelands (made up of builders, realtors, and bankers) has claimed that the "Commission has not gone far enough in that it still refuses to address the legislative directive to assess the effects of the plan on the beneficial use of private property."[35] This statement is difficult to evaluate.

First, the commission has recommended that the state legislature adopt a full tax equivalency payments program for those areas where land has been acquired by the state (and thus taken off local tax rolls). In addition, the commission has completed a study assessing the fiscal impact of the Comprehensive Management Plan on selected localities. The four chosen study areas were those that had experienced the largest recent increases in tax rates or declines in ratables in fiscal years 1981–82. The types of plan impacts examined were:

- how local land prices, revaluations, and reassessments were influenced by the private market perceptions of Pinelands plan effects on property owners
- private landowner appeals of reassessments based on claims that the

Pinelands plan had reduced land value
- land acquired by the state and thus removed from the ratable base
- changes in public service expenditures caused by the plan[36]

One of the study areas, Woodland Township, was determined to have suffered strong negative plan effects, primarily due to losses in vacant land values (which fell by 13 percent and 15 percent over the two years). Generally, though, the study found limited adverse economic effects due to the Pinelands program. However, it is probably still too early in the implementation process to make any firm conclusions about the plan's effects in any regard.

The study also explored the policy tools available to mitigate such effects. In addition the payments in lieu of taxes programs, receipt-sharing programs, grants, and tax-base sharing were mentioned. However, it is unlikely that the commission will seek to initiate such programs in the legislature.

Compensation at present therefore continues to rest with three programs, Green Acres, Development Credits, and the Pinelands Municipal Property Tax Stabilization Act of 1984. The Tax Stabilization Act provides for about $800,000 in support to Pinelands towns that experienced declines in ratables since 1980. Green Acres will provide tax equivalency payments to localities experiencing state land acquisition for thirteen years, the first year at full equivalency and subsequent years at a declining rate. The development credits program, if the market continues to develop, will provide potential financial relief to landowners in the preservation and agricultural production zones. However, landowners in the forest areas, also under severe development restrictions, will *not* be eligible to receive development credits.

The second major distributional effect of the Pinelands program involves the interaction of the Comprehensive Management Plan with casino gambling in Atlantic City. The plan has designated the majority of its regional growth areas near Atlantic City in anticipation of increased housing pressure. This has meant that these areas have been slated to receive the major portion of Atlantic City's growth, as well as a large portion of new development that might have been spread throughout the Pinelands region in the absence of the plan. Permit decisions under the Coastal Area Facility Review Act have also been similarly oriented: "The combined regional impact of the 3 state actions (Pinelands, casino gambling, coastal regulation) has been to redistribute growth eastward from the central Pinelands to the coastal area around Atlantic City. This shift in development patterns first became significant in 1980 and is expected to continue until State policy changes or until the housing demands generated by casino gambling are met."[37]

In one important sense, this result is nothing less than successful planning. Growth has been diverted from the essential "core" of the Pinelands to those areas where the inevitable development aroused by casino gambling (30,000 new jobs in five years) can best be handled with the minimum of environmental degradation. The Pinelands Commission has thus made the best of a potentially bad situation, since implementing its program would probably have been considerably easier without the casino phenomenon.

Yet it is important to consider the views of those communities most affected by these decisions. These communities (five towns and Atlantic County) have been the most stringently opposed to the Comprehensive Management Plan, because in the words of one local mayor, these communities have been designated "as the dumping ground for regional development."[38] They lament that higher-density development will mean increased public expenditures for services such as sewer lines and trash collection, even though a number of other communities no further away from Atlantic City are slated for much lower levels of development. Such communities however, are generally within the environmentally sensitive "core."

Terrence Moore's earlier comment that some people are going to get hurt is precisely the situation above. What must be asked, however, is whether this program—established at comparatively low costs to state and federal governments—asks too much of the affected localities. If protecting important natural resources is a concern worthy of state and national policy, it must be considered whether the costs of such programs must not also be borne or shared at these higher levels of government. Future national reserves must better address this issue if local support of such efforts is to be fostered.

G. State and federal consistency

The New Jersey Pinelands Protection Act provides that the Pinelands Commission shall issue guidelines to state agencies, counties, and municipalities to assure that capital investment and other agency decisions conform to the Comprehensive Management Plan. The provisions of the act are also considered to overrule other applicable state legislation in the event of inconsistencies (sec. 13:18A-27). State agencies also must receive a certificate of conformance from the commission to undertake capital projects. Examples of such occurrences involve the construction of a state prison within the Pinelands and the expansion of a sewage treatment system at a state school for the retarded within the "core" region.

At present the commission is moving toward formalization of a memorandum of understanding (MOU) with the Division of Coastal Resources (within DEP). The MOU would clarify each agency's responsibilities and powers with respect to areas of jurisdictional overlap and state coastal enforcement policy in those areas outside the state Pinelands boundary but within the federal national reserve. This agreement is expected to be entered later this year.

The commission also requires certificates of conformance from federal installations in the region, though it seems clear that the commission has no real powers to compel or prevent any federal action. The federal Pinelands act only "encourages adequate coordination of all government programs affecting the land and water resources" of the area (see sections 502[b][5] and 502[f][4]) and does not include a consistency component similar to the Coastal Zone Management Act's section 307.[39] New Jersey's consistency powers do extend to those parts of the Pinelands within the state coastal boundaries, and presumably activities outside these boundaries that could be shown to "directly affect" state coastal resources might also be controlled. There have been no major controversies along these lines, however. The commission has received and certified the Lakehurst Naval Air Station's master plan but has yet to receive any plan from Fort Dix Army Base, the largest federal holding in the region.

The Interior Department continues to play an active role in overseeing Pinelands management activities. One voting member of the commission is an Interior designate. Interior reviews land-acquisition proposals before funding these efforts (generally under a $1 state/$3 federal formula). Interior representatives also are working with commission staff on a resource extraction study, and with the State Advisory Council for Historic Preservation in identifying preservation sites.

Finally, the Environmental Protection Agency has not yet designated the Cohansey/Kirkwood aquifers as sole source under the Safe Drinking Water Act. The commission had recommended this action as part of the Comprehensive Management Plan.

Conclusion

By the end of 1985 the Pinelands Commission expected to certify the majority of local plans and has begun reviewing the original Comprehensive Management Plan for possible revision. The Pinelands has also recently been designated as an international biosphere reserve by the United Nations

Educational, Scientific and Cultural Organization. Thirty-eight sites (mostly national parks and forests) have already been so designated in the United States.

The short history of the commission has generally demonstrated the feasibility of the national reserve concept. A surprising number of localities have improved their local planning and regulatory output in a short period of time, and the commission has succeeded in limiting development in the most sensitive region of the Pines. This has been accomplished in the face of the enormous growth pressures aroused by the introduction of casino gambling in 1977, two years prior to the commission's creation.

In balancing its preservation mandate with the growth needs of local residents, the commission has generally favored the former. Though testimony to managerial fortitude, this tendency points out an important lesson for future efforts of its kind: that state or national policies of land preservation must fairly distribute the costs of preservation among all beneficiaries, not just local residents who are directly affected. The advantages of this approach are at least twofold: (1) this approach will yield a more equitable distribution of land preservation costs, and (2) this approach will promote greater local support for land management policies from landowners and residents within the preservation area, by eliminating the argument that nonlocal policy is imposing costs borne only at the local level. A corollary concern would involve the selection of proven tools to help distribute these costs, for it remains uncertain whether the development credit program will accomplish this end for the Pinelands.

Another important consideration in creating future national reserves is the development of mechanisms that can ensure adequate coordination of federal and state activities within the reserve. By creating the Pinelands National Reserve, the Congress declared a national interest in its preservation and management, but provided no assurance that federal activities must conform to the state-developed plan. In this sense it can be argued that federal activities at Fort Dix and through regulatory actions provide as much of a threat to Pinelands resources as local recalcitrance. A federal consistency requirement, similar to the Coastal Zone Management Act's, has been mentioned here as one possible remedy.

Finally, it should be emphasized that the Pinelands program remains in relative infancy, and new lessons and problems are likely to emerge in the next several years. These lessons will provide important background for any similar attempts at collaborative land management, just as the experiences of the Adirondack Park Agency have been used extensively within the Pinelands.

Urban Parks:
Are They Successful or Unrealistic?

Conservation Foundation Staff

As an alternative to expensive large-scale land acquisition, the Congress has encouraged the development of national recreation areas in regions in or around urban areas. The management of these "urban parks" has tested the National Park Service's original mission to keep national parks—in the words of former NPS Director Newton B. Drury—"unsullied and intact . . . not for commercial use of their resources but because of their value in ministering to the human mind and spirit." This is because the success of urban recreation areas is measured not just by the quality of the parks' natural resources but by the quality and quantity of recreational experiences they offer to the public. The staff of the Conservation Foundation reviews the nation's grand experiment with national parks in urban areas in this reprint from the Conservation Foundation Letter.

Many words have been written to articulate the meaning and central mission of the national parks. However inspiring and poetic, the words also have had a static quality as the authors attempt to make a timeless statement about parks that do not exist in a vacuum, but inevitably reflect a changing nation. Since Yellowstone was established, the national parks have provided a setting against which a dynamic society has continually reinterpreted its understanding of what resources should be protected and how they should be used.

Perhaps at no time have the concepts of protection and use undergone more change than in the past two decades. This has resulted in innovations that include the designation of man-made physical resources (impounded lakes, for example, and a wildlife refuge on a landfill) and nineteenth-century historic and cultural resources (Cuyahoga National Recreation Area and Lowell National Historic Park); protection of extensive scenic vistas (Blue Ridge Parkway); the "buying back of America" from unwilling sellers (Point Reyes National Seashore and Redwood National Park); the designation and management of extensive wilderness areas in a more pristine fashion than even early park advocates had in mind; the use of park creation as a deliberate economic revitalization tool

(Lowell and Redwood); the inclusion of unique natural areas heavily disturbed by man in order to restore the natural ecology (Redwood); and, of course, a focus on recreation and bringing "parks to the people." While many of these had some precedent back before the 1960s, only more recently have they become significant in national park policy.

The parks' "central mission" has been, in fact, a moving target. While this fact does not justify simple ad hoc responses, it does call for experimentation to deal with what are perceived as new priority needs—wilderness, energy, or social equity, for example.

An ambiguous mural is painted on the walls of the Fort Mason Center in Golden Gate National Recreation Area. Wild animals roam the San Francisco Freeway—a bear, a buffalo, a reindeer. Cars are stopped, their doors swung open. In one, the driver is asleep or dead. The other vehicles are empty. Billboards show only wilderness scenes; highway signs pointing out of the city are awry. The mural's message is unclear. Do park values return life to sterile urban environments? Or are they incompatible?

Like the mural, the Golden Gate National Recreation Area and other "urban parks" do not tell a finished story. Golden Gate, as one National Park Service official says, is "still too new to know what it is." The challenge of bringing national park philosophy, policies, resource management skills, and professionalism to national parks in urban settings has brought fresh thinking and vitality to the new parks and to the entire system; it has made the national park experience available in new places and to new audiences; it also has brought disturbingly high costs, questionable acquisitions, and unfulfilled grandiose promises.

The beginning of the push for urban parks is usually credited to the 1962 Outdoor Recreation Resources Review Commission's recommendations. Protecting open space around growing cities and accommodating nearby the recreation needs of a leisure-oriented population were prime concerns of the commission.

As the 1960s ended, two other concerns came to the forefront—equity and taming the automobile. The fact that national parks were primarily in the West and served white middle-class people who could afford to travel by automobile became prima facie evidence of discrimination and waste. Thus a major theme for the national parks' Second Hundred Years became the establishment of parks that car-less poor people could reach by mass transit. In addition, the idea was that more intensive, varied activities would be provided for. New types of units were acquired, using names like seashores, lakeshores, recreation areas, and historic sites —names coined earlier but now used more often to indicate areas that it was assumed would stress high-density recreation rather than nature preservation. In addition, the Land and Water Conservation Fund was established to help states and cities, as well as the federal government, acquire recreation land.

While there is no clear definition of a federal "urban park," major urban parks created under the new mandate include Golden Gate and the Gateway National Recreation Area (1972), Point Reyes National Seashore (1972), Indiana Dunes National Lakeshore (1966), Cuyahoga Valley National Recreation Area (1975), Lowell National Historical Park (1976), Chattahoochee River National Recreation Area (1978), and Santa Monica Mountains National Recreation Area (1978). These and others are extremely diverse in terms of urban setting, natural values, and ownership of land.

Golden Gate combines within its borders land on both sides of the Golden Gate Bridge, the federal Presidio, and an infamous federal island prison; the relatively undeveloped Marin Headlands; cattle and dairy ranches in the magnificent Olema Valley to the north; beaches previously owned by the state, as well as state parks expected to be transferred soon. Advocates were able to unify these opportunely available pieces — most of them threatened by speculation, development, or neglect — under two compelling concepts: "Gateway" and "Greenbelt."

The federal NPS presence in Golden Gate can take credit for giving reality to this unity and for enhancing the use of many of the resources. There is now a virtually unbroken coastline accessible to public use around San Francisco and its environs, along which many residents jog at day's end; old, often historic military buildings have been surveyed, repaired, and reused (or demolished), often with the aid of nonprofit groups; and an extensive interpretation and environmental education program serving school-age groups, the Chinese community and other minorities, and the elderly and other special populations, has been developed; the community has been heavily involved in planning; there is much improved maintenance and protection of beaches and trails, reduction of overgrazing on the Marin Headlands, and simple cleanup of debris. Funds spent for development have been minimal.

Problems include:

- *High maintenance costs and lowered federal appropriations* The top cultural priority is historic ship repair — $5 million for one rotting ship alone.
- *Tricky relationships with the Army, the state, the city, and local residents* The city is building a major sewage treatment facility and road

adjacent to one beach within Golden Gate, causing a considerable hassle. NPS, on the other hand, is razing a two-block area within its boundaries and adjacent to the well-to-do North Beach neighborhood, but delayed congressional appropriations for landscaping have stirred up local ire.

- *Continued acquisition pressure* To the south, Sweeney Ridge has been added to the park despite NPS objections, and despite local disputes over fair valuation, over the extent of development threats, and over the appropriateness of expanding Golden Gate in this area.
- *Ranchers* What does the future hold for ranches now owned by the feds and leased for twenty-five-year periods? In the north, land is very productive, and lessees will probably want to continue. Should the Park Service phase out productive land?

Gateway National Recreation Area began as a dream of the brilliant planning director of New York's influential Regional Plan Association, the late Stanley Tankel, who in 1962 described the 3½ miles of relatively undeveloped beachfront between Riis Park and Breezy Point as "the most important stretch of oceanfront in the entire world." Envisioning another Jones Beach, Tankel wrote that this peninsular area "has the potential for serving more people than any facility in the region." Pointing to the ten million people in a twenty-mile radius, Tankel argued that 2,500 small homes located on Breezy Point should be razed. "Access will need careful study. Perhaps another bridge . . . a subway link . . . buses on the parkway . . . maybe ferries from Coney Island."

By the time Gateway was created, after heavy political pressures, four separate land sections were included: Breezy Point, including Fort Tilden; Jamaica Bay, including a wildlife refuge, a landfill, and an obsolete airfield; Sandy Hook, in New Jersey, including abandoned Fort Hancock and heavily used state beaches; and Staten Island, to include Wadsworth at the base of the Verrazano Bridge, linked to a coastal belt of several city beaches ending at Great Kills Harbor.

The legislation specified intensive use of most of these areas. In fact, however, new intensive recreation activities have not been introduced to Gateway. Its areas of highest usage—the beaches—predated the park's creation. Instead, federal management kept Breezy Point from high-rise development and resulted in the demolition of two high-rise structures halted by the park's creation; it also has prevented residential development of Floyd Bennett Field.

Federal recreational accomplishments include cleaning up the wildlife refuge, a major East Coast bird sanctuary where sighted species have increased from 63 in 1953 to more than 300 today, and introducing creative environmental education and overnight camping activities as well as interesting interpretations of the Coast Guard and military installations at Sandy Hook.

This is how environmental writer Robert Cahn described Gateway, in a series of articles on the national parks that appeared in the *Christian Science Monitor* from 14–18 June 1982:

> Gateway is far more than a tangled mass of humanity on Riis Beach, as critics sometimes portray it. The Sandy Hook unit in New Jersey is a small national park in itself, with rugged beaches, havens for many species of birds, the unique 260-acre Holly Forest, historic Fort Hancock, and well-used fishing beaches. The Breezy Point unit, which includes Jacob Riis Beach and Park, also has Fort Tilden, another historical landmark, plus a popular fishing area at the point. The Jamaica Bay unit is highlighted by the 9,100-acre wildlife refuge with seven miles of trails, two large ponds, and marshlands and bay for sighting some of the 318 species of birds known to use the area."
>
> And other features of the park serve great numbers of people: Canarsie Pier, for example, where senior citizens gather daily, and Floyd Bennett Field with its Ecology Village set amid a grove of young pine trees. For many inner-city teachers and school children, an overnight camping experience here provides a first encounter with the outdoors.

The four units of Gateway remain separate and local, however, not only in attendance but in "feel." And it must be said that some of Gateway's natural resources do not clearly bespeak "quality," much less national distinctiveness. To create quality here will require more dollars and more consensus than have been available so far. One target would be cleaning up Jamaica Bay.

Floyd Bennett Field and its hangars once were slated for a $300 million museum, but now, with federal funds evaporated, there are plans for a large recreational development to be created in partnership with the private sector.

Other problems at Gateway:

— *Vandalism.* The park staff is especially bothered by abuses against resources. They say vandals, when confronted, do not always respect the rangers, who they know have no authority to make arrests.
— *Transportation.* This remains, in local eyes, the major obstacle preventing the park from fulfilling its potential. Ninety percent of Gateway

users come by car in a region where one-third of the people are car-less. Yet there is adamant opposition by residents to major land transportation projects. So water travel is seen as the only possible way to unify the detached park units and meet the "people mandate." But estimated costs for waterborne traffic are very high.
- *Erosion.* The park's major natural resource threat is the erosion of Sandy Hook beaches. NPS has asked for beach nourishment money, even though park policy generally is to allow the play of natural forces. If the "hook" detaches from the mainland, however, people will have difficulty reaching this popular beach.
- *Threat of incompatible use.* The city has proposed a shelter for homeless men at Floyd Bennett Field. Gateway's objections, at first criticized as selfish, have prevailed.

Lowell National Historical Park clearly owes its parentage to former Senator Paul Tsongas, once a Lowell city councilman. Created in 1978, this park has used federal designation as a way of revitalizing an obsolete city. To a surprising extent, or at least as much as a few years can reveal, it seems to have worked.

The federal "park" has authority to acquire by purchase or condemnation only six properties. In an extension of tools developed for natural areas, the legislation created a "protection" preservation district around the proposed federal properties and an agency, the Lowell Historic Preservation Commission, with a life of ten years, to administer the district. Its role includes making grants and loans to stabilize and revitalize properties in the area and developing cultural projects. Another commission task is to assist local government to put in place appropriate zoning, preservation, and other policies to complement the federal investment.

NPS has established an interpretive program from its headquarters in a downtown storefront office building. It features a popular three-hour canal and mill tour that combines a trolley ride, barge trip, and walking tour with an explanation of the second industrial revolution and Lowell's contribution, the role of the river and lock system, the importance of preservation and diversity in an urban setting, and the links between Lowell and Yellowstone.

Much renovation, especially in Lowell's downtown, has occurred, aided by public money used to leverage private dollars. However, local NPS personnel take care not to justify their presence by this revitalization —which might not be viewed as a legitimate national park purpose—but rather by Lowell's "national significance."

Lowell's problems include:

- *Crime.* A major lock beautifully restored for the bicentennial, located in the city's toughest neighborhood, was torched in late 1981 by a local gang, which also has pelted park rangers and visitors. The lock is still privately owned although renovated by the state. (The gang's identity is known, and one observer suggested they be put in public pillory as part of a "Living History" exhibit.)
- *Money.* The superintendent says his chief challenge is "money-gathering." Ambitious development plans depend on money—plans such as buying and fixing up the old city hall and making grants and loans, and restoring the parklands along the canals.
- *Complex concept.* Fred Faust, once Senator Tsongas's assistant and now head of the Lowell Historic Preservation Commission, wonders whether "we didn't do something too complicated. We have a hard job explaining what we are." It is difficult to specify how the commission differs from a city economic development authority, and turf questions between federal government, state, and city have called for a unique collaboration.

It has been important to bear in mind that these urban parks are new. Still, experience with them speaks to certain major park issues that, while often evident in traditional parks, do seem to present themselves more sharply in these so-called urban parks.

What kinds of opportunities should the federal government provide under the label of "recreation"?

One of the most interesting aspects of the urban parks is that each has been created in the name of providing recreation for the masses, and then—often after intense citizen involvement—seems to end up with more emphasis on protection and preservation than on new intensive uses. The Park Service has found itself advocating development, in response to a presumed mandate, against the wishes of constituencies that originally lobbied for national park designation. The citizens' views largely prevailed, for example, at Point Reyes National Seashore, the Jamaica Bay Wildlife Refuge at Gateway, and Indiana Dunes National Lakeshore.

In *Sand County Almanac,* Aldo Leopold argued that outdoor recreation was mistakenly linked to intensive recreation, and proposed instead that we should view outdoor recreation as "what we bring to the out-of-doors." Following this line of thinking, an area with distinctive natural qualities can provide a contemplative experience just as rewarding to the urban resident as an intensively developed area.

To a surprising extent, in the places where urban parks work best, one can see the influence of traditional park values on various urban resources. The Jamaica Bay Wildlife Refuge, although an artificial landscape on filled land around a polluted bay, is a prime example. Park development plans were squelched. Now no picnicking, smoking, or camping is permitted. Use has increased, however, to 125,000 visits per year, and local constituencies are pressing NPS to limit use.

The Breezy Point Tip, from which Tankel viewed New York City, remains undeveloped. Fishermen continue to fish, but their parking is controlled so it does not ruin the dunes. Tern nesting grounds are protected. To Terence Benbow, New York chairman of Gateway's Citizens Commission, "it is entirely appropriate for an urban park to provide diverse experiences for city residents. Thus, leaving the Tip undeveloped to provide the rare rural experience is consistent with the concept."

This limited use in some areas may seem paradoxical in view of the reported large numbers of visitors to urban parks. Figures citing millions of visitors are somewhat misleading. Most numbers come from areas already heavily used when the Park Service got involved—at Golden Gate, for example, this means the beaches, Cliff House, the Maritime Museum, and Fisherman's Wharf (where "visitors" may not know they have entered the park). Others come from new, controlled group activities like festivals, environmental education programs, classes, and specialized tours like the one to Alcatraz.

While Gateway's limited use can be called the result of impasse between NPS and the politically powerful Breezy Point community, which has resisted park plans for attracting more recreational use, in Golden Gate the officials and the Citizens Commission seem to have evolved an intelligent, serious response to the challenge of developing a "national park in an urban setting." As Citizens Advisory Commission head Amy Meyer says, "Let the neighborhood parks have the swings and the slides and the ballfields, or grassy lawns for senior citizens. We seek here to provide that special experience which only a national park, with its quality resources and quality management, can provide."

Where federal involvement in urban parks succeeds, there is a combination of quality natural or historic resources, quality management, and quality interpretation/education—an experience recognizably the unique contribution of the Park Service.

What is nationally significant?

In Lowell and in Gateway, some staff have questioned whether what they are doing involves nationally significant resources. This question is posed in congressional committees too, of course, and has been rekindled by former Secretary of the Interior James Watt.

However, significance cannot be assessed simply on the basis of numbers of visitors or the distance they have come, first, because visitation patterns change and, second, because even older traditional parks, whose place in the system is not questioned, often have predominantly local or regional visitation. But the resource should be outstanding—an area that a local resident could show an out-of-town visitor as a must-see sight, or an area that an out-of-town visitor would be pleased to have his or her tax dollars used to support.

It seems central to the health of the National Park Service that its resources not be second-class or dependent on fulfillment of grandiose plans to become first-class. The NPS staff needs to perceive that they are protecting natural or historic resources of importance to the nation.

True, the boundaries of traditional national parks are arbitrary to some extent; to get a "prize" the feds may have to take some inferior goods. But the maintenance costs of inferior goods can be high, and some of the "bargains" have not worked out. The feds may need to be more careful in acquisition—which is not the same as stopping it.

What other urban park experiences illuminate management
problems and opportunities in the entire park system,
or in urban parks managed by states or cities?

- Newer parks in or near urban areas have to deal with development in a way unlike the traditional national parks that were carved out of often inaccessible wilderness. Many of the buildings involved are viewed as having a cultural and historic distinction that puts them in need of surveying, rehabilitation, reuse, and interpretation. In fact, respect and appreciation for distinctive buildings as a valid component of the natural landscape is an important trend notable in all the parks. The costs are high, however, and the Park Service has not been adequately staffed for this purpose. Policies that for decades aimed at "restoring the natural landscape" do not yet adequately reflect the nation's new interest in cultural assets.
- Extensive use can be made of nonprofit community groups for interpretation and programming. These groups can be housed in vacant historic buildings, helping to maintain them in return for favorable leases and rentals. The Fort Mason Center in Golden Gate has been a model in this respect, and the San Francisco Foundation has planning funds for a promising new use of obsolete military structures on the Marin

Headlands for artists and cultural activities.
- Affirmative action and minority involvement can be linked readily to urban recreation, though there are ways to do it and not to do it. In Golden Gate, where success in programming seems most evident, NPS staff emphasize providing the opportunity for involvement and have developed creative ways to do this as federal grants for such purposes have waned. Minority staff in some parks reflect some dissatisfaction at being "typed" for urban parks, however.
- New perspectives on appropriate recreation and environmental education for an urban population are useful in traditional parks, which serve visitors from cities as well as other visitors who stay a short time. (Urban parks do not have "captive" overnighters, so they must reach out more to the populace.)
- New techniques are being developed for natural resource management in despoiled settings—to bring more of an "outdoor experience" to city dwellers.

Providing a national park experience for urban dwellers in nontraditional areas has presented more problems than anticipated but has had many positive results. These seem to be the most important general prerequisites for a valid experience worthy of NPS identification and national involvement:

1. It must involve a resource of outstanding quality. Hundreds of millions of development dollars should not be required to provide a high-quality experience.
2. Outdoor recreation for urban populations using urban resources need not be intensive or involve creation of another Jones Beach. On the other hand, federal dollars and NPS resources should not be called in to protect areas of less-than-distinguished quality, where little if anything of wider public benefit takes place.
3. The experience should involve top-notch resource management and interpretation. The main purpose should not necessarily be to provide geographic equity or recreation solely for the poor.
4. Land near urban areas is expensive to buy outright, and, where used, condemnation can be costly in dollars and antagonism toward the Park Service. Given the increased respect for established communities and local decision making, the Park Service needs to work collaboratively with local and state governments to encourage protection of the scenic and resource values through other land protection mechanisms—such as zoning, easements, and tax incentives.
5. Parks in urban settings should be brought closer in resource standards

and management, staff, and programs—to the traditional national park system. At the same time, lessons from urban parks should be shared with traditional NPS parks and with state and local parks.

6. To make urban parks "work" requires—to a greater extent than traditional parks—considerable local private as well as public support —from individuals, voluntary groups, corporations, and foundations. Urban parks, more than most traditional parks, have been able to leverage this kind of commitment.

Along with the many advantages of NPS involvement and the excellent example of Park Service resource management traditions—as well as the positive potential of urban parks—one should note the substantial problems that have arisen. Urban parks can involve NPS in a mixture of difficult or inhibiting situations—revitalization, garbage dumps, unfulfilled expectations, mass transportation, crime, vocal citizen groups, and drawn-out political hang-ups with local governments. The opportunities and possibilities are exciting, but the headaches and costs should not be minimized.

Urban park commitments, finally, should not be viewed as a means by which people are steered away from western national parks. People may be precluded from visiting them for various reasons, including the costs of travel and pinched budgets, but it is doubtful that urban parks make any significant dent in visitation. In the long run, it could well be that a National Park Service presence in urban settings induces greater visitation to western parks.

Impasse on the Upper Delaware

Glenn Pontier

Intense recreational activity along the Upper Delaware River brought trespassing and litter problems, and consequently demands by local residents for limitations on river access. The Upper Delaware Clearinghouse, composed of town officials from the five affected counties, helped enact federal legislation providing for limited land purchases along the river and cooperative land-use controls for the majority of the region. However, the National Park Service's traditional top-down planning ran into local opposition, in part because of local distrust of big government. This reprint from Planning *magazine (August 1984) describes the problems faced and lessons learned from the Upper Delaware River management effort.*

The Upper Delaware River flows between Hancock and Sparrow Bush, New York, through a relatively isolated valley, with few people and little industry. Not only is the area set apart from the mainstream, but the communities within it are isolated from each other. Yet the valley's culture is easily discernible by comparison with the larger cities and suburbs of the surrounding region. A considerable strain of nineteenth-century rural life has been retained, as much by habitat as by choice.

Local government, although part-time and overworked, still responds in a personal manner. Elected officials are "just folks," not lawyers, and have coffee every morning in the local restaurants. Their primary concerns are keeping the roads patched and the trucks operating. Annual budgets—including salaries, equipment, highway repair, insurance, courts, constables, and everything else—may not total much more than $250,000 a year. Change is traditionally slow to come, and slower to be accepted.

So it is not surprising that the arrival of a large federal bureaucracy, the National Park Service, was met with something less than all-out approbation. With a congressional mandate to protect the area, backed by an annual budget of over $1 million and a trained, uniformed staff, the agency began in 1978 to manage the river valley, including its recreational activities, land use, law enforcement, and trash removal.

Unlike other scenic rivers and national parks, however, the Upper Delaware is not owned by the Park Service. Virtually all of it remains in local hands. That meant that the bureaucracy's expertise—gained through years of managing areas it owns—was out of step in this area. Severely limited in its land acquisition, the NPS had to learn to deal with other political entities and to heed the advice of local residents.

Because of the unique nature of the law governing the Upper Delaware, a sophisticated planning process was called for. The Park Service arranged for planners from its Denver Service Center to fly in every month to captain a cumbersome, thirty-nine-member planning team. That team, now disbanded, included state and county planners, but no one from the fifteen riverfront towns. From the point of view of local residents, the situation was comparable to the Roman legions entering the land of Palestine.

All of this helps to explain the well-publicized conflict between the residents and the NPS—a conflict that culminated in the scrapping of the Park Service's original plan for the area.

The valley

The best path to understanding the Upper Delaware River Valley is to realize that the area is at the end of everyone's delivery route. From fuel and product distributors, right down to state and local agencies, the valley is last to obtain the normal supply of goods and services provided to other regions.

The river forms the border between Pennsylvania and New York. Along its banks is a sparsely settled area of small villages, scattered houses, large woodlots, and a few farms. Once the valley linked the communities, serving as a conduit for lumber rafts and coal barges. Later, as the fifteen municipalities and five counties developed, their dependence on the river lessened. Highways, the railroad for a time (Jay Gould brought the Erie Railroad down the valley in the mid-1800s), and modern life in general led to a decline in the river as a transportation artery, even as its commercial use for recreation took on greater significance.

Yet the valley never developed the strong tourist and second-home industries that washed over the Pocono Mountains to the west or the Catskills to the east. Instead, it remained rural, noted, if at all, for its fishing and hunting and summer camps. The cause is a phenomenon described by Sandra Hauptmann, a regional Park Service planner and now assistant park superintendent for the Upper Delaware, as "the principle of intervening opportunities." While the valley is only two hours from the New York metropolitan area and not much farther from Philadelphia,

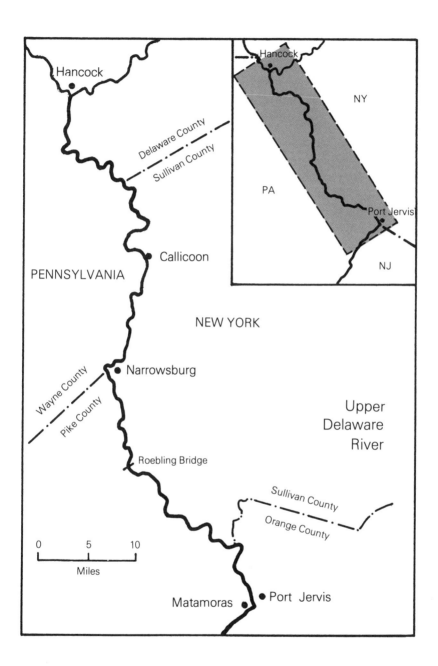

10.1   Upper Delaware River Regional Location Map

visitors have always been sidetracked by similar recreation centers before they reach the Upper Delaware.

The valley's living tie to the past cannot be overstated. Long bypassed by government authority, commercial development, and population growth, its fifteen towns remain small, with most residents centered in tiny hamlets. Total permanent population in the seventy-two-mile-long river corridor is less than seven thousand.

The people

Until the last decade most people who lived in the valley were born there. Staunchly independent, they are descendants of the Connecticut colonists who settled the land over two centuries ago. Mary Curtis, historian of the town of Delaware, New York, whose family was among the first in the valley, describes the early colonists as people who did not like government or authority. It is a trait passed on for generations and reinforced by the lack of attention given the valley by all layers of government over the years.

While recently the balance of natives to newcomers has tipped in favor of the latter, values have not changed significantly. Many of the newcomers are refugees from urban areas, people who have fled tight land-use controls and bureaucratic restrictions for a place with less government and fewer constraints.

After modest beginnings in the 1960s commercial canoe outfitters (called liveries) began introducing packaged canoe trips to the nearby city markets. By the mid-1970s they were flooding the river with thousands of canoes filled primarily with city youths interested in having a good time. The industry brought seasonal employment, development of new river access sites, and associated businesses like campgrounds, restaurants, and taverns. The customers also brought serious trespassing problems, illegal camping, drunkenness, drugs, disorderly conduct, and mountains of litter on summer weekends.

The canoe liveries have grown in size and number until at least two dozen now fill the seventy-two-mile stretch of river with about five thousand canoes, kayaks, and rafts at a time. The liveries also acquired economic and political clout beyond the control of local governments, whose tax base is inadequate to provide the increased services that are needed to handle the influx of visitors.

Federal law

The 1968 Wild and Scenic Rivers Act named the Upper Delaware as one of twenty-seven free-flowing rivers to be studied for preservation. The old federal Bureau of Outdoor Recreation (BOR) first proposed the outright purchase, through fee-simple acquisition and the procurement of scenic easements, of at least fifteen thousand acres of choice riverfront land. Restrictions, including a ban on growing row crops, were proposed for thousands more acres.

It was the time of the controversial Tocks Island Dam proposal, when the Army Corps of Engineers and the National Park Service were already buying up thousands of homes along the Middle Delaware for what eventually became the Delaware Water Gap National Recreation Area. (See "The Tocks Island Dam Is Dead, But the Delaware Gap Widens," December 1976, and "Local People Join Forces to Save the Upper Delaware," November 1977, in *Planning*.)

The BOR's proposals got a negative reaction in the valley. In fact, says LaRue Elmore, a Damascus, Pennsylvania, resident long active in river issues, the agency's arrogant manner so aroused local people that they organized themselves into several river associations.

At the start these groups opposed any sort of federal involvement. "But as time passed and river use increased, with all its turmoil," says Elmore, "people began to think federal management might be acceptable if it could be reconstructed in a way that would protect private property rights."

Although hesitant at first, the BOR indicated a willingness to work with local leaders to come up with alternative proposals. One of these alternatives, restricting federal condemnation of land in communities that had valid land-use controls to protect the river, was allowed in concept by a provision of the Wild and Scenic Rivers Act.

County planners formed the Upper Delaware Clearinghouse, composed of representatives of the five counties (Delaware, Sullivan, and Orange in New York; Wayne and Pike in Pennsylvania), the New York Department of Environmental Conservation, the Pennsylvania Department of Environmental Resources, the Delaware River Basin Commission, local officials, and private citizens, including canoe livery operators. "The Clearinghouse also began to develop zoning guidelines, reasoning that it was better to initiate them locally than to wait for the federal government to impose its own," recalls Elmore.

The local people worked hard to shape a law that would protect the valley's traditional values. In 1978 the area's congressional representatives wrote, and got passed, legislation unique to the National Park Service as part of the omnibus National Parks and Recreation Act, PL 95-625. While providing for NPS management of river recreation and protection of the valley's environment, it kept NPS land purchases to a minimum (1,450 acres in a river corridor of about 79,000 acres) and established a cooperative approach among all the levels of government.

The law required the municipalities to develop and enforce land-use controls that "substantially conform" to standards outlined in the land- and water-use guidelines approved by the secretary of the interior in September 1981. These guidelines were based on the proposal developed earlier by the Clearinghouse. If a municipality did not substantially conform to the guidelines and, as a result, land development occurred that threatened the river corridor, then the law allowed one hundred acres a mile to be acquired for condemnation.

To help put these land-use controls in place, the legislation provided funds for technical assistance. It also authorized federal payments to the towns to cover the cost of police protection and litter collection. An Upper Delaware Citizens Advisory Council was created to advise the NPS and other partners.

It was an enlightened law, a sensible alternative to the approach on other scenic rivers where thousands of acres of riparian land have been purchased; and in general, local residents were pleased. A large federal buyout had been averted; rangers would patrol the river to control the canoeists, and now things could get back to normal. Most people gave little thought to exactly what the river management plan might entail, supposing implementation to be years away.

The legislation required that the plan be developed within three years. When the land-use guidelines were delayed almost that long (although the law called for their adoption within eighteen months), everyone knew the plan itself would take a lot longer. And when the NPS assembled its planning team, representing all the affected parties, the fifteen towns were not included—even though the towns would be responsible for much of the implementation.

Planning from afar

The NPS's planners flew into the area from their Denver office for periodic meetings, but most of the writing was done in Colorado. For several years the town supervisors and planning boards, on whose cooperation the plan rested, had no direct participation. County planners, who understood local needs, were told that the NPS required that certain provisions be included in the plan and that a specific format be followed.

The result was a draft plan published in October 1982, a year late, that did not come to grips with local needs and values. Written by and for professional planners, in a jargon foreign to the Upper Delaware, the draft proved such a chore to read that some town officials are still unfamiliar with it. The draft also drew significant criticism from regional and national conservation groups, which felt it went overboard in promoting recreational development on an already abused river. "Although we are in no way opposed to the public enjoyment of the river, there are serious resource management problems—litter, public safety, shoreline degradation, water quality deterioration—that are not being adequately addressed by the proposed plan," said Chris Ballantyne of the Sierra Club. Studies of the river's carrying capacity and an assessment of the plan's effect on land values were never done.

A revised draft, reworked by the same planning team and published in October 1983, had the same flaws. It got an even stormier reception. Angry citizens took center stage, some declaring that the plan was a smoke screen for the NPS, which was plotting to take over the entire river corridor.

Although some of the local criticism was unfair and inaccurate, telling points were made about the failure of the NPS planning team to deal with such traditional local activities as hunting, timbering, and eeling, and about its failure to establish a working relationship with town planning boards. Overuse of the river by the canoe liveries and the plan's emphasis on recreation development were major concerns. "All the restrictions are on the property owner and none on the canoeists," was one commonly heard reaction.

The plan did a poor job of laying out some very good ideas. In addition to reiterating the law's basic concepts, it urged creation of an Intergovernmental Coordinating Council to plan policy along the river. The nineteen-member body—which would include the fifteen riverfront towns, the two states, the Delaware River Basin Commission, and the National Park Service—would be formed from an unofficial group—the Conference of Upper Delaware Townships (COUP)—that had been created by the towns in 1981 to represent their interests concerning the river. The federal power of condemnation would be tied to the council's recommendations. The Citizens Advisory Council was retained to provide for public participation, and the NPS education and law-enforcement programs on the river would be continued. Facilities would be developed to meet visitor needs and direct existing use. The plan also advocated placing restrictions on recreational river users and commercial canoe liveries if a carrying capacity study demonstrated such a need. Future management options outlined in the plan included the adoption of a permit system for canoeists.

Ambiguities and contradictions

The problems with the plan were many. It was poorly organized and filled with ambiguities and contradictions. More important, it did not tie the land-use guidelines to specific language that described potential threats to the river. The plan said "thou shalt not" when it should have been positive, recognizing and encouraging the valley's traditional activities—hunting, fishing, lumbering, farming, as well as canoeing. Nor did it adequately address the issue of how to direct new growth to existing settlement areas and make it compatible with the valley's character. The plan could have headed off some of the criticism simply by mentioning its own limits. It should have stated, for instance, that non-river-related businesses were never intended to be regulated. It never did.

What went wrong?

The National Park Service arrived in the valley in 1978 ready to plug into an operating structure that could carry out the local end of the bargain. To some degree, the law anticipated a need for local input and created the Citizens Advisory Council to advise the NPS. Yet no real linkup was available.

In fact, there has never been a regional organization in the valley. Ironically, it took hostility to the NPS, the common foe, to spur the formation of COUP.

Planning process as forum

COUP's existence is due in large measure to the foresight of Herbert Fabricant, then chairman of the Citizens Advisory Council, and a couple of the more progressive town officials. While publicly decrying the establishment of another layer of government, the popular line at the time, Fabricant harped on the need for a valleywide forum. But he also understood something that the Park Service seemed to miss; that the valley towns, for varied, even contradictory, reasons, did not want to change. They were in general, and remain today, largely opposed to government, bureaucracy, development, or anything new, whatever the effect.

While NPS and state officials tried to cajole the towns into adopting zoning ordinances to preserve the area, local residents saw the ordinances themselves as changing their way of life. Planners said that the towns should form an intergovernmental council to give themselves more power. The locals saw this as more bureaucracy.

In fact, the very tools suggested by the law and the planning team to help the local communities keep their way of life would lead to changes in that way of life. Yet the planners were right in their assessment of the situation. The valley was already changing, and the NPS's plan was the result of these changes, not the cause. "I think the plan got caught up in its own implementation," says Keith Dunbar, one of the NPS Denver Service Center's planners. "The planning process itself became a forum for the future of the valley."

Where the NPS went astray was in its inability to recognize and anticipate its own effect on the valley. This situation calls into question the ability of a large federal apparatus to deal with innovation in a case where it cannot own all the land or control all the details. The bureaucratic structure may simply not be capable of allowing competent individuals to do the job. Some of the officials involved on the Upper Delaware have, in fact, been top-notch, but too often the weight of federal codes and regulations has gotten in the way of intelligent and timely responses.

For example, the Denver Service Center's role is based on the theory that it can put together a team capable of planning in any situation in any place. Thus, the plan was written two thousand miles away by people who were also working on other projects. When a local reporter suggested that the planners should take a month and attend every school board meeting in sight, one NPS staffer responded, "Why would I want to go to a school board meeting? It has nothing to do with the river."

"True," answered the reporter, "but you need to understand how the people work and communicate when you do not have any power over them."

The advice went unheeded.

A fundamental error

The NPS made a second fundamental error. It got caught in the middle of long-standing conflicts, alienating people on both sides of each issue. There are conflicts between canoeists and riparian owners. Some towns want more development, while others want to return to the way they were thirty years ago. People cannot even agree on whether placing rest rooms along the river is a good idea.

The NPS was blamed by people on both sides, who then tended to forget their own disagreements. What the NPS should have done from the beginning was to take a position as a mediator and work to resolve the disputes. It should also have taken strong stands on some matters—for instance, a noncontroversial proposal to set up a single emergency phone number for the valley (which has several phone companies and area codes). The NPS ignored the issue, a critical one in an area where many visitors do not know what state they are in.

Likewise, the NPS never made any real headway in helping clean up the only toxic landfill in the river corridor. This most serious threat to the river has been the center of a dispute for over ten years and is now the subject of a $40 million federal lawsuit brought by New York State and one of the towns. The NPS has tried to stay out of the controversy publicly, opting instead for behind-the-scenes pressure. But that hasn't worked, leading some local folks to grumble: What good is the NPS if it can't even clean up the dump?

The Upper Delaware has been the subject of articles in the *New York Times*, the *Philadelphia Inquirer*, *National Parks*, and other publications. But few of the writers seem to understand the fundamental conflict in values that lies beneath the clash between the NPS and the residents of the valley.

Those who oppose the National Park Service don't have this problem. Two different groups have managed to parlay their knowledge of the situation into national publicity, although they are both small in size and not representative of the majority of residents.

One organization, the Coalition of Concerned Citizens, based in Damascus, Pennsylvania, is headed by individuals who are philosophically and politically opposed to the NPS, zoning, and government regulations. Although the valley is largely conservative and wary of big government, many in this group go further. Some are right-wing zealots pushing a whole agenda, of which fending off the Park Service is only one part. "Citizens Unite to Rid Our Valley of the National Park Service. Our homes, farms, schools, churches, even our lifestyles are in danger of falling prey to NPS," stated one of their flyers.

These "tin horn tyrants," as one local columnist called them, discovered a powerful tool to support their case in a public television program narrated by the late Jessica Savitch and aired nationally in 1983. The program, "For the Good of All," claims to show how the NPS ran roughshod over property owners in the Cuyahoga Valley near Cleveland in creating a national recreation area in the 1970s. Tapes of the program have been shown throughout the Upper Delaware inflaming audiences against the NPS.

Last winter the group drew over 350 residents to a meeting referred to unofficially by NPS officials as "the Monday night massacre." By the end of the evening the audience was clamoring for the NPS to "go away and leave us alone." Referring to the Park Service and the management plan as socialistic, the coalition is now pushing actively for "deauthorization" (repeal) of the law. Some of their rhetoric has fallen on fertile ground, with five of the fifteen towns adopting resolutions in support of deauthorization.

The inholders

Some of the canoe liveries are also active opponents of the NPS. Sobered by mounting public censure of their operations and by the determination of the NPS to license their businesses, the liveries have mounted a concerted effort to focus criticism squarely and solely on the NPS.

In February 1983 the liveries sponsored three boisterous meetings, marked by the appearance of Charles Cushman, a Sonoma, California, activist with years of experience attacking the NPS and other federal land-management agencies and head of the National Inholders Association, which he claims has nine thousand members working to protect the rights of private landowners within federal lands. Cushman, dressed in a buckskin vest and hiking boots, spoke to packed meetings, one of almost a thousand people. His theme was that NPS "perceives its goals to be the removal of people from a wilderness area." The NPS would "regulate everything to keep it natural," he added, "and they do not consider you as natural." Although he said he supported the Upper Delaware legislation ("as good a law as has been written to protect a river"), Cushman urged that the towns be given funding by the Park Service so that they could hire an independent planner to rewrite the management plan. "You've got to create a good plan and a political force to make it stick," he said.

Backed by the canoe liveries, Cushman helped to found a group called the "Upper Delaware Citizens Alliance." Alliance members have dominated several public meetings, sometimes shouting insults at NPS personnel or local officials with whom they disagree. Their attacks led to the resignation of one of the valley's most respected supervisors, Donald Scheetz of Lumberland, and provoked a fistfight between the vice-chairman of COUP and one of the liverymen.

NPS response

The Park Service's response to the criticism of the management plan was made in the winter of 1983–84 by James W. Coleman, Jr., the mid-

Atlantic regional director. He agreed to extend the planning process for six months, until July 1984, "in order to try to reach consensus on the plan among as many as possible." Encouraging all parties to contact the NPS with questions or concerns, Coleman instructed local park officials to set up a task force of valley residents, including citizen activists, to review the document.

"Part of the difficulty was that we did not have the local governments directly represented on the planning team," says John T. Hutzky, NPS superintendent for the Upper Delaware. "Had we done that right from the beginning, we would have had a better reading on what the towns would have accepted." "We simply made mistakes in designing the original planning effort," admits Donald Castleberry, another NPS official.

Soon after, COUP, the valleywide group described earlier, picked up Charles Cushman's idea of allowing the towns to hire their own planner to revise the plan. The NPS agreed to provide funding.

So, after spending $1.5 million on the draft plan, the NPS has now hired three separate groups of planners for a new one. Tom Shepstone, a planning consultant in Honesdale, Pennsylvania, who had served on the original planning team, was selected to rework the federal land- and water-use guidelines. (Shepstone is the author of the 1977 *Planning* article on the Upper Delaware.) Michael Presnitz and Charles Hoffman of St. Paul, Minnesota, were chosen to revise all those sections of the plan not having to do with river recreation. (Presnitz had previously served as a paid negotiator for the canoe liveries.) The Urban Research and Development Corporation of Bethlehem, Pennsylvania, was named to work on river recreation and carrying-capacity studies.

With the towns now taking the lead through COUP, the NPS has stepped back from an active role in the planning, confining most of its visible activities to operations on the river.

Lessons

There are several planning lessons to be learned from the Upper Delaware. The clash of two value systems was inevitable and is likely to occur in other planning situations. But the anger and panic could have been avoided. Had the NPS understood the people as well as the special interests and the ideologues did, it might have diffused the issues more quickly.

The law needed a bottom-up planning effort, beginning with the towns. Instead the NPS employed a traditional top-down approach, which did not work. For a genuine partnership to exist, the focus must be on conserving all the resources of an area, not just the ones an agency is used to protecting.

Most local residents are not opposed to the NPS. They want to see the river preserved, and they want to do what is right. But their natural instincts don't dovetail with what they see as the NPS's standard operating procedure in other places—full-scale acquisition and complete management. Their fear is that steps taken to preserve the area's natural resources could destroy the very cultural qualities that the law is meant to protect.

Local government enforcement of land-use standards, federal funding for law enforcement and trash removal, technical assistance to town governments—these are strange items for a national park's agenda. They are the tools of a new concept in park planning and operation, and they thrust the most basic and traditional values of a democratic nation into the center of the National Park Service's operations. Real grass-roots involvement is messy—with all of its pressure groups, tooth-and-nail struggles, and pragmatic compromises. The National Park Service got caught up in this ferment when its initial management plan failed to reflect the needs of the valley. Only time will tell if the new Upper Delaware plan will have more success. Events are still hot, still unfolding. It may be years overdue, but change comes slowly along the river.

Montgomery County Agricultural Preservation Program

Melissa Banach and Denis Canavan

Although a significant portion of Montgomery County, Maryland, is actively farmed, development pressure in the Washington, D.C., area has threatened the continued use of this land for farming activities. To balance the value of protecting farmland with the need to accommodate growth, the Montgomery County Planning Board has undertaken a unique and highly successful agricultural preservation program.

Since the inception of the program five years ago, Montgomery County has protected approximately 89,000 acres using transferable development rights (TDR) in conjunction with a preferential agricultural zone. The program represents a politically palatable and economically feasible solution to the problem of farmland disappearing at the urban fringe.

The preferential agricultural zone gives strong preference to agriculture, forestry, and other open-space uses, as well as allowing a wide variety of agriculturally related commercial and industrial uses. It discourages residential uses other than farmhouses by restricting residential development to one dwelling unit per 25 acres (one-acre minimum lot size).

The TDR system provides the opportunity for an economic return to farmland placed in this zone. All landowners in the preferential agricultural zone are eligible to sell their development rights to people interested in building new developments in county-designated growth areas at higher than normally allowed densities. The purpose is to make it possible for land included in the preferential agricultural zone to be maintained in agricultural use, without denying landowners the option to take advantage of the prior development value of their land.

The disappearance of farmland and open green space began to worry people throughout the country in the late 1950s. Both city dwellers and farmers viewed the loss of agricultural acres to subdivision as an economic, environmental, cultural, and social problem. People of many areas started to review their planning and zoning practices with an eye to preserving vital farmland while they addressed the urban needs for housing, commercial, and industrial development.

Maryland was the first state to try to cope with the issue when in 1956 the general assembly enacted a preferential agricultural tax assessment in an effort to encourage the tillers of the fields to stay behind their plows. Since then, forty-nine other states have adopted similar legislation. But despite these tax incentives, development pressure continued to entice farmers; farmland continued to erode; and state and local governments have intensified efforts to slow the conversion of farms to nonfarm uses.

Agricultural restrictive zoning has been the most popular and common method used to prevent the loss of agricultural land to nonagricultural purposes. In the last decade at least 270 jurisdictions have approved large lot requirements to protect their farmlands.[1] Agricultural zones are often combined with community plans, urban boundary agreements, or voluntary or mandatory state easements. Thus, agricultural zoning is often part of a larger program.

In certain situations zoning may not be an appropriate technique. For example, it may prove politically unfeasible to restrict zoning drastically in places where development pressure is high and it is evident that landowners would be deprived of substantial value. Moreover, experience has shown that many officials are reluctant to deny developers the right to ply their trade and landowners the right to profit. In response to such concerns, and reflecting a feeling that such uncompensated restrictions on development as embodied in agricultural zoning are unfair to owners of farmland in rapidly urbanizing areas, many public policy makers have turned to the idea of acquiring less-than-fee interest in land in order to control its use.

Purchase of Development Rights programs have been successful in attracting landowners who wish to participate. To date, more than 10,000 acres throughout the United States have been enrolled in Purchase of Development Rights programs.[2] However, the main problem with such programs is not effectiveness but rather the difficulty in developing and maintaining enough public and political support to appropriate large sums of money necessary to make the program work.

While the actual purchase of an interest in land is the most permanent way to prevent its development, it is often also the most expensive. Several techniques have been proposed or tried that are designed to reduce the cost, such as the right of preemption and land banking.[3] The right of preemption allows a government to match an open-market price and buy agricultural land only when it is actually on the market.

Yet another technique is the donation of development rights in perpetuity. This is made possible by section 170(h) of the Internal Revenue Code, which permits a landowner to deduct from his income the value of land, or of interest in land, that he donates to a public body or a qualified private nonprofit corporation.

The last predominant technique involves the establishment of a private land trust: a private, nonprofit, charitable (and tax-exempt) entity set up to acquire and manage lands in the public interest.

One of the newest and most promising techniques to limit development in agricultural areas is the transfer of development rights (TDR). This method gives farmland owners access to capital without forcing them off the land and gives developers more room to build where needed public services are available. Moreover, the taxpayers do not have to pick up the tab for the program in the form of a direct subsidy. The change of value is made between the farmland owner and the developer, with the government acting only as referee and keeper of the records of transaction.

TDR systems rely on working with private landowners to retire development rights by shifting the responsibility for purchasing them from the government to private developers. In a typical TDR system a preservation district is identified (the sending area), as is a development district (the receiving area). Development rights are assigned to owners of land in the preservation district in a systematic manner. However, owners of land in the preservation district are not allowed to develop intensively, but instead may sell their development rights to owners of land in the development district, who may use these newly acquired development rights to build at higher densities than normally allowed by the zoning. TDR systems are intended to compensate the owners of the preserved land for the loss of their full development potential. The owner of land in the preservation district has the option of either developing at low densities or selling the development rights to the land and then restricting development by easement. Thus, the TDR system encourages farming by compensating the owners of the preserved land for the loss of the right to develop. Developers are not deprived of the opportunity to build and everybody can continue to glory in the "amber waves of grain."

Although the TDR concept has been discussed for more than a decade, few municipalities have adopted TDR systems for the preservation of farmland. The National Agricultural Lands Study report in 1981 stated that TDR programs had saved only 184 acres of farmland *nationwide*. TDR critics cited these statistics and proclaimed TDR too complex a procedure to effectively preserve farmland. The skepticism about TDR spread. The statistics, however, do not indicate that TDR cannot work; they simply indicate that TDR cannot work in all situations. If applied in appropriate areas, usually in the metropolitan fringe, TDR can work.

Now, however, the most extensive TDR system designed to help implement a comprehensive agricultural preservation program has been successfully developed and applied in Montgomery County, Maryland, a rapidly growing suburban area of Washington, D.C. The TDR program was implemented as part of a comprehensive rezoning that established a preferential agricultural zone for an expansive rural area of 89,000 acres. Since Montgomery County formally launched the program five years ago, it has (*a*) significantly reduced the development potential on the 89,000 acres with the use of the preferential agricultural zone, and (*b*) permanently restricted development on portions of it by transferring the development rights to other lands targeted for growth. As a result of these efforts (which are described in this chapter), the speculative value of farmland has been removed in Montgomery County and for the first time in decades farmers can now buy farmland valued as farmland.

Development of an action program to retain farmland

Without a county farmland preservation program, the future of farming in Montgomery County appeared bleak. Between 1964 and 1974 about 40,000 acres of farmland were consumed. Current trends indicated that in five years approximately 7,000 acres of additional farmland would be lost and in ten years another 14,000 acres would be lost to suburban growth. Given these trends, in seventy years, no farmland of any significant size would remain in the county, and the viability of the county's farm industry would be diminished even faster.

As a result of these alarming trends, the Montgomery County Council directed the Montgomery County Planning Board in 1978 to develop a plan to preserve farmland at no cost to the county in terms of implementation. In addition, the plan had to be completed within a year. The planning board was the lead agency in the preservation effort.

Fearing that a considerable amount of land would be lost to nonagricultural uses during the one-year planning period, an interim moratorium on the subdivision of selected farmland areas was imposed. This moratorium did not preclude development; instead it significantly reduced the development density from the existing level of one dwelling unit per five acres to one dwelling unit per twenty-five acres.

Prior to initiating the plan itself, the planning board first considered the need for farmland preservation, overall preservation goals, and the various alternative methods available to preserve farmland. The planning board developed an issues and alternative report to serve as a vehicle for discussion among representatives of relevant agricultural, legal, development, political, and community interest groups. The discussion document contained no recommendations but simply identified need, verified issues, and presented alternative preservation methods. With this approach, the issue of agricultural preservation could then be discussed by all opposing groups without the immediate fear of winning or losing—a potentially explosive planning issue was diffused early on.

As a result of this discussion process, it became evident to the planning board that there were only three alternative ways to preserve farmland —buy it, zone it, or TDR it. Given Montgomery County's location in the Washington, D.C., metropolitan fringe, the purchase of farmland was prohibitively expensive. In contrast, an effort to place more restrictive zoning requirements on farmland would involve a bitter political battle that could easily extinguish the entire preservation program. TDR, used in conjunction with a preferential agricultural zone, appeared to be the most desirable technique to all members of the discussion groups. The application of the preferential agricultural zone would result in the reduction of full development potential, while the TDR mechanism would compensate the farmland owner for the loss of development potential. If a TDR mechanism were developed effectively, everyone involved in the land-use game could recognize a benefit: not only would the farmer have his equity concerns addressed, developers would realize that TDR is not a no-growth strategy. Development would simply be *shifted* to areas better able to serve increased density. Politicians also recognized that while a TDR program itself is low in operating costs, the farmland preserved remains on the tax rolls. A county TDR program used in conjunction with a preferential agricultural zone therefore emerged as the strategy of choice.

With political consensus achieved on its preservation strategy, the planning board next focused on the orchestration of a countywide preservation program consistent with the county's existing growth management system. Master planning, zoning, subdivision, and the control of public facilities provided the framework for the preservation program. Before a plan was initiated, overall goals needed identification, the public purpose objectives needed definition, and the geographic area to be affected needed a boundary.

A. Goal setting

Based upon review of local, regional, and national conditions of agriculture at the urban fringe, planning board staff concluded that there is no single all-encompassing panacea that will assure the retention of farmland, especially in urban fringe areas. For instance, local government itself can do little to influence food-pricing policies, the economics of a farm operation, or the commitment of a family to farm. Providing indirect economic incentives through the TDR proposal and overall county growth policies may be the most that can be done by local government. Preserving farmland and contributing to a favorable climate for farming, therefore, involve the concerted pursuit of a series of actions and policies aimed at

- stabilizing land value
- minimizing development pressures in rural areas
- avoiding premature and fragmenting subdivisions
- improving agricultural support services
- maintaining a critical mass of agricultural land
- relating county farmland preservation efforts to those of neighboring counties

The comprehensive master plan, completed in 1980, provides the policy framework to meet these objectives and to enable the continuation of farming in the county.[4]

B. Public purpose

To develop a meaningful farmland preservation program it is critical to clearly define the need for such a program in terms of the public interest. The definition of the public interest provides the basis for future government action and makes those actions more defensible and understandable. After all, fairness in public policy deals not only with equity among similar individuals, but between interests of private property owners and those of the public. Land-use policy and regulations designed to preserve farmland by development limitations must properly serve the public interest or risk strong political opposition. The county agricultural preservation program was therefore designed to complement existing public goals or programs.

First, the program is structured to help control public costs and prevent urban sprawl—to complement existing county planning efforts. Studies conducted by the planning board,[5] the Council of Governments, and other planning bodies suggest that there is substantial benefit in the compact form of growth encouraged by the Montgomery County General Plan. Specifically, the *Metropolitan Growth Policy Statement*, published by the Metropolitan Washington Council of Governments in 1977, calls for a compact growth pattern that will conserve the region's air, water, land, and energy resources by promoting development in specified growth centers with particular emphasis on areas served by mass transit. The prevention of urban encroachment into agricultural areas to be preserved also promotes compact urban development in designated growth areas as called for in the published statement.

The energy and fiscal implications of urban sprawl have been well documented.[6] Sprawl costs money, and with limited fiscal resources it is important that nonrenewable land resources be preserved, thereby encouraging orderly development and growth. This is especially true in an era of cost consciousness and in-depth examinations of government services and related costs. If development that would have occurred in the agricultural areas can be partly guided in terms of location and timing through a farmland and open space preservation program, the county could maintain additional control of public costs and urban sprawl, while preserving a viable agricultural industry.

Second, the program is designed to adhere to the county's ongoing growth management efforts. The county growth management system makes it possible for officials and the public to understand the relationships that exist between growth and facilities, and the consequences of each on the General Plan's proposed development pattern. (See discussion under Planning and Management Framework for an explanation of the General Plan.) One element of this system, the Comprehensive Staging Plan, places interim limits on growth that are keyed to the provision of additional public facilities, so that a relatively constant level of public service can be maintained over time. Montgomery County offers a full range of residential, commercial, and industrial development alternatives within its water and sewer envelope. More than fifteen separate zones permit a variety of residential densities in excess of two units per acre. There is sufficient vacant or easily redevelopable land for approximately 140,000 additional dwelling units exclusive of the areas designated for preservation. Using a high dwelling unit forecast for the county, total dwelling unit capacity is enough for the next thirty-five years of growth. Employment opportunities within the water and sewer envelope could easily double without exceeding the total zoned capacity.

Since the Comprehensive Staging Plan is consistent with General Plan recommendations, no new major development will occur in the agricultural preservation area with the exception of Clarksburg, a new community. The preservation program, then, carries out the intent of the General Plan, the Montgomery County growth management system, and more specifically the recommendations of the Comprehensive Water Supply and Sewerage System Plan.

Third, the developed program helps preserve regional food supplies. Preserving farmland plays a significant role in food production in the state. Montgomery County's contribution is necessary for the state to maintain its current level of producing 55 percent of the food needed by state residents. The importance of agriculture within the state is well documented in *Agricultural Revolution: Maryland Agriculture 1776–1976*, written by the Maryland Agriculture Week Committee, January 1976.

The significance of Montgomery County agriculture increases, when viewed as part of a larger regional agricultural community.[7] For example, the dairy economy and the dairyland itself of Montgomery County help support the dairy community in Frederick County, which is the top milk-producing county in the area. Because most of the supply dealers are now located there and because the agricultural community is stronger, the Montgomery County farming establishment relies upon, and is an integral part of, the dairy community of the neighboring jurisdiction. The demise of farmland here will affect neighboring farm areas by reducing the number of productive acres and by pushing the urbanizing fringe farther and farther out, thereby threatening productive farmland in adjoining Howard and Frederick counties. The loss of agriculture in Montgomery County will increase development pressures in Howard County and Frederick County at a time when citizens, farmers, and decision makers there are struggling to retain a viable farm community.

Fourth, the agricultural preservation program helps improve energy conservation efforts. When farming is located in proximity to primary markets, urban centers, or international ports (Baltimore), energy is conserved by reducing transportation costs to the marketplace and, in turn, can influence the cost of the product to the consumer.

In addition, greater use of public transportation is made possible if a compact growth pattern is implemented. According to the *Metropolitan Growth Policy Statement,* overall energy conservation is reduced without a compact form of growth. A dispersed pattern of growth decreases reliance upon public transportation and encourages automobile travel. The statement concludes that "automobile travel demand . . . would increase beyond the capacity of existing and currently programmed highways, and the facilities required to satisfy such a demand would cost far more than can currently be expected. . . . [P]er capita energy consumption would continue to climb, as would overall regional energy consumption."

Fifth, the farmland preservation program protects the rural environment, especially sensitive headwater areas, wildlife habitats, conservation areas, floodplains, etc., from the impact of development. It also serves as a "clean air shed" to clean the atmosphere as well as a mechanism to protect the quantity and quality of water resources. A large share of urban flood problems stems from a decrease in areawide infiltration and retention due to paving and building development with the resulting increase in stormwater runoff. Urbanization, with its alteration of both natural contours and permeability of the soil, also increases the irregularity of the surface water flow, thereby lessening its reliability as a water supply source. While properly managed farmland is not as effective as thickly forested land, it is superior to dense and extensively paved suburban areas.[8]

Sixth, the preservation program helps maintain open-space lands. The open-space qualities of farmland preservation are significant. It provides productive, privately maintained agricultural open space with environmental benefits that include rural aesthetics and water quality.

Similarly, the significance of open space, as a result of large-lot, residential, clustered development, cannot be underestimated. These open-space areas are vital to the buffering of the agricultural preservation areas and can also provide leaseback arrangements for interested farmers as well as protecting environmentally sensitive areas.

Finally, the program helps preserve rural life-styles. The county has a rich agricultural heritage, a blend of two cultural traditions, one stemming from English planters who arrived in the eighteenth century, the other from Pennsylvania German and Quaker farmers of the nineteenth century. These two farming and cultural traditions are reflected in the blend of building materials and types evident in the county. The entire agricultural scene describes a culture and is as instructive as a museum. Preservation encourages and fosters a rural life-style important to Montgomery County. It is still possible today to see vestiges of Montgomery County's agrarian heritage in the rural villages. It is a viable land-use alternative for those who desire such a life-style.

C. Area definition—the "critical mass"

Montgomery County identified an 89,000-acre area as a "critical mass" of farmland; this area provides the framework for the preservation program. Critical mass is defined as an area that contains a diversity of activities and land uses necessary to sustain a viable agricultural industry. Specifically, it contains a significant percentage of land in which large and small farms, scattered rural residential settlements, as well as necessary agricultural support services can operate. Once the critical mass of farmland is eroded by incompatible land uses, the agricultural industry declines.

Also located within this critical mass is a wide range of topographic and geographic features that directly or indirectly support and define the area to be preserved. Woodlots, stream valleys, and productive soils (not necessarily prime soils) are found throughout the preservation area; these features are considered vital to the cohesiveness of the area. If these less than highly productive areas were permitted to develop, they would threaten the desired land-use element—farmland. A climate would be created, identified by the New Jersey Commission on Agriculture, as the impermanence syndrome—the feeling by farmers that farming is doomed in their area. This psychology is seen as a key factor, perhaps more so than direct economic conditions, for the decline of agriculture in urban fringe areas such as Montgomery County.

The impermanence syndrome results from the convergence of many factors: development pressures, rising taxes, departure of support industries for stronger markets, loss of political influence, nuisance laws and health laws that inhibit sound or necessary agricultural practices, rising labor costs in the face of urban employment opportunities, and land speculation. The syndrome is manifested in an agricultural community that increasingly sees no future for itself and its children, that regards eventual overunning by the suburbs as inevitable. Such an attitude becomes a self-fulfilling prophecy as farmer after farmer succumbs to fear, frustration, and almost unbelievable land prices and moves to a more stable agricultural area or leaves farming altogether. The critical mass of farms and services necessary to sustain a socially and economically viable community crumbles.

Farming, particularly family farming, is not simply an economic enterprise. It is a way of life, an ethic of people and land that is at the same time hardy and fragile. Economics alone probably can neither sustain nor destroy it. Very human qualities such as hope are essential to it. That is why farmland preservation is a very complex social problem that requires a wide variety of measures if it is to be successful at the urban fringe. In contrast, those areas deemed appropriate for rural open-space preservation are those farmland areas abutting suburban development where the critical mass of farmland has already been eroded by subdivision activity. The preservation of farmland, in an appropriate combination with very low density residential development, is the objective.

Region's existing planning and management framework

All land-use planning in Montgomery County is based on the General Plan. Adopted in 1964, the plan envisioned development radiating outward from Washington, D.C., in a series of corridor cities along the major transportation corridors with wedges of lower density between them (see figure 11.1). The General Plan seeks to prevent urbanization of the agricultural and open spaces—the wedges—that now exist between the radial corridors it describes. However, the General Plan did not detail a specific implementation strategy; it treats the wedge as one large area without distinguishing between agriculture and rural open-space areas. Existing regulations and area land-use plans were not specifically designed or intended to protect farmland; farmland preservation was not an articulated public purpose.

The wedge portions of the county were generally included in the rural zone, a zone designed to limit nonagricultural uses and restrict any residential lots to five acres or more. The rural zone did not require that farming continue, or even prevent five-acre lots from preempting farmland. A review of rural subdivision plans submitted throughout the county showed that lot sizes were ranging from four to fifteen acres. Thus, even the lowest residential density available in Montgomery County, five acres, only slowed but did not stop farm conversion.

In addition to the General Plan, Montgomery County has a well-articulated growth management program. The county's program focuses on the orchestration of a variety of management tools designed to guide the locational aspects of growth as well as its timing and costs in a manner that is responsive to the public interest. A number of actions have been taken toward the development of a countywide growth management program.

- The General Plan identified areas where development should be delayed or severely restricted and those areas where development should be encouraged. (1964–69)
- The Capital Improvements Program schedules projects for construction for the upcoming budget year and five succeeding years.
- The Ten Year Water Supply and Sewerage System Plan has required the county to identify sewer service areas in terms of the time at which service should be extended.
- The Germantown Master Plan (1973) and subsequent area master plans demonstrated how the staging of development, both private and public, could work to benefit the overall objectives of the General Plan and growth management program by encouraging development in areas where a public facility infrastructure is available.
- The Adequate Public Facilities Ordinance (1973) allows the planning board to disapprove a subdivision if it finds that existing facilities plus those contained in the Capital Improvements Program are inadequate to serve it.
- The Annual Growth Policy Reports have been developed to describe the existing public facility conditions, define objectives, determine the capacity of existing public facilities, project needs, analyze the costs,

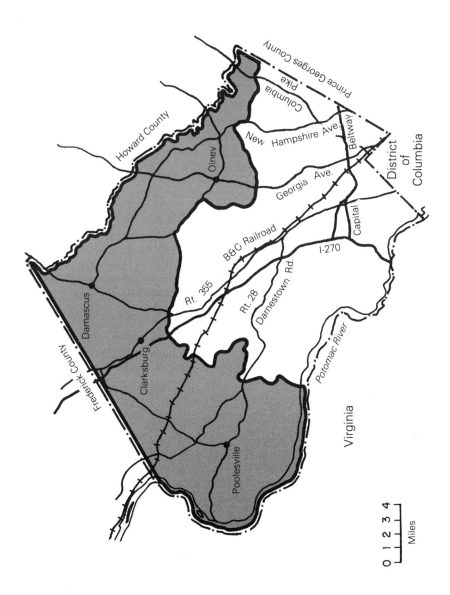

11.1 Montgomery County Agricultural Preservation Study Area

and propose the tools to establish a growth pattern to carry out the concepts of the General Plan within the framework of responsible expenditure of public funds. (Table 11.1 describes these efforts to preserve agricultural and open space in greater detail.)

The growth policy reports specifically recognize the goal of maintaining the rural character of the area defined as the critical mass. The first report focused on General Plan concept recommendations and noted that "to allow extensive development in these areas would obviously be ruinous to the concept of the General Plan" in that widespread, scattered development would "constitute the classic definition of sprawl, the very phenomenon that the General Plan was adopted to control."

The preservation program is built upon the policy framework established by the growth management strategy and becomes an implementation element of the General Plan. The preservation program is based on private sector regulation and public facility planning within a coordinated public policy context.

The preservation plan: management tools and techniques

A comprehensive farmland preservation program is one that meshes a broad spectrum of policy tools of government. According to the National Association of Counties' Research Foundation Study, *Disappearing Farmland*,

> Any one approach to farmland preservation is not likely to be effective, if other government programs or policies are inconsistent with it. For example, agricultural zoning can be undercut, if the local capital improvement plan calls for the extension of urban services into prime farming areas. Similarly, agricultural districting and the purchase or transfer of development rights can help preserve farmland, but may not succeed in preserving farming itself, if state or local policies do not support agriculture as an ongoing enterprise. And state and local initiatives themselves may be rendered ineffective if federal actions are not consistent with them.[9]

Since the thrust of the preservation program focuses on land-use policy and regulation, a master plan was chosen as the most appropriate vehicle to guide the program. *The Functional Master Plan for the Preservation of Agriculture and Rural Open Space*[10] therefore embodies all elements of a comprehensive preservation program, with emphasis on implementation. In addition to the county's complementary growth management strategy,

Table 11.1   Chronology of county farmland preservation efforts

12/64   Adoption of countywide General Land Use Plan proposed a development
        pattern consisting of "development corridors" separated by "open space
        wedges." This plan, while advocating rural economy, permitted residen-
        tial development at a density of one dwelling unit per two acres. The plan
        concentrated on future development of urban areas and allowed for
        scattered subdivisions in the rural areas.
8/74   Based on the revised 1969 General Plan containing specific statements
        favoring the continuation of agriculture in the rural wedge area, this
        rural area was "downzoned" by establishing a minimum lot area of
        five acres. Among the fundamental purposes was to avoid the intrusion
        of a mixture of conflicting land uses into the agricultural area.
9/78   The county council, recognizing the continual depletion of farmland by
        residential subdivision activity, mandated the planning board to study
        various alternatives to preserve the agricultural areas without a large
        expenditure of public funds.
3/79   First of several "white paper" reports indicating farmland was a viable
        land use for the county.
7/79   Issues and alternatives report documented that there was a continual loss
        of farmland acreage through residential activity and that it was threat-
        ening the "critical mass." The report stated there were various alternatives
        to preserve it, one of which was the use of the transfer of development
        rights concept, in conjunction with the preferential agricultural zone.
10/79   Interim zoning legislation—allowing one dwelling unit per twenty-five
        acres—was set in place for one year to prevent the further subdivision
        of land in the rural zone during the preparation of an Agricultural Preser-
        vation Master Plan.
2/80   A public education program was initiated and carried on throughout the
        plan-making process and subsequent implementing ordinances to reach
        all segments of those affected by the TDR program.
6/80   County council adoption of the Olney Master Plan. This advocated the
        preservation of agriculture for a small portion of the county's rural area.
        This prototype plan utilized, for the first time, the transfer of develop-
        ment rights process by recommending both sending and receiving areas,
        in conjunction with a preferential agricultural zone.
7/80   County council adopted zoning amendments creating the Rural Density
        Transfer Zone and Rural Cluster Zone and the transfer of development
        rights process for purposes of implementing the Olney Master Plan.
9/80   The county adopted the Functional Master Plan for the Preservation of
        Agriculture and Rural Open Space. This countywide plan provided for a
        comprehensive and cost-effective approach to the preservation of agricul-
        ture and rural open space utilizing traditional and innovative planning
        techniques.

Table 11.1—continued

10/80 The Olney sectional map amendment was adopted by the county council, thus comprehensively rezoning the area for the preservation of agriculture. It served as a prototype for a countywide transfer of development rights program.

1/81 The agricultural sectional map amendment was adopted by the county council. This implemented the land-use and zoning recommendations of the Agriculture and Rural Open Space Master Plan. This sectional map amendment established the Rural Density Transfer Zone (the preferential agricultural zone) as an area to be used primarily for agricultural uses having limited development potential and as a sending area from which residential development rights could be transferred. The plan did not establish any receiving areas. These areas were to be designated in future master plans covering the more urban areas of the county where residential growth was anticipated.

11/81 The Eastern Montgomery County Master Plan was adopted by the county council. This plan established the first receiving areas for the countywide TDR program. The accompanying sectional map amendment was passed 3/82.

5/82 The Damascus Master Plan was adopted by the county council and established additional TDR receiving areas. This plan was followed by a sectional map amendment adopted 9/82.

9/82 The Potomac Master Plan amendment was adopted by the county council and established additional TDR receiving areas.

10/82 Adoption of legislation creating the county TDR fund, envisioned since the conception of the TDR program. Its primary purpose is to loan money to farmers using TDRs as collateral.

1/83 The circuit court for Montgomery County upheld the county council's rezoning action in *Dufour et al.* vs. *Montgomery County.*

12/84 The Gaithersburg Vicinity Master Plan was adopted by the county council establishing additional TDR receiving areas.

7/85 The circuit court for Montgomery County upheld the application of the receiving areas in The Matter of the Application of Rock Run Limited Partnership for Approval of the Maryland National Capital Park and Planning Commission of Preliminary Subdivision Plan No. 1-84104, Avenel Farm, and The Matter of the Application of Rock Run Limited Partnership for Approval by the Maryland National Capital Park and Planning Commission of Site Plan Application Nos. 8-84095, 8-84107, 8-84108, 8-84109, and 8-84111, Avenel Farm.

a variety of innovative planning tools are used to implement the farmland preservation objectives. These include:

- Rural Density Transfer Zone and Transfer of Development Rights (TDR) Mechanism
- Rural Cluster Zone
- State of Maryland Agricultural District Easement Purchase Program
- Preferential Farmland Assessment

A. Rural Density Transfer Zone and TDR Mechanism

The new preferential agricultural zone is called the Rural Density Transfer Zone (RDT); it is applied in those areas of the county where little subdivision activity has occurred and a major effort to protect agriculture is warranted. This zone severely restricts development on the land itself while permitting a broad range of agricultural activities and agriculturally oriented special exception uses.

The RDT allows a density of one dwelling unit per twenty-five acres with a one-acre minimum lot size. However, as an integral part of the zone, the landowners in this zone have been assigned "development rights" equal to one development right per five acres, recognizing the density that land formerly zoned "rural" had before the new zone was adopted. This gives the landowners compensatory value for the presumed equity loss through downzoning. Officials, in adopting the zone, felt that this equity compensation was particularly important for the purpose of encouraging the maintenance of farming in the county since farmers often use their equity in the land to finance both their seasonal operations and the purchase of equipment. A strong equity position is vital to active farm use.

The TDR program is an optional, *voluntary* program; the owner still has the option to develop at the base density of one unit per twenty-five acres, thus the development value is not "wiped out." The farmland owners still retain title to their land, and they have something of value against which to borrow for needed improvements.

This approach, unlike traditional zoning techniques, offers farmland owners an economic incentive to resist development pressure, a fact that helps preserve farming activity as well as the land itself. The Rural Density Transfer Zone is referred to as the sending area from which development rights may be transferred.

Receiving areas are the designated sites to which development rights can be transferred. They must be specifically described in an approved and adopted area master plan, a process by which areas are screened to assure the adequacy of public facilities to serve them and to assure compatibility with surrounding development. Each receiving area is assigned a base density. Developers can build to this density as a matter of right. To achieve the greater density permitted under the TDR option, the developer must purchase development rights. No rezoning is necessary, but a preliminary subdivision plan, site plan, and record plat must be approved by the Montgomery County Planning Board.

Montgomery County has a wide variety of receiving areas well located from a marketing standpoint. They are strategically located in areas experiencing growth pressure that ultimately will translate into an active housing market. Since that is the case, and where the density bonuses are sufficient to justify the purchase of development rights, recent transactions have proved that the TDR concept will work. The Montgomery County Council has approved several area master plans that designate receiving areas:

Olney Master Plan[11]	1,800 TDRS
Eastern Montgomery County Master Plan	3,500 TDRS
Damascus Master Plan	400 TDRS
Potomach Subregional Master Plan	2,800 TDRS
Gaithersburg Vicinity Master Plan	2,200 TDRS

Additional TDR receiving areas will be designated as other area master plans are updated.

The value of development rights is determined solely through the private market. The incentive to sell is provided by the lower density allowed in the Rural Density Transfer Zone. On the demand side, everyone—real estate brokers, developers, investors, land trusts—may purchase development rights for use or speculation. The incentive to buy is bolstered by the simplicity of the process and the higher optional densities allowed in the receiving areas.

B. The TDR process

An example of an operational TDR process follows; farmer A owns six hundred acres in the Rural Density Transfer Zone. His development rights are calculated at one unit per five acres; therefore, he controls 120 development rights. If he wishes to develop some lots on the farm; his RDT permits farmer A to build lots at a rate that does not exceed one dwelling unit per twenty-five acres (each having a minimum of 40,000 square feet). Each lot created on the farm diminishes the total number of

TDRs by one. Farmer A is able to sell all or a portion of the 120 development rights at his discretion. After the development rights are sold and transferred, a restrictive easement on the property is filed among the county's land records limiting the development potential of the property to the number of rights retained.

A developer owns eighty acres in an area designated on a master plan as suitable for development with transferred development rights. His property is zoned RE-2 (one unit per two acres) with a recommended TDR density of two units per acre. Thus, he has the right to develop forty units under the base density or 160 units, if he acquires development rights. He approaches the farmer to purchase all 120 development rights or negotiates with another farmer for the additional rights needed. The developer then files a preliminary subdivision plan showing that he has forty units under the base zone and has acquired 120 more by purchase of development rights from the farmers. Thus, he is eligible to build 160 units.

The administrative process to shift development rights from sending to receiving areas is a simple mechanism that relies on existing subdivision procedures. First, a developer files a preliminary plan of subdivision, using at least two-thirds of the possible development rights allowed by the master plan. This represents the application for transfer. Once the preliminary plan is approved by the planning board, the developer then files a detailed site plan for the receiving area property. Following site plan approval, the developer then submits a record plat. Prior to record plat approval, an easement document limiting the number of TDRs on the area sending property must be prepared, recorded, and shown to the planning board. An easement document limiting future residential development in the sending area is prepared, conveying the easement to the county. Upon approval of the easement document and record plat by the planning board, the easement and the record plat are recorded in the land records and the transfer of development rights is complete.

The TDR mechanism uses private market incentives both to protect land and to provide financial compensation to landowners. It is an effective alternative to outright public acquisition of development rights and to noncompensable regulation. Moreover, it directs necessary growth away from productive farmland to more appropriate locations.

C. Rural Cluster Zone

The Rural Cluster Zone is applied to areas where subdivision activity already has eroded parts of the critical mass of farmland. However, the preservation plan deems it desirable to preserve some portion of these areas in a more open configuration and potential for small farms and other rural uses than would otherwise be possible by subdivision under the former five-acre rural zone.

Rural clustering retains open space by allowing residences to be grouped on a portion of the site and fosters a more compact development pattern than conventional residential development. Overall density as established by the rural zone would not be changed; it would remain at one dwelling unit per five acres with a cluster option of one-acre minimum lot sizes.

Two development options exist in the Rural Cluster Zone. The options include subdividing land into five-acre lots with large road frontage, or subdividing a portion of the land (approximately 40 percent) into 40,000-square-foot lots, while maintaining a density of one unit per five acres and preserving the remaining portion (approximately 60 percent) in agricultural or open-space use. Performance standards have been established for the subdivision of land using the 40 percent/60 percent formula.

D. Capital improvement program and nuisance regulations

In addition to the new Rural Density Transfer and Rural Cluster zones, capital improvements program policy and nuisance regulations are used to encourage the preservation of farmland. Essentially, there are three elements of this policy. First, community water and sewer service will not be extended into designated critical mass areas that have been affected by the Rural Density Transfer Zone. Second, rural roadways will be maintained in their present condition except for maintenance and safety projects. Finally, all final plats creating residential building sites in the Rural Density Transfer Zone include the following notice: "Agriculture is the preferred use in the Rural Density Transfer Zone. All agricultural operations shall be permitted at any time, including the operation of farm machinery and no agricultural use shall be subject to restriction because it interferes with other uses permitted in the zone." This latter policy is designed to prevent new homeowners from later seeking to institute nuisance regulations to restrict farm activities in their area.

E. Preferential tax assessment

Taxes have long been recognized as an important incentive to the retention of both farming and farmland. Farmland assessment, as practiced in Maryland, probably has little effect on the actual *amount* of farmland that is ultimately retained. It does, however, appear to affect the timing of conversion of some land. In some cases it has tended to hold land off the market. Also, it serves the public by making possible better-staged, large-scale development. Its most important beneficial effect on county agriculture, however, is that it has made it possible for some farmer-owners to retain their land rather than sell prematurely. At the same time it has made it possible for some land to be purchased as a speculative investment many years before development is timely. Much of this land is eventually leased to farmers, maintaining its eligibility for farmland assessment. Some is greatly underutilized for agriculture, since a loss on the investment reduces its owners' federal income tax.

However, some states provide for recapture by the state of the difference in taxes between the farmland and market rates of assessment at the time of sale if it is sold for a nonagricultural use. This provides a further disincentive to speculation. Maryland law provides for a 6 percent trans-fer tax on farmland to residential sales as a means of recapturing some of the lost revenues. This tax may be avoided, however, by postponing development for more than three years after sale. Maryland law also causes an owner to lose his farmland assessment if he requests that his property be rezoned to a more intense classification. There is also a rollback of tax liability at full value for one year when property is sold. Farmland assessments terminate when property is subdivided.

F. Maryland Agricultural Land Preservation Foundation

State-supported farmland district and easement purchases are recommended for use in Rural Density Transfer and Rural Cluster zones if the farm parcel meets the criteria established by both the state and the Montgomery County Agricultural Board and Committee. The state program is administered by the Maryland Agricultural Land Preservation Foundation of the Maryland Department of Agriculture. The foundation is an eleven-member body appointed by the governor.

The program is completely voluntary and involves the establishment of agricultural preservation districts in which the landowner agrees not to develop the land for at least five years. In exchange, normal agricultural activities (i.e., noise, odor, night operations, machinery operations, etc.) become protected in the district, and in districts involving more than one property landowners can assure self-protection from the encroachment of other land uses. For many landowners a district that provides agricultural land-use protection in addition to easement sale eligibility is an attractive option.

Once a farm has been accepted into a district, the owner is eligible, but not obligated, to sell a development right easement to the foundation. To sell an easement is to sell only one of many rights the property owner enjoys. When an easement is sold, the owner continues to own the farm or may sell it, but the owner and his heirs, or the new buyer, can be assured that the farm will remain undeveloped.

The sale of an easement results in exchanging a portion of equity in land for cash and easement sale eligibility, or even a gift of the easement to the state can be used effectively in estate planning through providing a means of equitably dividing an estate while saving the family farm.

Implementation strategy

Montgomery County has developed a preservation program that revitalizes and sustains its agrarian heritage in a way that is not only environmentally wise but legally and economically practical. By forming an effective partnership of private and public interests, rural and urban philosophies, new and old ideas, Montgomery County has developed and implemented a program to preserve farmland and rural open space.

It is one of the first comprehensive plans for the preservation of agriculture and rural open space in the United States that is an integral part of an established growth management strategy. The preservation plan presents a synthesis of findings, develops policy, identifies preservation techniques, and then recommends that all proposed zoning changes be implemented through comprehensive rezoning immediately upon the approval and adoption of the plan. The plan is open-ended, allowing for revisions and additions as individual area master plans are completed. The open-ended nature of the plan helps to fine-tune the new incentives and regulations.

Developing and implementing such a large-scale innovative program requires strong public planning, zoning, and courage. The implementation strategy evolved after planning board staff studied the strengths and weaknesses of farmland preservation and TDR efforts throughout the nation and identified certain basic features that are necessary to implement a management plan of this nature. It is hoped that the features described here will help others structure an effective implementation strategy.

A. Unique needs

Although a considerable amount of literature on the subject is available and TDR programs do exist throughout the country, staff chose not to rubber-stamp a "typical" TDR process for use in the county. Instead, staff identified the most common recurring problems inherent in TDR systems and sought to overcome them. As a result, Montgomery County's TDR system is (*a*) easy to understand and administer, (*b*) is applied to receiving areas with a strong development potential, (*c*) encourages developer participation because of adequate density options, and (*d*) results in receiving area development that is compatible with surrounding residential communities and the carrying capacity of planned or existing public services. The preservation program is designed to meet the unique needs of Montgomery County.

B. Public support and commitment

Early involvement of private sector interests in the technical aspects of plan development instilled a sense of partnership and cooperation. A high level of involvement was stressed early on in the plan-making process to help diffuse a possible early negative reaction to the idea of preservation and the techniques needed to preserve farmland. In developing and explaining the preservation program, Montgomery County officials and staff sought the active participation and counsel of leaders from the local agricultural, legal, and development community. This ongoing involvement, especially in the choice of preservation alternatives, helped the staff anticipate and avoid problems as the program began to take shape and has laid the basis for a system relatively free of inhibiting confusion.

In addition to technical involvement throughout the plan-making process, a public education program was initiated to explain the mechanics of the system to small groups of interested individuals throughout the county. Using this nonthreatening, informal format, the staff was able to satisfy the concerns of most people prior to initiation of the public hearing process.

C. Political support

Initially, the Montgomery County Council requested the Montgomery County Planning Board to "review elements of an effective program of agricultural land preservation that would preserve farm activity without a large expenditure of public funds." Also, the council requested the staffs of the Montgomery County Planning Board, Agricultural Preservation Advisory Board and Committee, and Office of Economic Development to identify those geographic areas of the county that should be considered for agricultural land preservation. These requests culminated in the preparation of the preservation plan.

Political support slowly evolved after many work sessions to justify a program that many people considered experimental and to satisfy questions as to its legality, economic feasibility, equity, and workability. It soon became apparent that (*a*) the program had no hidden agenda —farmland preservation was its principal objective, (*b*) the program was part of a comprehensive planning and zoning program that complemented the objectives of the General Plan and growth management strategy, (*c*) the program had some benefit to all those involved in the land-use game, (*d*) the program was carefully designed to be legally defensible, and (*e*) the preservation of farmland could be undertaken at little or no cost to the county.

D. Administrative simplicity

The Montgomery County Agricultural Preservation Program has been developed with simplicity in mind. The market for development rights is relatively unencumbered. The value of rights is determined in the private marketplace. Rezoning is avoided since the TDR density option, in receiving areas, is predetermined in area master plans. In addition, staff relied on *established* subdivision procedures to facilitate the transfer of development rights. (See pp. 260–61 earlier in this chapter for a detailed description.)

Since complexity of processing has a direct influence upon timing and development costs, developers feel that the use of TDR will not result in increased costs. As a result, developers find the simple administrative procedures an attractive aspect of the TDR system.

E. Clear objectives

Montgomery County offers one of the few TDR programs with farmland preservation as a principal objective. Typically, other programs have farmland as only one of many resources to be protected.

F. Comprehensive

By itself, TDR is not sufficient to protect extensive farmland. However, when used in conjunction with a preferential agricultural zone couched well within a comprehensive planning strategy, it can be highly successful.

G. Solid legal basis

The courts in Maryland have consistently upheld regulations that diminish property values so long as a reasonable use of the property remains. The preservation program was carefully designed to be legally defensible. It is based upon careful analysis both in documenting the public interest in farmland preservation and in selecting sending and receiving areas and appropriate development densities therein. The sending area density is based on careful economic research suggesting twenty-five acres as a minimum viable farm unit. Careful designation and staging in receiving areas prevents neighborhood incompatibility.

H. Strong development rights market

The nature of the development rights market is the critical determinant of TDR success. TDR is appropriate for areas with both an inventory of productive farmland and a vigorous housing market. Without a market for higher densities than presently allowed in receiving areas, development rights are unmarketable. Development pressures are strong in Montgomery County, and the program itself is designed to maximize the marketability of rights. In terms of the sending area, it is one of the only TDR schemes restricting density in the sending areas to a level below the pre-TDR density. This provides a strong incentive to sell rights, since it provides a greater financial return than development at the new, lower density. The program also provides a strong incentive for TDR purchase, since receiving area density options offer a high potential return on investment. Overall, the county has attempted to balance supply and demand to assure a vigorous and stable TDR market.

I. Development rights fund

Legislation has been approved that is designed to implement the development rights fund in Montgomery County. This legislation set up an earmarked fund to be directed and managed by a board of directors consisting of five members. The purpose of the fund is to provide a public financial resource to guarantee loans through private banking institutions using TDRs as collateral.

The board of directors of the fund is empowered to acquire, by easement purchase, development rights on farmland, hold these rights, and later sell them through auction to the highest bidder. Specific activities of the board are limited to the following:

– The first priority for use of appropriated funds shall be to guarantee loans.

- Loan guarantees may not exceed 75 percent of the market value of a farm including the development rights, less any improvement values as established by the board.
- No loan guarantee may exceed five years; however, a single-year extension may be granted for good cause.
- The board must determine the value of development rights to be purchased through two independent appraisals.
- The board shall acquire evidence from a private applicant that he has not been able to sell development rights to buyers in the private market.
- Before the board purchases development rights, it shall require evidence from the applicant that he is ineligible under the Maryland State Farmland Preservation Program.
- The board can purchase development rights and make loan guarantees only on land within the Rural Density Transfer Zone.

Legislation establishing the governing board of the fund and the development right fund itself is subject to interim sunset legislation whereby, unless otherwise provided by law, purchase powers shall expire after five years. The board shall, however, have full authority for a ten-year period to administer existing loan guarantees and sell previously acquired development rights.

Conclusion

Montgomery County challenged status quo thinking about the preservation of farmland and overcame typical local government political unwillingness and institutional inability to develop an innovative program to protect farmland and farming. By taking the institutional and educational initiative, Montgomery County has developed a highly successful agricultural preservation program within a fast-growing metropolitan area and encourages other local governments to undertake similar efforts tailored to meet their unique needs.

Conclusions

The case studies presented in this book demonstrate exciting new approaches for managing resource conflicts. They also describe the development of unique management tools and the use of the special area management process to guide resource management. These elements are discussed below.

Unique management tools fostered by the special area management process

The case studies have demonstrated the success of a number of unique management tools that other land-use practitioners may wish to consider using in their endeavors. These include:

- the use of steering committees, composed of all disputants, to plan future uses for an area through decisions by consensus (San Bruno, Grays Harbor)
- transfer of development rights programs, which allow landowners in development-restricted areas to be partially compensated for keeping their land in less-intensive use, such as agriculture (Pinelands, Montgomery County)
- land-classification techniques to guide management of large areas (Pinelands, the Adirondack Park, Grays Harbor)
- the co-op–conservancy approach, where private parties, interested in land preservation, support the goals of public protection programs through donations and their ability to act more quickly than government to protect crucial land parcels (estuarine sanctuaries)
- memoranda of understanding that facilitate interagency cooperation and allow plan implementation through reliance on an existing patchwork of legislation (Grays Harbor, Baltimore Harbor, San Bruno)
- habitat conservation plans, under section 10(a) of the Endangered Species Act, which provide for greater flexibility in managing critical habitat for listed as well as unlisted species (San Bruno, Key Largo)

The unique approach represented by each of the case studies has also aroused considerable attention. As noted, the Baltimore Environmental Enhancement Plan's techniques have been cited by the U.S. Army Corps of Engineers as a national model for others to use. The Grays Harbor effort was specifically cited in the 1980 amendments to the Coastal Zone Management Act, which encouraged the use and preparation of special area management plans by the states. Finally, the San Bruno Mountain Habitat Conservation Plan approach was also commended by the U.S. Congress for its ability to encourage "creative partnerships between the public and private sectors and among governmental agencies in the interests of species and habitat conservation." Section 10(a) of the Endangered Species Act was therefore amended to permit future San Bruno-style efforts to take place.

The common thread: special area management

Though each of the case studies presents its own particular set of management questions, they are linked by a number of common concerns and management challenges. This common thread, the special area management process, is discussed in this chapter.

Determining when special area management is appropriate and needed

All of the management experiences described in this book arose, in part, due to the failure of existing institutions and management routines to properly manage the area in question. In Grays Harbor, Washington, port development was stymied by conflicting regulatory policies. In Montgomery County, Maryland, existing management authority and state policies did not provide adequate incentives for the preservation of agriculture and open space. And in the Pinelands and Adirondack regions, existing local and state policies failed to consider regionwide development issues that threatened the integrity of these special areas.

While institutional failure is an important step in the problem-identification process, establishing the need for special area management also requires that management problems be well documented and recognized. Without this shared recognition, some parties will not understand the need for special management treatment, and bringing all the parties together will be more difficult (see Convening the Process below). In those cases where a new management authority is to be established, problem documentation is of course necessary to help tailor the agency's mandate as well as provide a first level of public support for the agency's mission.

Finally, because of the potential costs of special area management efforts (both dollars and time), two other elements are usually necessary to demonstrate the need for the process. First is the recognition that without special area management there will continue to be policy fragmentation, use conflicts—all the problems that characterize an area in need of special treatment. Second, in those areas experiencing piecemeal development whose management agencies are unable to deal with the cumulative effects of this development, the need for special area management will appear more acute. As the case studies have shown, an important attraction of special area management is that it offers the means to see the big picture that often may be lacking under the previous management structure.

Convening the special area management process

As noted in the introduction, it is often more difficult to convene a special area management process than to actually achieve the necessary compromises and decisions once the forum is established. This is because the task of convincing potential participants of the value of special area management involves instilling participants with the belief and understanding that they have something to gain overall. For mediation processes, participants must believe that the potential benefits of compromise will outweigh what they are likely to give up. In agreeing to come to the table most disputants have thus already tacitly made such a calculation, which is one important reason for the high rate of success for mediation that makes it to this stage. This observation is no less true for the process of creating a new management authority, though the benefits of creation are as likely to be politically (as opposed to rationally) calculated.

Two major obstacles to the convening process should be noted. Bureaucracies are typically risk-adverse, so that it is often difficult to persuade agencies to participate in innovative processes that imply compromises in agency discretion and power. More generally, regulatory and private interests to a mediation process (or those interested in drafting the mandate of a new agency) seek to maximize their leverage over the emergent management process, a tendency that inherently threatens the convening process. Assurance must therefore be provided that all parties' views will have an equal or mutually acceptable weight. This constraint also applies to the devised mechanism for later, more specific decision making, for parties will try to maximize their influence in this process as well.

Given these general observations and constraints, there are a number of situations likely to enable the process to convene.

Preexisting framework. Least likely is the existence of a mechanism by which special area management is mandated or encouraged. This possibility may strengthen, however, as the value of the process achieves greater recognition. At present, both the Coastal Zone Management and Endangered Species acts contain provisions encouraging special area management processes described in this book (Grays Harbor, San Bruno Mountain). To the extent that funding and other logistical support may otherwise impede special area management,* increased funding for the acts' provisions may help stimulate new management efforts that are now stalled.

All else has failed. Where the fragmentation of interests and other problems that characterize special areas have arisen, parties may come to sense that there is nothing to lose by participating in the process. The impetus to this realization is often the refusal of an agency to permit a desired development. In both Grays Harbor and Baltimore, federal agency permit denials of important dredge and fill proposals spawned a desire for a new management approach that could provide greater rationality and predictability. Objections by the states of Georgia and Alabama that the proposed estuarine sanctuary for Apalachicola Bay, Florida, would impede navigation also led to meetings of state and federal representatives to allay such fears. At the same time environmental interests and regulators may see nothing to lose in trying to seek longer-term preservation of areas where the alternative may be to lose habitat piece by piece.

Creation of new management focus. The convening process described here should be seen not just as a step toward a mediation/conflict-resolution approach (though it could be), but more generally as means of developing a revised management focus for an area. In this sense the creation of a new management entity may be the most desirable way to "convene" the special area management process. Though there are no steadfast criteria to assess when new authorities are most appropriate, some tentative conclusions can be offered.

Where there is a history of agencies working together (see directly below) or at least a historical perception of the area in question, together with adequate legal authority to implement a management program, it is probably desirable to focus on conflict resolution and improvement of

---

*This was precisely the case for the management effort for the lower St. Croix River until the Minnesota-Wisconsin Boundary Commission provided simple logistical support.

agency coordination rather than seeking new authority. Many coastal areas fit this description, where there already are many agencies and applicable legal mandates in place. The success of the San Francisco Bay Conservation and Development Commission, as an exception to this rule, may therefore be due to the large size of the Bay Area. For it is in large special areas that new management authorities appear to be most appropriate. Here, management fragmentation is as much due to the size of the area as it is to conflicting authorities, and a new authority will serve to codify regional concerns lacking in the previous management framework. This was clearly demonstrated by the Adirondacks and the Pinelands cases and was also an important element in the success of the Tug Hill Regional Commission in New York (see the selected bibliography for appropriate references). Much less clear is whether a new authority is more desirable where there is already significant planning and management experience (as in the New Jersey Pinelands) or where much new data and planning must be initiated. The Adirondack Park chapter indicates the range of approaches for the latter type of area. Finally, areas where development pressures are particularly intense seem to be another appropriate condition for creating new management authorities.

History of working together. In areas where agencies and interests have had a history of working together (and there is perhaps a temporary breakdown in this relationship), it may be easier to convene these parties for a new management effort. The Maryland-National Capitol Park and Planning Commission had gradually put in place a publicly supported planning program over two decades, so the decision to implement an agricultural preservation program could build on this base of support. The preservation program was also explicitly linked to existing plans and policies. Preexisting institutional focus on Baltimore Harbor was also an important factor in the parties' willingness to try and develop the environmental enhancement plan described in the Baltimore case study.

Catalytic individuals. In many cases there is someone (or some group of individuals) who seize the moment by clearly identifying the need for special area management and by convincing others of this need. Such leadership may come from the scientific community, as has occurred at several national estuarine sanctuaries, or it may emerge from key legislators drafting a new agency's authority. The new legislative authority, in the latter case, then serves to catalyze efforts to manage the special area properly.

The difficulties in beginning a special area management process may be overcome by some combination of the above factors. However, the size of this hurdle provides a strong argument for seeking new mechanisms of encouragement to insure that special area management efforts are not often derailed at this stage. Some of these mechanisms are reviewed in the second half of this chapter.

Moving the special area management process along

In some cases, a lead agency with important regulatory or permit powers over the special area may serve well as a leader in the management process. However, unless all participants agree to an unbalanced distribution of power tilted toward the lead agency (which is unlikely), it is advisable to seek a party or agency that can act as a neutral facilitator for the process. The Regional Planning Council, lacking legal authority, served this role effectively in Baltimore. Other special area management efforts have hired consultants for this purpose when funds were available. This role may be as small as providing needed logistical support, yet in such a case parties to the process should realize that their own work load and responsibilities will be greater. Other important issues for moving the process along include:

Nonthreatening forum. The process will best be fostered if participants perceive that they are on neutral turf. In this way the credibility of the effort can be established as participants begin developing mutual trust that all parties are bargaining in good faith. Clearly, where conflicts and disputes preceded the establishment of this forum, it will take time to develop this atmosphere.

Keeping participants in the game. A benign atmosphere created by good facilitation is essential to maintaining the integrity of the process. Details in this regard are noted in the Walters chapter. For special authorities requiring or needing the participation of local governments, the ability to keep participants in the game will tend to vary with the type of mandate possessed by the authority. The Pinelands Commission had the power to require local governments to prepare master plans and regulations as part of its overall implementation program. The Pinelands Commission also possessed the authority to take over planning functions from recalcitrant local governments. As a result, most Pinelands local governments stayed in the game and fulfilled their planning responsibilities rather than risk losing some of their power to a higher authority. By contrast, the Adirondack Park Agency lacked the authority to directly take over local planning functions. The absence of this strong negative incentive to elicit local participation has meant less local involvement and generally higher levels of political opposition. Thus, maintaining the special area management process will require different approaches depending on the type of process occurring (new agency versus mediation) and the nature of the participants.

Establishing the management team

In setting up a new agency, authority, or corporation, it is important to tailor the mandate to the management tasks at hand. The most visible part of the organization, such as commission membership, must seek to provide balanced representation of all legitimate interests. For large regional management agencies, balancing local and state interests is clearly a delicate political decision. Common formulas usually include county representatives together with gubernatorial appointees representing state interests. Advisory committees composed of local representatives are another alternative, though the success of this approach varies (from little participation in the Pinelands to a focal point of severe opposition for the Adirondack Park program).

Similar concerns apply to choosing the members of a management task force, as in the Grays Harbor and Baltimore examples. Two constraints must be accommodated. First, including too many individuals and agencies on the task force will tend to limit how much work can be accomplished, as consensus decisions become harder to reach. At the same time the failure to include those parties who can implement or subvert the plan implies a direct trade-off with the predictability and long-term viability of any agreed-upon plan. The exclusion of public interest, environmental, and important private groups may therefore ease the consensus process but invite later opposition (lawsuits, etc.) that could effectively wipe out earlier task force efforts.

Developing the plan

The first important step at this stage of the process is to figure out the ground rules. For a new agency this will involve defining the scope of authority and power and the agency's relationship to existing authorities. For a task force approach, it is essential to (a) define how decisions are to be reached (consensus versus majority vote), and (b) outline the implementation responsibilities of all the parties involved. Generally, this approach will work best through a process of "incremental commitment" as participating agencies agree to decisions or perform tasks toward a next step, then another step, etc.

Second, the content of the developed plan or other task force product will vary depending on unique circumstances and the area under study.

As noted earlier, larger-sized special areas will probably require greater management resources as well as limit the detail (and perhaps the predictability) of the developed plan. In these cases a stronger emphasis on outlining *how decisions will be made* rather than making hundreds of detailed decisions will probably be warranted.

Finally, despite this expected variance, it is essential that the task force decide early just what outcomes are being sought. Some special area management plans, such as Hilton Head Island, South Carolina, contain only a set of nonbinding recommendations. If greater outcomes are being pursued (such as contracts, new authority, specific implementation responsibilities), this goal must be clear to all parties.

Other important considerations

(*a*) *Simplicity*. A simple, understandable plan is always preferable to a complex approach. The advantages are ease of implementation and a greater likelihood of achieving public support. Montgomery County's formulation of its transfer of development rights program is a particularly good example.

(*b*) *Maintaining consensus*. There are a number of useful tools to either hold decisions in place or maintain the integrity of the special area management process through any plan amendments or changes.

1. *Maps* provide a fixed perception of how an area is or should be. The use of land-classification maps by the Pinelands Commission and the Adirondack Park Agency has served as a major tool in guiding local government and public investment decision making. The risk of this approach is to raise the ire of private landowners, but rational criteria for reclassification can help satisfy any seeming inequities while still preserving an agency's mapped intentions for future development.

2. *Estoppel* is an equitable legal concept that requires honoring of commitments made that others were intended to rely upon. This concept could be used in special area management efforts to bind the parties to their original agreement. However, where the dissenting party is a unit of government, courts may be reluctant to use this concept to limit the ability of a unit of government to exercise its police power (or enforce agreements that limit the future use of this power). Though such a result is probably desirable when environmental degradation is occurring under the agreed-upon plan, there is something to be said for demanding the same level of commitment from the public sector as is required of the private sector. Estoppel may be an attractive tool for the private sector to explore as a means of enhancing public agency responsibility. Probably

most crucial to maintaining agreements, however, is more administrative and policy consistency in the public sector.

3. Closely related to estoppel is the approach undertaken in the San Bruno Mountain Habitat Conservation Plan. Here, the agreement provided for *special rights and procedures* for the U.S. Fish and Wildlife Service to use in the event that the plan's operation threatened species' survival. Recognizing these rights (or statutory responsibilities) may serve to aid plan agreement without compromising a party's power if environmental conditions substantially change. Threshold tests or findings delegated to a lead agency may therefore be devised by the task force.* This is an important consideration, as often agreements are not reached in these circumstances.

4. *Memoranda of understanding* may also be devised to specify implementation responsibilities of task force participants. Though memoranda of understanding (MOUs) lack the legal force of a *contract* (such as in San Bruno), they do indicate an agency's willingness to commit itself in writing to a policy or course of action. In this sense, MOUs provide a level of assurance greater than that available before the special area management process began.

In choosing any of these tools and approaches, the key concern must be a resolution of the trade-off between plan predictability and plan adaptability. As environmental conditions or public purposes change, the plan must be able to respond adequately to the changes and still maintain the consensus and participation of the original parties. Anticipating these changes or providing flexible procedures to maintain plan agreement as changes occur is thus the mark of a well-developed special area management effort.

The future of special area management

Special area management requires different commitments and management techniques than presently undertaken in most areas. As a means of resolving both present and future public interest conflicts for either preservation, multiple use, or development, the special area management process has emerged as one important method for pluralistic decision making and regulatory improvement.

The case studies presented in this book have evidenced the success and promise of special area management, though the experiences have evolved

---

*This approach can also be likened to plan amendment procedures such as the hardship exemption test used by the Pinelands Commission.

(almost universally) in an ad hoc manner. It is therefore important to consider whether there is a need to convert the ad hoc development of the special area management process into a more systematic approach cognizant of the common elements laid out in the first part of this conclusion. If such a need exists, it will also be worthwhile to explore relevant constraints to such institutionalization.

With the decline of private property rights when weighed against increased public sector authority, there is demonstrable need to replace the illusory certainty of private property rights with new forms of assurances. New amendments to the Coastal Zone Management Act and the Endangered Species Act "encourage" special area management planning, which may include tools to provide greater public and private predictability. The National Environmental Policy Act's scoping process also presents opportunities for formalizing special area management efforts. However, further changes would be necessary to provide the proper tools, incentives, and institutional environment for special area management. These changes should preserve the integrity of congressional and state mandates, while permitting a flexible approach to management involving *all* relevant interests. Though any expectations of harmonious plan-making nationwide are unrealistic, developing the mechanism to enhance special area management could be possible.

A first level of change involves improving the clarity of regulations and policy decisions. Agencies should therefore develop uniform substantive guidance for field personnel with respect to key regulatory terms that affect permitting in potential special areas, or devise procedures for allowing agency participation in special area management efforts. Especially important in this regard are the development of "threshold" tests within the agency's mandate that will specify the conditions under which the agency can or cannot adhere to compromises pursuant to a special area management plan (see San Bruno case study for an example).

A second way to encourage special area management planning is through the development of local guidelines or technical assistance programs to enhance ad hoc management efforts as they emerge. The lessons and experiences reflected in this book are hopefully a good first step in such an effort, in that many important considerations and trade-offs for any special area management attempt are outlined here. The Office of Ocean and Coastal Resource Management, within the National Oceanic and Atmospheric Administration, for example, is actively pursuing this type of assistance at the time of this writing.

A third way to provide incentives for special area management would involve legislative changes to promote collaborative planning or to harmonize now-conflicting legislative mandates. These changes could enable or require agency representatives to develop and endorse formal plans for use in subsequent permit reviews. Two examples:

Coastal Zone Management Act (CZMA). Besides encouraging special area management, the act could be amended to fund and require state coastal programs to identify and undertake special area management in selected areas. Though it is difficult to establish criteria for area selection, the act could require special area planning for "areas of particular concern" or "coastal resources of national significance" already identified by coastal states. Success would depend, in part, on how special area management efforts can balance the act's competing goals of preservation and development.* Clearly, not all coastal area plans can maximize the CZMA's energy development goals and at the same time achieve the national coastal protection objectives set forth in the act's 1980 amendments. Further clarification of how the nation intends to use its coastal areas is therefore essential to both limiting federal and state administrative discretion and providing greater regulatory predictability in the future. Returning the CZMA to a greater resource protection focus (which was the impetus to its original passage) would also make coastal management more consistent with the applicable requirements of the Clean Water Act.

Clean Water Act. The conflict between section 404 (wetlands protection) requirements and special area management should be resolved. Such a decision by the Congress would be feasible, given adequate experience with Grays Harbor-type experiences. Key questions to answer:

– Is it acceptable to trade off wetland fills for preservation of the remaining area?
– Can there be firmer guarantees for preserved areas than now provided by plans such as Grays Harbor that could make this approach more feasible?

These questions are most appropriate for the Congress, not regulatory agencies, to answer.

However, there are a number of important constraints for efforts attempting to formalize special area management efforts.

1. A myriad of inconsistencies between federal and state statutes, which are unlikely to be easily resolved
2. Significant legal difficulties in trying to limit governmental authority through contracts

---

*Section 302 of the Coastal Zone Management Act states that there is a national interest in the effective management, beneficial use, protection, and development of the coastal zone.

3. Lack of available funds and resources for undertaking "new" management efforts
4. Scientific uncertainty for decisions involving multiple uses within areas
5. Difficulties in achieving full public participation and adequate representation of all relevant interests

It is important to note that part of the value of special area management lies precisely in its adaptability for many types of areas. In this sense, agencies should be given the power and encouragement to cooperate with other interests, but it is less clear whether they should be *required* to compromise at this time. For these reasons, work should continue toward providing agencies and local interests with guidelines and technical assistance for undertaking special area management and with continued monitoring of the success of these experiences. Given this nurturing process, any later efforts to formalize special area management will have the added benefit of extensive new experience in this field.

Notes

Planning in Coastal Areas

1. Lorraine Bodi and Charles Walters, in proceedings of *Coastal Zone '80* (New York: American Society of Civil Engineers, 1980).
2. See Nan Evans et al., *The Search for Predictability: Planning and Conflict Resolution in Grays Harbor, Washington* (Washington Sea Grant, 1980), 13–25.
3. Section 307 of the Coastal Zone Management Act requires that certain federal actions obtain a certification of consistency from the state's coastal management agency before they proceed. SAMPs that are incorporated into a federally approved state coastal plan could employ these consistency powers in implementation efforts. See, for example, Daniel S. Carol and David J. Brower, "Legal Considerations for Special Area Management," in proceedings of *Coastal Zone '83* (New York: American Society of Civil Engineers, 1983).
4. See Bodi and Walters, 1980.
5. The SAMP procedures discussed in sequence here represent an amalgamation of concepts from various SAMP efforts.
6. See chapter 4 for further discussion of the importance of land-water coupling in special area management efforts.
7. Nevertheless, Bodi and Walters have identified eight guidelines necessary to successfully complete a SAMP.
8. Grays Harbor would be an important precedent for the advanced designation concept, both *for* the use of dredged material disposal and its reciprocal, areas to be designated as *non*disposal areas. This concept is extremely important for future port planning efforts. It provides for future port development predictability, yet it also could be a major factor in preserving aquatic areas through de-designation. For further discussion, see Office of Technology Assessment, *Wetlands: Their Use and Regulation* (Washington, D.C., March 1984).

Environmental Mediation

1. Allan Talbot, *Environmental Mediation: 3 Case Studies* (Seattle: The Institute for Environmental Mediation, 1981), 1.
2. Kai N. Lee, "Intervention by 'Neutral' Third Parties: An Analytic Report," *Working Paper* (Institute for Environmental Studies, University of Washington), 1982.
3. The Institute for Environmental Mediation, brochure, 1982. For a more complete discussion of the intervenor's responsibility to the parties, see Gerald W. Cormick, "Intervention and Self-determination in Environmental Disputes: A Mediator's Perspective," *Resolve* (The Conservation Foundation, Winter 1982), 1ff.
4. Orville Tice, "But What Does a Mediator Really Do? The Pitch Mine Case" (The Institute for Environmental Mediation, August 1981).

5. This dispute and the mediation effort that led to its settlement is described in the case study, "The CREST Dispute: Negotiated Settlement Through Mediation," by Verne Huser.

6. This mediation experience and a series of workshops and discussions with persons involved in disputes over the management of solid waste were part of a study funded by the California State Solid Waste Management Board. The results of that study are reported in *Siting Solid Waste Management Facilities: Approaches to Dispute Settlement*, Recommendations to the State Solid Waste Management Board (The Institute for Environmental Mediation and The Wisconsin Center for Public Policy, October 1981).

Estuarine Reserves

1. John R. Clark, John S. Banta, and Jeffrey Zinn, *Coastal Environmental Management* (Federal Insurance Administration, 1980).

2. U.S. Department of Interior, *The National Estuarine Pollution Study* (U.S. Senate Doc. 91-58, 1970).

3. John R. Clark, "New Approach Needed for Protection of Estuaries," *Staff Memorandum* (Washington, D.C.: The Conservation Foundation, 1980).

4. Bostwick H. Ketchum, *The Water's Edge* (Cambridge, Mass.: MIT Press, 1972).

5. Bureau of Sport Fisheries and Wildlife and Bureau of Commercial Fisheries, *National Estuary Study*, vol. 1, Main Report (Washington, D.C.: U.S. Department of Interior, Fish and Wildlife Service, 1970).

6. Protection of estuarine environments also occurred under the general auspices of the Coastal Zone Management Act. Many of the states identified estuaries as special areas; some, like California and Florida, specified particular estuaries for critical attention. California went one step further and established a program to restore degraded wetlands and estuaries. See, for example, Scott McCreary and John Zentner, "Innovative Estuarine Restoration and Management," Proceedings of the Third Symposium on Ocean and Coastal Resources Management, *Coastal Zone '83* (American Society of Civil Engineers, 1983), and Scott McCreary and Renée Robin, "The Coastal Conservancy Experience in Wetland Protection," in Jon Kusler, ed., *Strengthening State Wetland Regulations* (Gainesville: Center for Government Responsibility, University of Florida, 1985).

7. Clark et al., *Coastal Environmental Management*.

8. U.S. Senate, Document No. 92-753, 1972; Ketchum, *Water's Edge*.

9. See regulations for the implementation of the Estuarine Sanctuary Program, *Code of Federal Regulations*, vol. 15, part 921.

10. Ketchum, *Water's Edge*.

11. John Clark and Scott McCreary, "Prospects for Coastal Resource Conservation in the 1980's," *Oceanus* (Winter 1980–81).

12. However, high salinities are often reported in central and southern California wetlands where freshwater flow is seasonal or intermittent. See OCZM, "Elkhorn Slough Estuarine Sanctuary" (Final Environmental Impact Statement) (NOAA, Office of Coastal Zone Management, and California Department of Fish and Game, 1979).

13. Thomas G. Dickert and Andrea G. Tuttle, "Elkhorn Slough Watershed: Linking the Cumulative Impacts of Watershed Development to Coastal Wetlands" (Berkeley: Institute of Urban and Regional Development, University of California, 1980).

14. Dickert and Tuttle, "Elkhorn Slough Watershed."

15. Ibid.
16. Tomales Bay subsequently became the focus of comprehensive estuarine, riparian, and watershed restoration through the efforts of the State Coastal Conservancy. See "Innovative Estuarine Restoration and Management," and Scott McCreary and Alyse Jacobson, *A Program for Restoring the Environment of Tomales Bay* (California State Coastal Conservancy, 1984).
17. See Nona Dennis et al., "Elkhorn Slough: The Making of An Estuarine Sanctuary," *Coastal Zone '80* (New York: American Society of Civil Engineers, 1980).
18. Elkhorn Slough Final Environmental Impact Statement.
19. Ibid.
20. Interview Alyse Jacobson, California State Coastal Conservancy, 1985.
21. Dickert and Tuttle, "Elkhorn Slough Watershed."
22. See California State Coastal Conservancy, *Work Plan: Elkhorn Slough Enhancement Plan*, 1985.
23. *Work Plan.*
24. Ibid.
25. Interviews with Thomas Dickert, University of California, (April 1982).
26. Office of Coastal Zone Management, U.S. Department of Commerce, *Tijuana River National Estuarine Sanctuary: Final Environmental Impact Statement* (1981).
27. Mike McCoy, personal communication, 1980.
28. Jim MacFarland, one of the NOAA hearing officers, called this the most positive hearing to date on a sanctuary proposal.
29. Tijuana River, Environmental Impact Statement (1981).
30. Alyse Jacobson, personal communication, 1985.
31. James Dobbin Associates, *Tijuana River Estuarine Sanctuary Management Plan* (prepared for U.S. Office of Ocean and Coastal Resource Management, 1985).
32. Alyse Jacobson, personal communication, 1985.
33. See Joy B. Zedler, "Salt Marsh Community Structure in the Tijuana Estuary, California," *Estuarine and Coastal Marine Science* 5 (1977), and Joy B. Zedler et al., "Salt Marsh Productivity with Natural and Altered Tidal Circulation," *Oecologia* 44 (1981).
34. See John R. Clark, "Progress in Management of Coastal Ecosystems," *Helgolander Meeresunters* 33 (1980); and H. M. Leitman et al., *Wetland Hydrology and Tree Distribution of the Apalachicola Flood River Plain*, Water Supply Paper 2196-A, University of Florida (1983).
35. U.S. Office of Coastal Zone Management, *Apalachicola River-Bay Estuarine Sanctuary: Final Environmental Impact Statement* (1979).
36. Steve Leitman, Florida Department of Environmental Regulation, personal communication, 1985.
37. Scott McCreary, "Estuarine Sanctuaries: A Strategy for Managing Coupled Ecosystems," *Proceedings of the 7th Annual Meeting of the Coastal Society* (1982).
38. The Conservation Foundation, "Apalachicola Symposium and Workshops" (unpublished working paper, 1979).
39. The Conservation Foundation, *Franklin County, Florida, Shoreline Development Strategy* (1980).
40. See R. J. Livingston and E. A. Joyce, eds. *Proceedings of the Conference on the Apalachicola Drainage System*, Florida Marine Research Publication No. 26, 6-15, April, 1977.
41. See *Franklin County Shoreline Development Strategy* and Scott McCreary and John

R. Clark, "Community Flood Hazard Management for the Coastal Barriers of Apalachicola Bay, Florida," in *Preventing Coastal Flood Disasters: The Role of the States
and Federal Response*, proceedings of a national symposium, Ocean City, Maryland,
23–25 May 1983 (Natural Hazards Research and Applications Information Center
Special Publication #7).

42. Pam McVety, personal communication, 1985.

43. Scott McCreary, "Strategy for Managing Coupled Ecosystems," 1982.

44. Lawrence Susskind and Scott McCreary, "Techniques for Resolving Coastal Resource
Management Disputes Through Negotiation," *Journal of the American Planning
Association*, special issue on coastal management (Summer 1985).

45. Personal communications, Earl Johnson, State of Oregon Division of State Lands
(1985), and Taber Hand, Hackensack Meadowlands Commission, New Jersey
(February 1985).

46. Scott McCreary and John Zentner, "Innovative Estuarine Restoration and Management," Proceedings of the Third Symposium on Ocean and Coastal Resources
Management, *Coastal Zone '83* (New York: American Society of Civil Engineers,
1983), and McCreary and Robin, "The Coastal Conservancy Experience in Wetland
Protection."

47. Personal communications, James MacFarland, Florida Department of Natural
Resources (1984), James Murle, Florida Department of Community Affairs (1984),
and George Stafford, New York Coastal Program Director, 1985.

San Bruno Mountain Plan

1. The Mission Blue butterfly (*Plebeius icarioides missionensis*) was listed as an
endangered species on 1 June 1976. 41 Fed. Reg. 22044.

2. The Callippe Silverspot butterfly (*Speyeria callippe callippe*) was proposed for listing
on 3 July 1978. 43 Fed. Reg. 28938. Critical habitat was proposed on 28 March
1980. 45 Fed. Reg. 20503. The critical habitat proposal alerted the landowners to
the endangered species issue on the mountain.

3. The Bay Checkerspot butterfly (*Euphydryas editha bayensis*) was proposed for listing
as an endangered species on 11 September 1984. 49 Fed. Reg. 39665. Waste Management of California, Inc., and the city of San Jose have prepared a habitat conservation plan to protect the Bay Checkerspot and to resolve issues relating to the development of a municipal landfill in the city of San Jose. The conservation plan and the
conservation agreement that implements the plan are modeled after the San Bruno
Mountain Habitat Conservation Plan.

4. The significance of this proposal was that section 7 of the Endangered Species Act
requires federal agencies to insure that any action "is not likely to jeopardize the
continued existence of any endangered or threatened species or result in the destruction or adverse modification" of critical habitat. 16 U.S. § 1536(a)(2). Section 7 has
been the subject of extensive litigation. The Supreme Court in *Tennessee Valley
Authority v. Hill*, 43 U.S. 153 (1978), settled any doubts that language of section 7
should be read literally and strictly in holding that section 7 precluded the completion of Tellico Dam because of the effect of the dam on the snail darter.

5. The requirements of section 7 of the Endangered Species Act are only imposed
directly on federal agencies. Section 7, however, refers to any action "authorized,
funded or carried out" by a federal agency. This language is exceedingly broad and
has been interpreted to encompass within it virtually any private action that requires

some form of federal authorization or approval. Nevertheless, the wildlife agencies have retained the fiction that the consultation under section 7 is between the federal agency and the wildlife agency. Congress, however, amended the act in 1978 and 1982 to encourage greater private sector participation in section 7 consultations.

6. Visitacion was also concerned that even though consultation under section 7 would not be triggered until some federal agency became involved in the development, section 9 of the Endangered Species Act prohibited the "taking" of any endangered or threatened species. The prohibitions of section 9 apply to any person whether or not there is any federal agency involvement in the activity. In addition, the prohibition applies to actions affecting individual animals, whereas section 7 applies to action affecting the population as a whole.

The Endangered Species Act defines the term "take" to include actions that "harrass, harm, pursue, shoot, wound, kill, trap, capture . . . or attempt to engage in any such conduct." 16 U.S.C. § 1532(19). The Ninth Circuit has held that section 9 prohibits habitat modifications in addition to actions that actually kill a member of a listed species. *Palila v. Hawaii Department of Land and Natural Resources*, 639 Fed.2d 495 (Ninth Cir. 1981). Accordingly, Visitacion realized that even if section 7 was never triggered for development on the mountain (which was unlikely) the development could be challenged pursuant to section 9 of the Endangered Species Act.

7. Cal. Fish and Game Code § 2062.

8. Endangered Species Survey, San Bruno Mountain Biological Study—1980–81 (May 1982).

9. San Bruno Mountain Area Habitat Conservation Plan (November 1982); Agreement with Respect to the San Bruno Mountain Area Habitat Conservation Plan, dated March 4, 1983, and recorded in the official records of San Mateo County on March 22, 1983 as Doc. 83026343.

10. 16 U.S.C. § 1539(a).

11. H.R. Rep. No. 412, 93rd Cong., 1st Sess. 17 (1973); Sen. Rep. No. 307, 93rd Cong., 1st Sess. 4 (1973).

12. In fact, in another context the Eighth Circuit has held that Department of Interior regulations permitting the sport trapping of the threatened Eastern Timberwolf was in violation of the Endangered Species Act. (*Sierra Club v. Clark*, 755 Fed.2d 608 (Eighth Circuit, 1985). The Eighth Circuit interpreted the definition of "conservation" in the Endangered Species Act to conclude that before the taking of a threatened animal could occur, a determination must be made that the "population pressures within the animal's ecosystem cannot otherwise be relieved." (*Id.* at 613.)

13. Tellico Dam received an exemption from the Endangered Species Act in a rider to the Energy and Water Development Appropriations Act of 1980.

14. H.R. Rep. No. 835, 97 Cong., 2d Sess. 30-31 (1982).

15. Pub. L. No. 97-304, § 6 (Oct. 13, 1982). The amendment is codified at 16 U.S.C. § 1539(a)(1)(B).

16. Joint Environmental Impact Report, Environmental Assessment prepared by the County of San Mateo and the U.S. Fish and Wildlife Service (1982).

17. Arthur M. Shapiro, Ph.D., professor of zoology, University of California at Davis; Paul R. Ehrlich, Ph.D., Bing Professor of Population Studies, Stanford University; and Ward B. Watt, Ph.D., University of California at Berkeley.

18. The decision of the Ninth Circuit should help to facilitate the preparation of habitat conservation plans. In upholding the finding of no significant impact by the Fish and Wildlife Service pursuant to the National Environmental Policy Act, the court noted

that "the extensive coordination and agreement between the state and federal government is a factor supporting the Service's decision. . . ." *Friends of Endangered Species, Inc.* v. *Janzen*, 760 Fed.2d 976, 987 (Ninth Cir. 1985). The court also noted that "even if the mitigation measures in the present case would not *completely* compensate for all adverse environmental impacts, the shortcoming would not be detrimental. In this circuit, so long as significant measures are undertaken to 'mitigate the project's effects,' they need not *completely compensate* for adverse environmental impacts." (*Id.* at 987, emphasis in original.)

Adirondack Park Agency

1. Adirondack Park Agency (APA), *Comprehensive Report—Adirondack Park Agency*, vol. 1 (1976), 1. Referred to hereinafter as *Comprehensive Report*.
2. Information Please Publishing, Inc., *Information Please Almanac—1978*, 725. This almanac states that New York State's total area is 47,831 square miles.
3. With respect to the growth in the size of the Adirondack Park since the 1890s, see Norman Van Valkenburgh, "The Adirondack Forest Preserve: A Chronology" (New York: Department of Environmental Conservation, 1968, unpublished), 302–3. For the legal definition of the boundary of the Adirondack Park, see New York State Environmental Conservation Law, New York Consolidated Laws Service, *NY Statutes*, vols. 12, 12A, and 12B, section 9-0101(1). Referred to hereinafter as NYS Environmental Conservation Law.
4. Adirondack Park Agency, *1977 Annual Report*, 7. Referred to hereinafter as *1977 Annual Report*.
5. APA, Temporary Study Commission on the Future of the Adirondacks, *The Future of the Adirondack Park* (1970), 26–27. Hereinafter referred to as *The Future of the Adirondack Park*; the Commission is hereinafter referred to as the Temporary Study Commission.
6. References to the "crazy-quilt" mixture of public and nonpublic lands in the park are common. See Lincoln Barnett, *The Ancient Adirondacks* (Boston: Time-Life Books, 1974), 24.
7. See New York State, *Adirondack Park State Land Master Plan* (1979), 38–63; Referred to hereinafter as *State Land Master Plan (1979)*. The original Adirondack Park State Land Master Plan was adopted in 1972; see NYS, *Adirondack Park State Land Master Plan* (1972).
8. See Richard Liroff and Gordon Davis, *Protecting Open Space: Land Use Control in the Adirondack Park* (Cambridge, Mass.: Ballinger, 1981), 14–15.
9. Adirondack Park Agency, *The Adirondack Park* (1977), 2. Referred to hereinafter as *The Adirondack Park*.
10. Ibid.
11. New York State Wild, Scenic and Recreational Rivers System Act, NYS Environmental Conservation Law, article 15, title 27.
12. See Temporary Study Commission, *Recreation (Technical Report No. 5)* (1970). In 1968 the New York State Conservation Department estimated approximately 8.4 million persons vacationed in the Adirondacks, *The Future of the Adirondack Park*.
13. New York State Constitution, New York Consolidated Laws Service, *NY Statutes*, vol. 42A, article XIV, section 1. Referred to hereinafter as NYS Constitution.
14. *State Land Master Plan (1979)*, 48. This system of designated wilderness areas makes up a very significant percentage of all designated wilderness areas in the

eastern United States. See U.S. Geological Survey map entitled "National Wilderness Preservation System and Principal Lands Administered in Trust by Federal Agencies" (April 1978) (prepared for the U.S. Forest Service); see also *The Adirondack Park*, 4.

15. Temporary Study Commission, *Private and Public Land (Technical Report no. 1*, vol. B (1970), 5–21, 53–59.

16. Section 1 of article XIV of the New York State Constitution contains specific exemptions from its general forever wild mandate allowing the construction of several ski areas, including the Whiteface Mountain and Gore Mountain areas in the Adirondacks and Belleayre Mountain in the Catskills.

17. APA, "Adirondack Park Economic Profile—Phase One" (referred to hereinafter as "Economic Profile") in *Comprehensive Report*, 2; Temporary Study Commission, *Recreation (Technical Report No. 5)* (1970); Temporary Study Commission, *Transportation and the Economy (Technical Report No. 4)* (1970), 24–27.

18. Temporary Study Commission, *Forest, Minerals, Water and Air (Technical Report No. 3)* (1970), 5–36; Liroff and Davis, *Protecting Open Space*, 14–15.

19. Temporary Study Commission, *Transportation and the Economy (Technical Report No. 4)* (1970), 24–25.

20. "Economic Profile," 3–8.

21. Barnett, *The Ancient Adirondacks*, 44–57; William Chapman White, *Adirondack Country* (New York: Alfred A. Knopf, 1967), 55–64; Nathaniel Sylvester, *Northern New York and the Adirondack Wilderness* (Harrison, N.Y.: Harbor Hill Books, 1973), 282–98.

22. White, *Adirondack Country*, 55–64; Sylvester, *Northern New York*, 298–304; Harrison Bird, *Navies in the Mountains* (New York: Oxford University Press, 1962).

23. Frank Graham, Jr., *The Adirondack Park: A Political History* (New York: Alfred A. Knopf, 1978), 9.

24. Liroff and Davis, *Protecting Open Space*, 24–26, 113; *Comprehensive Report*, 35.

25. Liroff and Davis, *Protecting Open Space*, 16–18.

26. *The Future of the Adirondack Park*.

27. *McKinney's 1971 Session Laws of New York*, chap. 706; the Adirondack Park Agency Act, as amended, is set forth in article 27 of the NYS Executive Law, New York Consolidated Laws Service, *NY Statutes*, vol. 14A. (Note there are two article 27s in New York's Executive Law. The other article 27 deals with public employee pension and retirement systems.) The Adirondack Park Agency Act is hereinafter referred to as the APA Act.

28. Liroff and Davis, *Protecting Open Space*, 124–29; APA, *Adirondack Park Land Use and Development Plan and Recommendations For Implementation* (March 1973), 1–2.

29. In 1973 the legislature made major amendments to the APA Act, including the addition of the Adirondack Park Land Use and Development Plan. See *McKinney's 1973 Session Laws of New York*, chap. 348; APA, *Comprehensive Report*, 12–13.

30. The Adirondacks have remained a significant issue in the state legislature since 1973. A good barometer of the vitality and seriousness of the issue over these years is the NYS Environmental Planning Lobby's "Environmental Voter's Guide." The guide is published annually by EPL, a statewide environmental lobbying organization. For a cross section of Adirondack issues over several years, see EPL's voter's guides for 1977, 1979, 1981, and 1982. The issues have ranged from trying to abolish the APA to attempting to alter its membership. See also Liroff and Davis, *Protecting Open Space*, 153–54.

31. See APA Act, section 803, as set forth in chapter 706 of the NY Laws of 1971, in which the two designated state officials on the original APA were the director of the Office of Planning Services and the commissioner of Environmental Conservation. The APA's membership was changed in 1973 with the major amendments made to the APA statute.

32. For further discussion, see Richard Booth, "Developing Institutions for Regional Land Use Planning and Control—The Adirondack Experience," *Buffalo Law Review* 28 (1980): 645, 663–66.

33. In spite of the fact that service on the APA brings no financial rewards (except for the chairman) and requires a great deal of work, APA commissioners can enjoy fairly high visibility in terms of environmental decision making in New York State. In the mid- and late 1970s two members of the APA became commissioner of the Department of Environmental Conservation, the state's highest environmental post. Through a 1984 amendment to the APA Act, the chairman of the agency now receives an annual salary of $30,000. See *McKinney's 1984 Session Laws of New York*, chap. 986, section 22.

34. APA, *Annual Report* (March 1983), 8. Referred to hereinafter as *Annual Report—1983*.

35. Booth, "Developing Institutions. . . ," 689–90; Liroff and Davis, *Protecting Open Spaces* 42–50. In spite of obvious strengths the APA staff has often faced criticism from both prodevelopment and environmental constituencies; see Liroff and Davis, *Protecting Open Spaces,* 53–54, 150–51; personal communications with the staff of the Adirondack Council, a private, umbrella organization representing environmentalists on Adirondack issues.

36. Discussions of the technical meaning of article XIV have occupied legal scholars for years. For two excellent discussions, see Robert Glennon, "State Acquisitions in the Adirondacks: The Inconsistent Purpose Doctrine and Related Legal Issues" (1982, available through APA); and Ralph Semerad, "Article XIV," in Temporary Study Commission, *Private and Public Land (Technical Report 1)*, vol. B (1970), 5–21.

37. APA Act, section 801 states in part: "Our forefathers saw fit nearly a century ago to provide rigid constitutional safeguards for the public lands in the Adirondack park. Today forest preserve lands constitute approximately forty percent of the six million acres of land in the park. The people of the state of New York have consistently reiterated their support for this time-honored institution."

38. *State Land Master Plan (1979)*.

39. See National Wilderness Preservation System, 16 *United States Code*, sections 1131–36. One of the leading works on management of wilderness areas is John Hendee, George Stankey, and Robert Lucas, *Wilderness Management* (U.S. Department of Agriculture, Forest Service, Misc. Publ. No. 1365, 1978).

40. Ibid., 23. For example, Valcour Island in Lake Champlain can never meet the acreage requirement for wilderness classification, but it superbly fulfills the purposes of the primitive classification; ibid., 53.

41. NYS Environmental Conservation Law, section 9-0105.

42. The lack of progress on unit management plans by DEC has been a constant source of tension between DEC and the state's environmental constituency. The limited progress of DEC in preparing unit management plans is reflected in *Annual Report—1983*, 5. See Richard Booth, "Adirondack Park State Land Master Plan," Report No. 14 in NYS Bar Association, Committee on Environmental Law, *Evaluation of Key Regulatory Programs Administered by the New York State Department of Environmental Conservation* (1981), 119–36.

43. See Ian McHarg, *Design With Nature* (Garden City, N.Y.: Doubleday, Natural History Press, 1969); Liroff and Davis, *Protecting Open Spaces*, 26–28.

44. *Comprehensive Report*, 16–17. Telephone conversation with George Davis, former assistant director, APA, 17 May 1983. Davis was the primary staff architect of the Land Use and Development Plan for the park's nonstate lands. He now works with the Adirondack Council, a private environmental organization that concentrates on Adirondack issues.

45. Liroff and Davis, *Protecting Open Spaces*, 126–29, 152; Richard Booth, "The Adirondack Park Agency Act: A Challenge in Regional Land Use Planning," *George Washington University Law Review* 43 (1975): 622–25; Arthur Savage and Joseph Sierchio, "The Adirondack Land Use Plan Confronts 'The Taking Issue,'" *Albany Law Review* 40 (1976): 447.

46. Authors typically express the density restrictions as "average lot sizes"; Liroff and Davis, *Protecting Open Spaces*, 32–33; *Comprehensive Report*, 19; Michael Heiman, "An Evaluation of State Land Use Planning and Development Control in the Adirondacks," Cornell University Water Resources and Marine Sciences Center (1974), 7.

47. Telephone conversation with George Davis, former assistant director, APA, 17 May 1983.

48. See APA Act, section 801; see also *Report of Citizens' Advisory Task Force on Open Space to the Adirondack Park Agency* (1980), 7–28. Referred to hereinafter as *Open Space Task Force Report*. See also *Comprehensive Report*, 16–17.

49. APA Act, at section 810(1)(b)(1), (c)(1), (d)(1), and (e)(1).

50. *Comprehensive Report*, 5–12.

51. Compare APA Act, section 810(1)(a) with section 810(1)(e) and section (810)(2)(d); see *Comprehensive Report*, 20–21, 35.

52. Ibid., section 809(6). See NYS Uniform Procedures Act, NYS Environmental Conservation Law, article 70.

53. Telephone conversation on 7 June 1983 with Edmund Lynch, deputy director at the APA.

54. Telephone conversation on 8 June 1983 with John Banta, APA director of planning. Banta also reported the APA disapproves approximately ten map amendment requests annually, covering a total of approximately 2,700 acres.

55. Ibid., Banta estimates 80 percent of Adirondack local governments have worked with the APA on local planning; *Annual Report—1983*, 6.

56. See NYS Department of State, *Local Government Handbook*, 3rd ed. (1982), 270.

57. APA Act, section 801; see APA, *Adirondack Park Land Use and Development Plan and Recommendations for Implementation* (March 1973), 11–14.

58. Liroff and Davis, *Protecting Open Spaces*, 116–19.

59. Section 801 of the APA Act reads in part as follows: "A further purpose of this article is to focus the responsibility for developing long-range park policy in a forum reflecting statewide concern. . . ."

60. The Temporary Study Commission certainly contemplated a planning and policy effort dealing with topics far beyond the scope of the State Land Master Plan and the Land Use and Development Plan. See generally *The Future of the Adirondack Park*.

61. *Open Space Task Force Report*.

62. See *Report of the Joint Government/Industry Steering Committee on Intensive Timber Harvesting in the Adirondack Park to the Adirondack Park Agency* (1981). Available at APA.

63. Liroff and Davis, *Protecting Open Spaces*, 57–58; Richard Booth and Theodore Hullar, "Has the Adirondack Park Agency Made a Difference?" *Amicus Journal* (published by the Natural Resources Defense Council) (Summer 1980).
64. For example, see Adirondack Park Local Government Review Board, *1977 Annual Report—Can There Be a Partnership with the Adirondack Park Agency?* (1977).
65. NYS Environmental Conservation Law, article 24.
66. NYS Tidal Wetlands Act, NYS Environmental Conservation Law, article 25.
67. Section 15-2701(3) of the Environmental Conservation Law reads in part as follows: "It is hereby declared to be the policy of this state that certain selected rivers of the state . . . shall be preserved in free-flowing condition, and that they and their immediate environs shall be protected for the benefit and enjoyment of present and future generations."
68. *State Land Master Plan (1979)*, 60–61.
69. 9 NYCRR Part 577.
70. See, for example, NYS Town Law, New York Consolidated Laws Service, *NY Statutes*, vols. 34 and 34A, article 16; and NYS Village Law, New York Consolidated Laws Service, *NY Statutes*, vol. 39, article 7.
71. NYS Environmental Conservation Law.
72. Ibid., for example, at articles 17 and 19.
73. Ibid., article 15, title 5.
74. Ibid., article 15, title 15.
75. NYS Public Health Law, New York Consolidated Laws Service, *NY Statutes*, vols. 25 and 25A.
76. See APA, Department of Environmental Conservation, and Department of Health, "Application For Permits in the Adirondack Park" (1977).
77. The APA participated as a party in the Public Service Commission's public hearings regarding the building of a 765 kV transmission line from the Canadian border to Marcy, New York. The preferred route discussed at the hearings would have crossed into the Adirondack Park in two places. The final route selected by the PSC avoided the park. With respect to the importance of transmission lines to the environment of the Adirondack Park, see the Opinion and Order of the NYS Energy Planning Board of 20 March 1980 in the state's "State Energy Master Planning and Long-Range Electric and Gas System Planning Proceeding," in State Energy Office, *New York State Energy Master Plan and Long-Range Electric and Gas Report—Appendices* (1980), 136.
78. NYS Environmental Conservation Law, article 51.
79. NYS Department of Environmental Conservation, "1972 Environmental Quality Bond Act Land Acquisition Status Report," (16 April 1982).
80. *The Future of the Adirondack Park*, 86–87; also see for this type of program (chapter 8) Pinelands.
81. Some of the most eloquent tributes to the contributions made by the Forest Preserve to the character of the entire Adirondack Park are contained in White, *Adirondack Country* 8, 238–46, 264.
82. See generally Van Valkenburgh, *Adirondack Forest Preserve*; see also Graham, *The Adirondack Park* 275–78; see, for example, *Helms v. Reid*, 394 N.Y.S.2d 987 (1977).
83. Liroff and Davis, *Protecting Open Spaces*, 156–75; Booth, "Developing Institutions . . ." 672–73 and 690–91; see for example *Wambat Realty Corp. v. State*, 393 N.Y.S.2d 949 (1977); see generally memorandum from Robert Glennon, General Counsel APA to agency members, dated 13 August 1981 and entitled "Significant

Litigation Involving The Adirondack Park Agency and/or the Adirondack Park Agency Act."

84. Booth and Hullar, "Has APA Made a Difference?" 15–16; *Comprehensive Report*, 20–23.

85. Barnett, *The Ancient Adirondacks*, 20–35.

86. The APA has had only four chairmen since it began: Richard Lawrence, Robert Flacke, Theodore Ruzow, and Herman Cole. All four lived in the park. Lawrence has been a longtime leader on many Adirondack issues. Flacke has been a successful businessman and a well-respected local official (and later commissioner of the Department of Environmental Conservation). Ruzow is a lawyer. Cole worked for the state in the Adirondacks before becoming chairman. All have been strong leaders and personalities. See Liroff and Davis, *Protecting Open Spaces*, 11, 63–65.

87. See generally Frank Popper, *The Politics of Land Use Reform* (Madison: University of Wisconsin Press, 1981); Robert Healy and John Rosenberg, *Land Use and The States*, 2d ed. (Baltimore: Johns Hopkins University Press, 1979), 186–88; and Savage and Sierchio, "The APA Act."

88. Many of the negotiations that surrounded the creation of the Adirondack Park Land Use and Development Plan focused on lands at or near shorelines because of their attractiveness for development and existing land-use patterns (personal recollections of author, who served on original APA staff). Several of the significant concessions made in the legislative process surrounding the amendment of the APA Act and the adoption of the Land Use and Development Plan in 1973 involved major reductions in the shoreline restrictions proposed by the APA. Compare APA, *Adirondack Park Land Use and Development Plan and Recommendations for Implementation* (March 1973), and APA Act, section 806. (It is interesting to note that the March 1973 plan proposal states the APA made approximately five hundred changes in its original land-use classification proposals; see pp. 1–2 of that document.)

89. *Annual Report—1983*, 6; see also APA Order for State Project No. SP81-15, adopted 29 March 1982 (on file with APA).

90. In 1982, nearly ten years after the initial State Land Master Plan was adopted, DEC had under way only four unit management plans, and those were not yet completed; *Annual Report—1983*, 5. That record has improved to some degree in the past two years. See Adirondack Council, *State of the Park 1986*, 10, 13.

91. Booth and Hullar, "Has APA Made a Difference?" 20–21; see Adirondack Council, "State of the Park—1982" (November 1982), 2.

92. See Environmental Planning Lobby, "New York Environmental Voter's Guide" (1981 and 1982).

93. For example, for the 1983 session of the state legislature, see Assembly Bill A1992/Senate Bill 1385 dealing with deadwood collection.

94. For example, for the 1983 session of the state legislature, see Assembly Bill 243/Senate Bill 219 dealing with Forest Preserve management.

95. For the 1983 session of the state legislature, see Assembly Bill 2277/Senate Bill 1625.

96. See, for example, statement by Robert Flacke, former APA chairman, comparing APA effort and effort by California and Nevada to preserve Lake Tahoe, *1977 Annual Report*, 8.

97. From a rapidly expanding body of literature, see Phil Weller et al., *Acid Rain: The Silent Crisis* (Between the Lines and the Waterloo Public Interest Research Group, 1980), 18, 24, 25; Robert Boyle and R. Alexander Boyle, "Acid Rain," *Amicus Journal* (Winter 1983): 22–37; Ralph Blumenthal, "Acid Rain in Adirondacks Dis-

rupts the Chain of Life," *New York Times* (8 June 1981); and Richard Lyons, "4,867 Feet High In the Adirondacks, Scientists Study Acid Rain," *New York Times*, 28 July 1982.

98. *Annual Report—1983*, 4; Graham, *The Adirondack Park*, 277–78; Booth and Hullar, "Has APA Made a Difference?" 20.
99. See generally, Temporary Study Commission, *Recreation (Technical Report No. 5)* (1970).
100. 9 *NYCRR* 573.7; See APA, "Newsline" (Fall 1982), 1.
101. *Annual Report—1983*, 4; NYS, *Energy Master Plan and Long-Range Electric and Gas Report—Final Report* (March 1982), 2:109–14, and also 1:70.
102. Graham, *The Adirondack Park*, 96–97.
103. *Open Space Task Force Report*, 100–101.
104. See APA, "Final Environmental Impact Statement—Revision of the Adirondack Park Agency's Rules and Regulations in Regard to Timber Harvesting That Includes Clearcutting" (13 September 1982), appendixes i, ii, and iii; statement of the Society of American Foresters, "Response to the Draft Environmental Impact Statement Concerning Proposed Revisions to the Adirondack Park Agency's Rules and Regulations in Regard to Timber Harvesting That Includes Clearcutting" (March 1982); and see also "Proposed APA Clearcutting Rules Spark Debate," *Plattsburgh Press Publican*, 26 May 1982.
105. See 9 *NYCRR* 573.7; APA, "Newsline" (Fall 1982), 1.
106. Section 2 of article XIV of the NYS State Constitution allows the use of up to 3 percent of the Forest Preserve for the construction and maintenance of reservoirs for municipal water supply and for the canals of the state. See Van Valkenburgh, *Adirondack Forest Preserve*, 104–200; Graham, *The Adirondack Park*, 197–207.
107. See APA Act, section 810; see also NYS Environmental Conservation Law, section 15-0503(6), prohibiting the state or any river regulating board from constructing reservoirs for any purpose on the Upper Hudson River and parts of the Boreas River, the Indian River, and the Cedar River.
108. *Annual Report—1983*, 4; Adirondack Council, 3; Adirondack Council, "Resolution on Hydro Development" (November 1981); APA staff memorandum of 28 March 1979 on APA jurisdiction regarding hydroelectric facilities.
109. Wild and Scenic Rivers, 16 *United States Code*, sections 1271–87.
110. Liroff and Davis, *Protecting Open Spaces*, 122–24, 147–49; Graham, *The Adirondack Park*, 268–72; see, generally, Charles Zinser, *The Economic Impact of the Adirondack Private Land Use and Development Plan* (New York: State University of New York Press, 1980).
111. Graham, *The Adirondack Park* 268–72; "Economic Profile"; Temporary Study Commission, *Transportation and The Economy (Technical Report No. 4)* (1970).
112. Adirondack Park Local Government Review Board, 11–12.
113. *McKinney's 1973 Session Laws of New York*, chap. 348, section 11; *Comprehensive Report*, 50–52.
114. See, in general, Catskill Center for Conservation and Development, Inc., *Property Taxation and Land Use* (1977); Temporary Study Commission, *Local Government (Technical Report No. 6)* (1970), 7–18, 33–39; Natural Resources Defense Council, *Land Use Controls in New York State* (New York: Dial Press, 1975), 315–24.
115. In a rapidly expanding body of literature, see, generally, Council on Environmental Quality, *Untaxing Open Space* (1976); Richard Dunford, "An Overview of the Open Space Taxation Act in Washington" (Pullman: Washington State University, 1979);

and Mark Lapping, Robert Bevins, and Paul Herbers, "Differential Assessment to Preserve Missouri's Farmlands," *Missouri Law Review* 42 (1977): 369.

116. Only New York's Agricultural Districts Law, NYS Agriculture and Markets Law, New York Consolidated Laws Service, *NY Statutes*, vols. 1 and 1A, article 25AA, appears to be a major, feasible effort by New York State in the real property taxation field. That law has a number of features that go far beyond real property tax reform in an effort to protect farmlands. See Ken Gardner, "Agricultural District Legislation in New York as Amended Through August 1982" (Cornell University, 1982).

117. See Assembly Bill A2323A/Senate Bill S1997A that was considered in the NYS Legislature in 1983. Similar legislation was proposed for years in New York but failed. See Environmental Planning Lobby, "New York Environmental Voter's Guide" (1982), 8. Conservation easement legislation was finally passed in 1983 but had to be immediately amended in 1984. See *McKinney's 1983 Session Laws of New York*, chap. 1020, and *McKinney's 1984 Session Laws of New York*, chap. 292. New York State has not pushed the implementation of its conservation easement legislation, but private groups are eagerly exploring possibilities.

118. Environmental Planning Lobby, "Environmental Voter's Guide" (1982), 7.

119. Adirondack Council, 2.

120. Ibid.

121. *Annual Report—1983*, 6; APA Order for State project No. SPB1-15 adopted 29 March 1982.

122. In 1982 the NYS Department of Health (DOH) determined to stop providing funding to Adirondack towns for aerial pesticide spraying to combat blackflies. DOH issued an environmental impact statement relative to that funding proposal and subsequently decided to halt the program. Adirondack Council release entitled "Toxic Chemicals Are Once Again About to Shower the Adirondacks" (22 January 1982); Adirondack Council, 2.

123. Adirondack Council, 3; NYS, *Energy Master Plan and Long-Range Electric and Gas Report—Final Report* 1 (1982): 29–39. In 1984 New York State finally took significant action to curb sources of acid rain within its own borders. When fully implemented, New York's State Acid Deposition Control Act will hopefully effect a 30 percent reduction in New York's sulfur dioxide emissions from 1980 levels. See *McKinney's 1984 Session Laws of New York*, chaps. 972 and 973.

124. Adirondack Council, 4.

125. Ibid., 3.

126. Ibid., 4. New York's 1987 budget contains appropriations for building two visitors' centers in the Adirondacks.

New Jersey Pinelands Commission

1. N.J. Pinelands Commission, *New Jersey Pinelands Comprehensive Management Plan* (adopted November 1980), 12.

2. Ibid., 94.

3. Gary R. Letcher, "New Jersey's Pine Barrens: Strategies for Protecting a Critical Area," *Journal of Soil and Water Conservation* (September–October 1979): 211.

4. Two excellent accounts of the Pine Barrens' rich history and its residents (the "Pineys") are Henry Charlton Beck's *Forgotten Towns of New Jersey* (1936) and John McPhee's *The Pine Barrens* (1968).

5. Letcher, "Strategies," 212.

6. See Hearings on Pinelands National Wildlife Refuge before the House Subcommittee on Fisheries, Wildlife Conservation and the Environment, Committee on Merchant Marine and Fisheries, Print No. 95-35, 1978.
7. A 1979 study of twelve Pinelands municipalities also revealed that if these local plans were fully implemented, they would result in over one million residents in the twelve townships alone. See *Airola, 1979*, in *Final Environmental Impact Statement, Proposed Comprehensive Management Plan for the Pinelands National Reserve* (Washington, D.C.: Heritage Conservation and Recreation Service, Department of the Interior, 1980), 549.
8. *New Jersey Pine Barrens: Concepts for Preservation* (Washington, D.C.: Bureau of Outdoor Recreation, U.S. Department of the Interior, 1975).
9. *National Urban Recreation Study, Technical Reports, Volume 1: Urban Open Space: Existing Conditions, Opportunities and Issues* (Washington, D.C.: Heritage Conservation and Recreation Service, Department of Interior), 43–44.
10. The notion of greenline parks was initially proposed by Charles Little in *Greenline Parks: An Approach to Preserving Recreational Landscapes in Urban Areas*, report prepared by CRS for the Subcommittee on Parks and Recreation of the Senate Committee on Interior and Insular Affairs, 1975. This idea relied upon a number of well-known applications, such as the Adirondack Park Agency, wild and scenic river programs, and the English national parks, all of which established resource management programs within the context of mixed public-private ownership.
11. Ibid., 79. Other sites identified in the report included the Lowell, Massachusetts, Heritage Park, the Hudson River Waterfront (New Jersey), the Platte River and Hogback Corridors in Denver, and the Delaware River Waterfront in Philadelphia.
12. *National Urban Recreation Study*, 68.
13. Ibid., 69.
14. Letcher, "Strategies," 214.
15. Sec. 502(a)(6) of the National Parks and Recreation Act of 1978, P.L. 95-625, 10 Nov. 1978 (16 U.S.C. 471i).
16. Executive Order No. 71. Membership of the commission is composed of seven representatives appointed by the governor, one federal representative, and representatives (one apiece) chosen by each of the Pinelands counties.
17. N.J.S.A. 13:18A-1.
18. N.J.S.A. CAFRA is the primary legislative base for New Jersey's federally approved coastal management program. 13:19-1 et. seq.
19. The state's coastal policies are codified at N.J.A.C. 7:7E-1.1 et seq.
20. *New Jersey Statewide Water Supply Master Plan* (Division of Water Resources, Department of Environmental Protection, April 1982), 15.
21. N.J.S.A. 58:1A-7.1.
22. *Comprehensive Management Plan*, 221.
23. Ibid., 171.
24. Alan Mallach Associates for New Jersey Department of Community Affairs, "Social and Economic Factors Influencing Pinelands Development" (1980).
25. Devon Schneider et al., *The Carrying Capacity Concept as a Planning Tool*, Planning Advisory Service Report, American Planning Association (1979).
26. *Comprehensive Management Plan*, xiii.
27. However, the recent New Jersey Supreme Court decision in the *Mt. Laural II* case has caused some uncertainty as to how low-income housing should be provided. For the moment, the commission is requiring new housing developments to include percent-

ages of low- and middle-income housing based on the supreme court's income definitions, but has suspended such requirements for municipalities in regional growth areas.

28. Jonathan Berger, "Planning the Use and Management of the Pinelands: A Historical, Cultural and Ecological Perspective" (University of Pennsylvania).

29. See N.J.S.A. 40:55D-1 et seq.

30. "Pinelands: Develop or Preserve," *Philadelphia Inquirer*, 1 August 1982, p. 1C.

31. Conversation with Alice D'Arcy, Pinelands Commission, 22 March 1983.

32. New Jersey Pinelands Commission, *Legislators Update* (January 1983), 2.

33. Conversation with Robert Bembridge, Pinelands Commission, March 1983. The reported price was $20,000 per credit. One credit is worth four additional dwelling units above nominal densities in regional growth areas.

34. New Jersey Assemblyman Robert Myers of Medford has been most vocal in this matter.

35. Testimony of Peter Hibbard, New Jersey Builders Association on Pinelands Commission, *Draft Analysis of Fiscal Impact of the Pinelands Comprehensive Management Plan on Selected Municipalities* (1982).

36. Government Finance Associates for Pinelands Commission, *An Analysis of the Fiscal Impact of the Pinelands Comprehensive Management Plan on Selected Municipalities* (September 1982).

37. "The Disparate Effects of CAFRA, the Pinelands Act, and Casino Gambling on Residential Development in Southern New Jersey," Staff Issue Paper by Allan B. Campbell, Division of Coastal Resources, N.J. DEP (September 1981), 35.

38. Pinelands Commission, *Legislators Update*.

39. Under sec. 307 of the CZMA, federal activities must be consistent "to the maximum extent practicable" with federally approved state coastal management programs. Relevant federal activities are those that "directly affect" a state's defined coastal zone.

Montgomery County Agricultural Preservation Program

1. National Agricultural Lands Study, "The Protection of Farmland" (Washington, D.C.: U.S. Government Printing Office, 1981).

2. Lands Study, "Protection of Farmland."

3. Land banking is the stockpile of publicly owned land, the result of a program under which a government buys land and holds it for future use as needed.

4. Montgomery County Planning Board, *Functional Master Plan for the Preservation of Agriculture and Rural Open Space* (October 1980). The Functional Plan amends the county General Plan.

5. Montgomery County Planning Board, *Fiscal Impact Analysis*, second annual growth policy report (1975).

6. Real Estate Research Corporation, *The Cost of Sprawl* (Washington, D.C., 1976).

7. A case for farmland preservation in the Washington Metropolitan Area was made very strongly in a report entitled *Farmland Retention in the Washington Metropolitan Area*, by Dallas Miner (June 1976).

8. Montgomery County Planning Board, *The Functional Master Plan for Seneca and Muddy Branch Basins* (1975).

9. National Association of Counties, Research Foundation Study, *Disappearing Farmlands* (Washington, D.C., December 1979), 15.

10. This Functional Master Plan represents a synthesis of findings expressed in the General Plan and various area master plans—especially the Olney Master Plan. The Olney Master Plan was a prototype agricultural preservation plan for a 30,000-acre area. This area master plan utilized the transfer of development rights technique in a "closed-circuit" situation so that all development rights sending and receiving areas were identified and operational. Using the experience learned in the Olney Master Plan, the Functional Master Plan then utilized and expanded the agricultural preservation techniques on a countywide basis while adding still another innovative technique, the county development rights fund.

11. The Olney TDR program is a closed-circuit system whereby TDR sending and receiving areas serve *only* the Olney planning area.

A Brief Bibliography of Special Area
Management Experiences

I General

Bodi, L., and C. Walters. "Special Area Management—The Big Gamble." In *Proceedings of Coastal Zone '80*. New York: American Society of Civil Engineers, 1980.

Carol, D., and D. Brower. "Legal Considerations for Special Area Management." In *Proceedings of Coastal Zone '83*. New York: American Society of Civil Engineers, 1983.

Corbett, M., ed. *Land Conservation Trends for the Eighties and Beyond*. Washington, D.C.: National Parks and Conservation Association, 1983.

Davis, Gordon. "Special Area Management: Resolving Conflicts in the Coastal Zone." *Environmental Comment* (October 1980).

Dickert, T., and J. Sorensen. *Collaborative Land Use Planning for the Coastal Zone: A Process for Local Program Development*, vol. 1. Berkeley: Institute of Urban and Regional Development, University of California, March 1978.

Environmental Comment. Special Issue on Urban Waterfronts. (April 1981).

Kolis, A., ed. *Thirteen Perspectives on Regulatory Simplification*. Research Report no. 29. Washington, D.C.: Urban Land Institute, 1979.

Marsh, Lindell. "Focal Point Planning." Paper presented at the American Planning Association Annual Conference, Dallas, 1982.

Smithsonian Institution. *Planning Considerations for Statewide Inventories of Critical Environmental Areas: A Reference Guide*. Washington, D.C.: Center for Natural Areas, Office of International and Environmental Problems, the Smithsonian Institution, 1974.

U.S. Congress. Senate. Committee on Commerce, Science, and Transportation. *Report on P.L. 96-404 (Coastal Zone Management Act, 1980)*. Report no. 96-783.

U.S. Department of the Interior. *National Urban Recreation Study, Technical Reprints, Vol. 1—Urban Open Space: Existing Conditions, Opportunities and Issues*. Washington, D.C.: U.S. Department of the Interior, Heritage Conservation and Recreation Service, 1978.

U.S. Office of Coastal Zone Management. "Improved Coordination for Planning and Permitting for Special Areas." In *Federal Coastal Program Review*. Washington, D.C., 1981.

II Conflict Resolution

American Arbitration Association and Clark-McGlennon Associates. *Proceedings of a Workshop on Environmental Conflict Management*. Prepared for U.S. Congressional Research Service. Washington, D.C.: American Arbitration Association, 1980.

Boschken, Herman L. *Land Use Conflicts—Organizational Design and Resource Management*. Urbana: University of Illinois Press, 1982.

Environmental Comment. Special Issue on Conflict Resolution. (May 1977).

Susskind, Lawrence, et al. *Resolving Environmental Disputes.* Cambridge, Mass.: Massachusetts Institute of Technology, Environmental Impact Assessment Project, 1978.
Talbot, Allan R. *Settling Things: Six Case Studies in Environmental Mediation.* Washington, D.C.: Conservation Foundation, 1983.

III   Grays Harbor, Washington

Chasan, Daniel. "The Grays Harbor Estuary Management Plan." *Amicus Journal* 4, 1 (Summer 1982).
Coastal Society Bulletin 4, 4 (1978).
Conservation Foundation. *Coastal Zone Management '80 — A Context for Debate.* Washington, D.C., 1980.
Evans, Nan. "Conflict Resolution: Lessons from Grays Harbor." In *Coastal Zone '80.* Proceedings of the Second Symposium on Ocean and Coastal Management. New York: American Society of Civil Engineers, 1980.
Evans, Nan, et al. *The Search for Predictability: Planning and Conflict Resolution in Grays Harbor, Washington.* Seattle: Washington Sea Grant, 1980.
Shapiro and Associates, Inc. *An Analysis of Wetland Regulations and the Corps of Engineers Section 404 Program in Western Washington.* Prepared for U.S. Office of Technology Assessment. Washington, D.C.: U.S. Government Printing Office, 1982.
Wilsey and Ham, Consultants. *Grays Harbor Estuary Management Plan.* Draft prepared for the Grays Harbor Estuary Task Force. Grays Harbor, Wash.: Grays Harbor Regional Planning Commission, 1982.

IV   Coos Bay, Oregon

Coos County Board of Commissioners. "Coos Bay Estuary Management Plan." In *Coos County Comprehensive Plan,* vol. 3. Coos Bay, Oreg., 1982.
Davis, Gordon E. "Principles and Techniques for Special Area Management: The Grays Harbor and Coos Bay Experience." In *Coastal Zone '80.* Proceedings of the Second Symposium on Coastal and Ocean Management. New York: American Society of Civil Engineers, 1980.
Grile, William P. "Environmental Mediation: Lessons from the Coos Bay Estuary Planning Process." Paper presented at the American Planning Association Annual Conference, Dallas, 1982.

V   San Francisco Bay, California

Baum, Alvin. "San Francisco Bay Conservation and Development Commission." *Lincoln Law Review* 5 (June 1970).
Davoren, William. "Tragedy of the San Francisco Bay Commons." *CZM Journal* 9, 2 (1981).
Dolezel, J., and B. Warren. "Saving San Francisco Bay." *Stanford Law Review* 23 (January 1971).
Fay, Dennis. "Discussion of the San Francisco Bay Area Seaport Plan." In *Coastal Zone '83.* Proceedings of the Third Symposium on Coastal and Ocean Management. New York: American Society of Civil Engineers, 1983.
Odell, Rice. *The Saving of San Francisco Bay.* Washington, D.C.: Conservation Foundation, 1972.
Schoop, E. Jack. "The San Francisco Bay Plan." *AIP Journal* (January 1971).

Swanson, Gerald C. "Coastal Zone Management from an Administrative Perspective: A Case Study of the San Francisco Bay Conservation and Development Commission." *CZM Journal* 2, 2 (1975).

VI Pinelands Commission, New Jersey

Letcher, Gary. "New Jersey's Pine Barrens: Strategies for Protecting a Critical Area." *Journal of Soil and Water Conservation* 34 (September-October 1979).
National Parks and Recreation Act, P.L. 96-625 (16 U.S.C.A. 4711); see section 502 of the act.
New Jersey. *Pinelands Protection Act*. New Jersey Statutes Annotated Section 13: 18A-1.
New Jersey Pinelands Commission. *New Jersey Pinelands Commission Annual Report*. New Lisbon, N.J., 1981.
———. *The Pinelander*. Newsletter of the New Jersey Pinelands Commission. 1982–85.
———. *Pinelands Comprehensive Management Plan*. New Lisbon, N.J., 1980.
———. *Pinelands Development Credits: A Landowner's Guide*. New Lisbon, N.J., 1981.
Sinton, John. "Opportunities and Problems in Planning the New Jersey Pinelands and Coastal Zone." In *Coastal Zone '80*. Proceedings of the Second Symposium on Coastal and Ocean Management. New York: American Society of Civil Engineers, 1980.
U.S. Department of the Interior. *Final Environmental Impact Statement on New Jersey Pinelands Protection Plan*. Washington, D.C.: Heritage Conservation and Recreation Service, 1980.

VII Tug Hill Commission, New York

Dyballa, Cynthia, et al. *The Tug Hill Program: A Regional Planning Option for Rural Areas*. Syracuse: Syracuse University Press, 1981.
The Future of Tug Hill Programs. Albany: Report of the Temporary State Commission on Tug Hill, 1980.
Hahn, A., and C. Dyballa. "State Environmental Planning and Local Influence." *APA Journal* (July 1981).
Marsh, Elizabeth R. *Cooperative Rural Planning: A Tug Hill Case Study*. New York: Cooperative Tug Hill Planning Board, 1981.
Tug Hill Commission Newsletter. 1981–84.
The Tug Hill Region: Preparing for the Future. Albany: Report of the Temporary State Commission on Tug Hill, 1976.

VIII Adirondack Park Agency, New York

Booth, Richard. "The APA Act: A Challenge in Regional Land Use Planning." *George Washington Law Review* 43, 2 (1975).
———. "Developing Institutions for Regional Land Use Planning and Control: The Adirondack Experience." *Buffalo Law Review* 28, 4 (Fall 1979).
Buschman, Charles. "Preserving Scenic Areas: The Adirondack Land Use Program." *Yale Law Journal* 84, 8 (1975).
Davis, L. Gordon. "Land Use Control and Environmental Protection in the Adirondacks." *New York State Bar Journal* 47 (April 1975).
Hahn, A., and C. Dyballa. "State Environmental Planning and Local Influence." *APA Journal* (July 1981).

Lewis, Sylvia. "New York's Adirondacks: Tug of War in the Wilderness." *Planning* 42, 9 (1976).

Liroff, R., and G. Davis. *Protecting Open Space: Land Use Control in the Adirondack Park.* Cambridge, Mass.: Ballinger, 1981.

Savage, A., and J. Sierchio. "The APA Act: A Regional Land Use Plan Confronts the Taking Issue." *Albany Law Journal* 40, 3 (1976).

IX   Patuxent River Commission, Maryland

Bunker, S. M., and G. V. Hodge. "The Legal, Political and Scientific Aspects of the Patuxent River Nutrient Control Controversy." Presentation to the Atlantic Estuarine Research Society, Baltimore, 1982.

Clark-McGlennon Associates. *Patuxent River Nutrient Control Strategy Charrette: A Report.* Boston: Clark-McGlennon Associates, 1982.

X   Bolsa Chica, California

EDAW, Inc. *Draft Report to the Bolsa Chica Study Group: Background Issues and Considerations in Planning for the Long Range Uses of the Bolsa Chica Area.* San Francisco: EDAW, Inc., 1978.

Marsh, Lindell. "Bolsa Chica—A Case Study of Coastal Planning and Conflict." In *Coastal Zone Management.* ALI-ABA Course Materials. Philadelphia: American Law Institute, American Bar Association, 1981.

XI   Hilton Head Island, South Carolina

South Carolina Coastal Council. *Hilton Head Island Special Area Management Plan.* Charleston: 1982.

XII   La Tortuguera, Puerto Rico

Puerto Rico Coastal Management Program. *La Tortuguera Special Area Management Plan.* San Juan, 1982.

XIII   Apalachicola Bay, Florida

Conklin, E. "Apalachicola As Special Area Management." In *Coastal Zone '80.* Proceedings of the Second Symposium on Ocean and Coastal Management. New York: American Society of Civil Engineers, 1980.

Conservation Foundation. "Coastal Zone Management '80—A Context for Debate." Washington, D.C., 1980.

Final Environmental Impact Statement: Apalachicola Bay River and Bay Estuarine Sanctuary. Washington, D.C.: U.S. Office of Coastal Zone Management, 1979.

XIV   Tahoe Regional Planning Agency, Nevada and California

Baxter, Laurence D. *Draft Environmental Impact Statement for the Establishment of Environmental Threshold Carrying Capacities, Tahoe Regional Planning Agency.*

Research Reports 29–30, EQ Series Reports 21–22. Davis: University of California at Davis, Institute of Government Affairs, 1982.

XV South County Salt Ponds, Rhode Island

Collins, Clarkson. "The Design of a Land Use Element for Rhode Island's Coastal Ponds Special Area Management Plan." In *Proceedings of Coastal Society 8.* Baltimore, October 1982.
"Tidal Gates Urged for Salt Ponds." *Narragansett Times* (8 July 1982).

XVI Columbia River Estuary Study Task Force
(CREST), Oregon and Washington

Columbia River Estuary Data Development Program. Annual Report. Vancouver, Wash.: Pacific Northwest River Basins Commission, 1979.
Columbia River Estuary Regional Management Plan. Astoria, Oreg.: CREST, 1979.

XVII Providence Harbor, Rhode Island

Providence Harbor: A Special Area Management Plan. Providence: Rhode Island Coastal Zone Management, 1983.

XVIII Urban Recreation Areas

Fahey, Kathleen. *National Parks in Urban Areas: An Annotated Bibliography.* CPL Bibliography no. 90. Chicago: Council of Planning Librarians, 1982.
Foresta, Ronald. *America's National Parks and Their Keepers.* Knoxville: University of Tennessee, 1984.
"Urban National Parks—For People or for Plants?" In *Resources.* Washington, D.C.: Resources for the Future, 1984.

XIX Baltimore, Maryland

City of Baltimore. *The Baltimore Harbor.* Baltimore: Department of Planning, 1985.
Dolan, Mary. "A Baltimore Harbor Enhancement Plan." In *Proceedings of Coastal Zone '85.* New York: American Society of Civil Engineers, 1985.

XX Philadelphia, Pennsylvania

Wapora, Inc. *Philadelphia/Camden Port: Environmental Enhancement Plan.* Prepared for the U.S. Environmental Protection Agency, Region III. Washington, D.C.: U.S. Government Printing Office, 1984.

Index

About the Editors and Authors

David J. Brower (coeditor), a lawyer and planner, is Associate Director of the Center for Urban and Regional Studies at the University of North Carolina at Chapel Hill where he specializes in managing the growth of urban areas and coastal zone management. He is the coauthor (with Daniel S. Carol) of *Coastal Zone Management As Land Planning*, published by the National Planning Association in 1984.

Daniel S. Carol (coeditor and author) was formerly a policy analyst with the U.S. Congressional Budget Office, where he wrote policy studies on hazardous waste management, electric utilities, and the effects of budget reductions at the Environmental Protection Agency. Previously, he was an environmental investigator for the City of Philadelphia Law Department. He currently works as a consultant with National Strategies and Marketing Group in Washington, D.C.

Melissa C. Banach has had extensive experience in urban planning, both in private consulting and in public agencies. During the past six years she has been planner-in-charge of development of a transfer of development rights program to preserve rural open space and farmland in Montgomery County, Maryland.

Gail Bingham is a senior associate at the Conservation Foundation, specializing in dispute resolution. She facilitates policy dialogue and negotiation groups, provides technical assistance and training, conducts research in dispute resolution, and edits the newsletter *Resolve*.

Richard Booth is an Associate Professor in Cornell University's Department of City and Regional Planning, where he teaches courses in environmental law, environmental politics, historic preservation, and administrative law. He is currently on the board of directors of the Environmental Planning Lobby—and served as its president from 1979 to 1982—and the Adirondack Council, two of New York's leading environmental organizations.

Denis D. Canavan has been a practicing planner since 1970 and has worked in a number of public agencies in the state of Maryland and as a consultant representing both private developers and civic organizations. He is a team participant in the preparation of the Montgomery County transfer of development rights program and was responsible for drafting the implementing ordinances including zoning text amendments and subdivision ordinance revisions.

John R. Clark has worked as a research scientist for the U.S. Fish and Wildlife Service and Bureau of Commercial Fisheries at Woods Hole, Massachusetts, and Sandy Hook, New Jersey, and as a senior associate with the Conservation Foundation, focusing on coastal resources planning and management, research policy, and demonstration programs. He is currently coastal resources advisor to the International Affairs Office, National Park Service, Washington, D.C., and is responsible for research, planning, and training projects dealing mostly with tropical coastal development and renewable resource planning and management for developing countries.

Gerald W. Cormick is executive director of the Institute for Environmental Mediation in Seattle, Washington. He has mediated labor, environmental, and other social disputes in both the United States and Canada.

Mary G. Dolan works at the Regional Planning Council in Baltimore, Maryland, implementing the recommendations of the Baltimore Metropolitan Coastal Area Study, a component of the Maryland Coastal Zone Management Program. In her previous work as an environmental planner with Barton-Aschman Associates, she took part in a broad range of land-use, transportation, and community development projects, and she has worked with a team of planners and architects at Skidmore, Owings and Merrill to study the impacts of greatly increased patronage for the Northeast Corridor Amtrak service.

Lindell L. Marsh is an attorney and partner in the Orange County, California, office of Nossaman, Guthner, Knox & Elliott, which specializes in land-use and natural resources law. A member of the National Policy Council of the Urban Land Institute, he is also a lecturer and member of the Dean's Council, University of Southern California, Graduate School of Urban and Regional Studies, and visiting lecturer on public planning and control of urban and land development, School of Law, University of California at Los Angeles.

Scott McCreary is a Ph.D. candidate in the Department of Urban Studies and Planning at MIT, specializing in environmental dispute resolution and international coastal resources management. He coauthored *Coasts: Institutional Arrangements for the Management of Coastal Resources,* published by the U.S. AID (1984), and is the author of numerous articles on coastal resources and other environmental policy subjects. He has recently served as a consultant to the New York Academy of Sciences, the UN Ocean Economics and Technology Branch, and U.S. EPA.

Glenn Pontier is managing editor of *The River Reporter,* a nonprofit community newspaper published in Narrowsburg, New York. He also leads canoe trips sponsored by the National Park Service on the Delaware River and was one of several local residents hired by the NPS to assist in the revision of the river management plan.

Robert D. Thornton specializes in environmental law as a partner in the firm of Nossaman, Guthner, Knox & Elliott. He has represented private sector interests on sensitive resource issues including wetlands and endangered species and has participated in the development of two habitat conservation plans under the provisions of the Endangered Species Act of 1973. Formerly counsel to the House of Representatives Subcommittee on Fisheries and Wildlife Conservation and the Environment, he took part in drafting the 1978 and 1979 amendments to the Endangered Species Act.

Charles K. Walters is currently special assistant to the Northwest regional director of the U.S. National Marine Fishery Service, with primary responsibility for the Pacific Salmon Treaty with Canada and related international issues. Previously, he worked with the U.S. State Department on international fishery issues, taking part in negotiations with Canada, Japan, Taiwan, and other nations. His prior service with the NMFS involved stints as national coastal zone coordinator in Washington and as Northwest Coastal Zone Management coordinator in Portland, Oregon.